MODERN LOVES

MODERN Loves

THE ANTHROPOLOGY OF
ROMANTIC COURTSHIP & COMPANIONATE MARRIAGE

JENNIFER S. HIRSCH AND

HOLLY WARDLOW, *Editors*

The University of Michigan Press   Ann Arbor

Copyright © by the University of Michigan 2006
All rights reserved
Published in the United States of America by
The University of Michigan Press
Manufactured in the United States of America
⊗ Printed on acid-free paper

2009   2008   2007   2006   4   3   2   1

A CIP catalog record for this book is available from the British Library.

Library of Congress Cataloging-in-Publication Data

Modern loves : the anthropology of romantic courtship and companionate
    marriage / Jennifer S. Hirsch and Holly Wardlow, editors.
        p. cm.
    Includes bibliographical references and index.
    ISBN-13: 978-0-472-09959-7 (cloth : alk. paper)
    ISBN-10: 0-472-09959-0 (cloth : alk. paper)
    ISBN-13: 978-0-472-06959-0 (pbk. : alk. paper)
    ISBN-10: 0-472-06959-4 (pbk. : alk. paper)
        1. Companionate marriage—Cross-cultural studies.   2. Courtship—
    Cross-cultural studies.   3. Man-woman relationships—Cross-cultural
    studies.   I. Hirsch, Jennifer S.   II. Wardlow, Holly.
    HQ803.M63   2006
    306.81—dc22   2006015255

To our modern loves,

JOHN & KEN

JSH and HW

CONTENTS

ILLUSTRATIONS

FIGURES

ACKNOWLEDGMENTS

Over the many years it has taken to bring this volume to fruition, we have taken to referring to it as our labor of love. While this might seem at first like just the sort of silly pun that people who work with words for a living rely on to amuse themselves, the idea of a labor of love is in fact resonant on many levels with the work we present here. First of all, this volume is a demonstration of our love for our work; as anyone who has ever produced an edited volume can attest, the amount of work required to go from a panel at a professional meeting (in our case, the 1999 American Anthropological Association meeting in Chicago) to a physical volume is both great and greatly out-of-proportion to the rather modest professional reward that even the finest edited volumes generate. Our commitment to seeing this project through draws in no small part from our love for our discipline. That is the "love takes work" part of the labor of love.

Next, of course, comes our love for our colleagues—and to express our gratitude for a group that has stood by us for six years (at least), holding back papers that they might have more quickly published in a journal, love is perhaps not too strong a word. Certainly we are grateful as well to Laura Ahearn and Yunxiang Yan, whose outstanding service as discussants at that panel and whose seminal work in the anthropology of love laid the groundwork for the research presented here. The fact that we had given our word to these valued colleagues about this volume also kept us going; another face of love, in our part of the world, is commitment.

Most profoundly, of course, this volume is a labor of love because it is the complicated forms of love we have seen among our informants in the field—and the love we feel for them—that motivated us in the first instance to consider the anthropologies of love. In that regard, Holly would especially like to thank Mary and Michael Parali, Anna and James Samkul, and Margaret and Peter Ekopia. These couples welcomed her into their households, allowing her to witness their times of laughter, affection, frustration, and anger. Without their candor and generosity, she would not have gained an intimate understanding of the contemporary stresses and strains on Huli marriages. Mary has been an especially wonderful friend, keenly interested in thinking about love and marriage herself and always eager to share her thoughts with her.

Jennifer was particularly moved to reconsider love and migration through her friendships with Estela Mata, Marta García, and Silvia Rodriguez. She also notes with special fondness and admiration those to whom she lived in greatest proximity during her two long-term stays in Degollado, the Lujambio family; it is an honor and a pleasure to count Evita, Pepe, Blanca, Alan, and Patti as her family in Mexico. It is the love that we saw among our friends in the field—and the nagging feeling that we had initially gone to the field without quite having the conceptual apparatus to think in critical ways about how love is a social and cultural construct—that led us to persist with this volume.

Finally, there is the love that has, in many ways, sustained us. In Papua New Guinea special thanks go to the Papua New Guinea Institute of Medical Research and all its staff for their assistance, friendship, and intellectual companionship. In Mexico we would like to thank our colleagues at the Colegio de Mexico for their intellectual support and companionship. We would also like to gratefully acknowledge those who supported this project in various material ways. This includes the National Science Foundation (SBR-9510069) Program in Cultural Anthropology, which supported the Mexico fieldwork; the Emory AIDS International Training and Research Project (#1 D43 TW001042–06), which provided salary support to Jennifer during the years in which the majority of this volume was conceived and written; the Center for Gender, Sexuality, and Health at Columbia University's Mailman School of Public Health; and the Love, Marriage, and HIV project (NIH R01 HD041724), which functioned as a sort of auxiliary brain trust for us as we were working on the introduction to this volume. Harriet Phinney and Shanti Parikh deserve a special thanks in this regard since their ideas have helped us refine our thinking over the years, but none of their writing is represented (except in the references) in the pages herein. We include as well in our thanks Maria Sullivan, Mayra

Pabon, and Ellen Stiefvater, who provided crucial administrative support at various moments along the way. We would like to thank our editor, Raphael Allen, his assistant, Christy Byks, and our initial contact at the University of Michigan Press, Ellen McCarthy, as well as two anonymous reviewers, for their interest in and support of this project.

INTRODUCTION

Holly Wardlow and Jennifer S. Hirsch

In Singapore, young women melt down the jewelry given to them by their in-laws, refashioning the gold into rings and necklaces in more modern styles—or else they sell it, using the cash to buy a computer so the couple can get ahead. In rural western Mexico, young couples walk hand in hand in the plaza, or even dance together in the dark corners of the town disco, rather than courting as their parents had, in secret whispers through a chink in a stone wall—and the intimacy these couples share during courtship is only a taste of what is to come later, as they luxuriate in the privacy of neolocal residence, newly accessible through hard-earned dollars from men's sojourns in the United States as migrant laborers. Among the Huli of Papua New Guinea, young spouses often live together, rather than in the separate men's and women's houses of the past, claiming that "family houses," as they are called, are the "modern" and "Christian" way for loving couples to live. In Nigeria, although marriage is still very much regarded as a relationship that creates obligations between kin groups as well as between individuals, courtship at least has been transformed into a moment for young men and women to demonstrate their modern individuality. Around the world, young people are talking about the importance of affective bonds in creating marital ties, deliberately positioning themselves in contrast to their parents and grandparents.

This volume discusses how women and men from Mexico, Papua New

Guinea, Brazil, Pakistan, India, Nigeria, North America, and Singapore negotiate courtship, love, and marriage. Collectively we show how people in a variety of settings are coming to emphasize emotional intimacy as the source of the ties that bind. The chapters explore similarities and differences in shifting expectations for marriage, the growing perception that intimacy and pleasure are fundamental elements of modern relationships and modern personhood, the cultural forms—popular videos, advertisements, Christian tracts—that facilitate the globalization of a companionate marriage ideal, and the ways that these claims of modern love relate to changing gender ideologies. Our intent here is not simply to show women and men doing the work of love but rather to link interpersonal experiences of intimacy to the surrounding social and political context.

This volume seeks to raise questions about why similar companionate ideals have emerged and been embraced in such different contexts. While we recognize the importance of a global *ideological* shift in marital ideals, the contributors also address what Nancy Scheper-Hughes (1992) has referred to as the "political-economy of emotion"—that is, the ways in which the meanings, values, and very experience of emotion are shaped not only by culture but also by material structures of power. While the forms and idioms of modern love may on the surface appear to be similar around the world, those similarities are a product not just of cultural globalization but also of specific economic and social transformations. Some economic formations facilitate or even promote companionate marriage (Collier 1997; Rebhun 1999 a,b; Ahearn 2001; Yan 2003), while others make marriage of almost any kind nearly impossible (Hunter 2005; Gregg 2003). Thus, in addition to describing the varied local permutations of the globally available ideology of marital love (Jankowiak 1995; Jankowiak and Fischer 1992), we locate these ideologies of intimacy in relation to the material and demographic conditions of people's lives, looking at the ways in which the organization of production and consumption enables or impedes various kinds of conjugal ties, as well as the different strategic advantages men and women see (or don't) in their particular local version of companionate marriage.

Taking a cue from Connell's characterization of gender regimes as composed of labor, power, and affectivity (1987), we view emotion—marital love in this case (as well as other sentiments generated by marriage)—as a key component of gendered experience. The anthropology of gender in the 1980s and 1990s exposed the degree to which marriage and the "private" and "domestic" spaces that it supposedly inhabits are highly charged political arenas in which gendered persons negotiate labor, sex, reproduction, consumption, mobility, health, and the care of older and younger dependent generations. These explorations of gendered axes of power were vital for demonstrating that realms of experience that previous generations of (largely male) anthropologists had disregarded as trivial or personal were actually sites of complex strategizing and struggle. To think about couples only in terms of power, however, is to miss the fact that men and women may also care for the conjugal partners with whom they are simultaneously involved in daily battles over bodies, power, and resources. (This emphasis on conflict and inequality, to the exclusion of love and tenderness, is particularly notable in public health research on gender inequality and sexuality. Sexuality has been largely invisible as a category of interest in public health except in terms of commercial sex, sexual violence, and bargaining around contraceptives or condom use—all moments when the gendered optic is invoked in terms of conflict or domination, rather than pleasure or affect.) We argue that to study gendered relationships it is necessary to attend both to the socially, politically, and economically structured inequalities within which couples negotiate *and* to the possibilities for tenderness, pleasure, and cooperation that exist in spite of these inequalities. Incorporating this dual focus of attention—without simplifying matters by, for example, asserting that love is an ideology that seals men and women into various relations of inequality—may seem like a stretch theoretically, yet it is no more than many of us do in our own daily lives, in our own intimate relationships.

Keeping this dual focus in mind, the chapters point out that it is one thing to marry for love and another to stay married for love. In other words, romantic love is not the same as companionate marriage. While romantic love may be something that companionately married couples strive to maintain during married life—indeed, this is a defining aspect of companionate marriage in many of the cases discussed here—privileging romantic attraction and individual choice when selecting a spouse is, in fact, quite different from being able (and wanting) to prioritize the ongoing affective primacy of the conjugal unit. For one, parents, siblings, and other kin may dispute the centrality of the marital bond, insisting on the equal or greater value of their own emotional and economic claims, making love both a practice through which kin ties are constructed and, at times, a force in tension with those same ties. Relatedly, economic interdependence—between women and men, between the generations, and between affinally related groups—continues to exist, often in tension with newer ideologies of personal connection. Equally important, partners' expectations within marriage may conflict with gendered performances outside of marriage, as when an expectation of mutual fidelity is at odds with the prestige (more often for men than women) generated by extra-marital partnerships. Keeping these complexities in mind, some of the authors consider the ways in which companionate marriage may falter or fail in the face of poverty, gender asymmetry, or resistance on the part of those who benefit from more "traditional" ways of organizing family life.

In the remainder of the introduction, we first sketch out a brief conceptual exegesis and history of companionate marriage and review some recent work on the economic and demographic changes that seem to underpin shifts in the nature of marital ties. We then discuss links between companionate marriage and key dimensions of modernity: individualism, commoditized social relations, and narratives of progress, particularly the way in which gender is deployed as a trope to represent progress or its lack. We close the introduction by providing an overview of the chapters and an explanation for the book's organization.

"LOVE MAKES A FAMILY": HISTORICAL AND CROSS-CULTURAL PERSPECTIVES ON THE COMPANIONATE IDEAL

We draw the term *companionate marriage* from the English-language social science literature on marriage and family change (Simmons 1979; Skolnik 1991). In this literature companionate marriage is generally defined as a marital ideal in which emotional closeness is understood to be both one of the primary measures of success in marriage and a central practice through which the relationship is constituted and reinforced. The term *companionate marriage* has also been used in this literature to refer to a form of kinship in which the conjugal partnership is privileged over other family ties. In addition to these associations, we also use the phrase *companionate marriage* to suggest two core themes. The first is the idea of companionship as a deliberate goal of marriage and, more generally, the idea of marriage as a project, the aim of which is individual fulfillment and satisfaction, rather than (or in addition to) social reproduction.[1] Some of the chapters in this volume demonstrate the way that people put these ideas into practice, fundamentally changing the meaning and experience of marriage; in other cases, what is new is the way people evaluate their experiences of love and marriage in relation to this emerging global ideal. A second theme is the way the modern discourse of love provides a window into emerging concepts of individuality—for example, the idea that one particular person would be a more satisfying and pleasurable partner than any other because of his or her specific characteristics.

In the historical literature on love and marriage, most of which has focused on Europe, the term *companionate marriage* implies a constellation of associated ideals and practices, some (but not all) of which can be found in the cases examined in this volume: marriage based on a prior romantic relationship, individual choice in spouse, monogamy (as opposed to polygamy), sexual fidelity within marriage, nuclear family households, neolocal residence, the idealization of verbal over instrumental expressions of attachment (e.g., saying "I love you" rather than washing his clothes or fixing her car), preferring the company of one's spouse over familial or same-sex sociality, viewing marital sex as an expression and symbol of emotional attachment, and viewing marriage as "the presumptive venue of emotional gratification" (Kipnis 2005:88). Anthropologists, not surprisingly, have been quick to problematize these characteristics. De Munck (1998), for example, effectively demolishes the neat opposition between love marriage and arranged marriage, exposing the orientalist binary oppositions that inform these categories. Cynthia Dunn, for her part, points out that although companionate marriage can be said to predominate in both North America and Japan, in North America "the work of marriage involves working on the relationship itself to improve the couple's compatibility and emotional satisfaction. By contrast, [in Japan] compatibility and emotional fulfillment were much less emphasized (although not totally absent) . . . The focus was as much outward on the couple's place in society as it was inward on the couple's relationship with each other" (2004:365).

The contributors to this volume similarly complicate the Euro-American narrative about companionate marriage, showing that emotion, courtship, intimacy, companionship, sexuality, and fidelity interrelate differently in different places. In Nigeria, for example, courtship is a time marked by intimacy, with the implication that the development of this intimacy is a key preamble for a successful marriage. However, as Smith argues, postnuptially the affective qualities of the relationship decline in importance, to be replaced by a much more "traditional" emphasis on the fulfillment of reproductive obligations to kin. In Mexico, in contrast, ideologies of companionate marriage frame not just courtship but also marriage itself as an affective project (Hirsch 2003). In both the Gregg and Erickson chapters, furthermore, a central concern is the *tension* between ideologies of love-based marriage and the reality of marriage under circumstances of persistent poverty and gender inequality. In some of the cases presented here, companionship is centrally expressed through sexual intimacy, whereas in still other cases sleeping together under the same roof (rather than "sleeping together") is the principal expression of marital intimacy and is considered a somewhat racy departure from the past, acceptable only because of its associations, via missionary teachings, with Christianity. In some contexts, polygynous marriage is entirely incompatible with companionate marriage, whereas in others, the two can coexist, albeit uneasily at times. Our point, then, is not so much that marriages around the world are actually becoming more companionate—and far less that companionate marriage looks the same everywhere—but rather that the companionate ideal has grown in prominence as a part of the repertoire of concepts on which people draw when crafting their complicated lives, and that part of what is particularly hard for some is the very impossibility of building relations structured primarily around affect, pleasure, and satisfaction.

Although we recognize the Eurocentric nature of the historical narrative that we provide here, it is primarily these models of love and marriage that have been, and are being, globalized—through missionization, through mass media—and thus our goal in sketching out these fragments of history is to provide some sense of the eras and movements that influenced the American/Western European ideal of companionate marriage, which has been subsequently refracted and transformed around the world in ways that we address throughout the volume. Our goal is not to lead our readers to evaluate which marriages are more or less companionate along any one single scale but rather to encourage reflection about how these images of marital romance and intimacy are deployed symbolically—and used strategically—around the world.

Just when, and in what social group, one should date the development of the companionate ideal in Europe is far from clear. Some social historians posit that the ideal of companionate marriage had its origin in the *amour courtois* of eleventh-century Provence in which, ironically, the partners were expected *not* to marry. As Ian Watt states, "Courtly love is in essence the result of the transfer of an attitude of religious adoration from a divine to a secular object—from the Virgin Mary to the lady worshipped by the troubadour" (1987:136). In this scenario, elements of courtly love became embedded in marriage, and wealthy elites were the first to adopt this marital form because, being financially secure, they could afford to marry for love (Reilly 1980). Watt adds that in England, Puritanism, with its emphasis on "the God-given unity of marriage," was also crucial in the development of the "idea that love between the sexes is to be regarded as the supreme value of life on earth" (1987:135). Arguing that literature played an important role in promoting the companionate ideal, he observes (rather ethnocentrically) that "the Puritanism that is already strong in [Spenser's *Faerie Queene*] finds its supreme expression in *Paradise Lost* which is, among other things, the greatest and indeed the only epic of married life" (137).

Other perhaps less literarily-minded historians propose an alternative origin story for companionate marriage in Europe in which the poor, having little stake in ensuring ties with the "right" families, were the first ones to marry for love rather than lineage or property, while the landed aristocracy lagged behind (Benton 1966; Zeldin 1973). Historian Jean-Louis Flandrin, taking issue with the courtly love theory, argues that marriage in which personal sentiment took precedence over other considerations was a literary fantasy that only started shaping actual practice "when wealth became less a matter of land or other forms of real property and more one of cultural capital. Only then would the love marriage cease to threaten the social order" (in Illouz 1997:213).

In the North American context, magazines and court documents concerning divorce suggest that marriages predicated on romantic love—and divorces predicated in part on its absence—occurred as early as the late 1700s or early 1800s. Lantz, for example, cites a case from 1842 in which the Connecticut State Legislature granted a divorce to one Jabez Phelps from his wife, Laura, based on her desertion and neglect of duty, among other things, which Phelps himself attributed to her lack of love for him: "about the time of said desertion, she declared that she did not love her husband, that she never did, and never could, and never would love him . . . that she had nothing against him, he had always used her well, but she . . . had rather go to the poor house, and be supported by the town, than to live with him and all his property . . . only she did not love him" (Connecticut Session Laws, 1842: 16–17, in Lantz 1982). Of course, such documents do not tell us the social position of those involved, what options Laura may have had, or even what Laura herself actually said, thought, and did (the preceding transcript was based on her husband's testimony). Nevertheless, that concern about love was so elaborated in this document and in others analyzed by Lantz, and was, moreover, juxtaposed with economic security as a basis for marriage, suggests at the very least that love was a possible, if contested, rationale for marriage.

Both archival and more ethnographic observers of life in North America and Europe documented a shift, dated variously from the mid-eighteenth to the early twentieth century, toward a marital ideal characterized by a pronounced emphasis on emotional, social, and sexual intimacy (Stone 1977; Bott 1957 [1971]; D'Emilio 1999; Trimberger 1983). Participants in these companionate unions argued that they were inherently more satisfying and pleasurable than more traditional forms of union, but another aspect of companionate marriage's appeal seems to have been the way people used these gendered performances to signify their own modernity (Stansell 2000). Similarly, many of the chapters in this volume depict young couples arguing for the superiority of affectively oriented relationships by emphasizing the break with tradition, and so it seems worth noting how the deliberate crafting of a more modern gendered self was part of the cultural apparatus of these earlier shifts in marital ideals.

Around the kitchen table and between the sheets, men and women may make the history of love, but of course they do not make it as they please. Addressing questions of causality, Skolnik explores how demographic, economic, and cultural factors came together to cause a marked shift toward a companionate ideal in the late-nineteenth- and early-twentieth-century United States. Demographic transformations included declining fertility and infant mortality, so that couples had fewer children, more of whom survived. Combined with gains in life expectancy, these demographic transformations (which were themselves the product of broader economic and political changes) meant that couples spent a relatively larger proportion of their married life together without young children in their care. Skolnik suggests that intimacy-building stepped into the vacuum created by the decline in the relative proportion of their married years that couples spent caring for children. Urbanization and the spread of wage labor also promoted a nuclear family ideal by reducing people's access to and dependence on their own extended families and by increasing the privacy and mutual interdependence of the conjugal unit (for a discussion of similar changes in Mexico, see de la Peña 1984). Along similar lines, D'Emilio in his work on the history of gay sexuality in the United States (1999) argues that rural to urban migration and industrialization, along with a decline in household production, were the key material changes that made modern sexualities possible. Eva Illouz makes a parallel argument, saying that the expansion of the labor market in the first decades of the twentieth century enabled some women to become less financially dependent on potential husbands, which had the further consequence of shifting women's expectations of marriage from economic security to emotional fulfillment (1997).

But the increasing importance of romance within marriage in the United States cannot be attributed solely to economic and demographic shifts; the rapid spread of new images of and narratives about marriage also played a crucial role. Illouz's reading of popular magazines of the period, for example, shows that Hollywood was singled out and chastised for peddling improbable images of marriage: "Attributing the new definitions of romance to the enthralling power of the new media of film and advertising to shape fantasies, the articles argued that the new romance was the figment of an overexcited imagination . . . In short, marriage was perceived to be under the assault of women's increased autonomy and of Hollywood fantasies, which led to unrealistic expectations of marriage as an arena of hedonistic satisfaction" (1997:50–51). Increasing divorce rates in the early decades of the twentieth century were framed as a "crisis" in American moral life, and one response was the marriage education movement, which was institutionalized on college campuses from the 1930s through the mid-1960s (Bailey 1987). This movement sought to combat the supposed deleterious influence of Hollywood by assembling a cadre of experts, primarily sociologists, to conduct research on "typical" families and to provide youth with a kind of vocational training for matrimony. While the content of these courses varied, they shared a general "hedonistic-therapeutic model" (Illouz 1997:53) that attempted to integrate seemingly opposed discourses about marriage: it should be romantically thrilling but should also be based on scientific principles and hard work. In this brief history we see a complex chain of economic and demographic changes, media technologies, and state policies shaping American desires, possibilities, and moral evaluations of companionate marriage.

Ideas about marital companionship—although not necessarily romantic love—do seem to have a longer history in Western Europe and North America than, say, Nigeria, Papua New Guinea, or rural Pakistan, and one of our goals here is to trace out the mechanisms through which the companionate ideal has come to prominence—and been transformed and used locally—in these very different contexts. Recent ethnographic research in other world areas suggests that ideological and emotional shifts in the bonds of marriage are similarly tied to material and demographic transformations, as well as being shaped by media technologies and discourses linking new marital practices with notions of progress.[2] Drawing on ethnographic fieldwork in Spain and China, respectively, Collier (1997) and Yan (2003), for example, both argue that the shift away from family-based agricultural production toward wage labor was a critical aspect of the structural terrain in which companionate ideals grew in prominence. Collier also suggests that the consequent focus on individual achievement and consumption as markers of success reshaped people's attitudes toward intimate relations.

As in the North American context, however, the increasingly widespread conviction that love is the legitimate basis for marriage cannot be attributed solely to material or structural changes. The globalization of images and "proto-narratives of possible lives" (Appadurai 1996) has also shaped people's desires and worked to link this conjugal form to ideologies of modern progress. For example, Larkin asserts that Hausa viewers interpret imported Indian films as illustrating an attractive alternative to both Western modernity and Nigerian traditionalism in the realm of romantic relations (1997). Similarly, Wardlow observed while living with Papua New Guinea nurses that they often spoke of Harlequin and Mills and Boon novels—particularly those concerning relationships between doctors and nurses—as instructional manuals for how to conduct their romantic lives (see also Wardlow 1996). Importantly, economic transformations often work in concert with, and partially structure, globalized cultural forms: that these women were nurses meant that they were literate enough to read romance novels, had the money to buy them or were embedded in social networks that exchanged them, and were sometimes financially independent enough to resist the less companionate arrangements their kin or boyfriends tried to foist on them. Similarly, the Mexican telenovelas that have played such a central role in teaching women more modern forms of desire are only accessible to them because migrant remittances have made satellite dishes an affordable luxury—and because the Salinas administration, to shore up the ruling party's fragile hold on political power, worked hard at installing electrical power in towns throughout rural Mexico.

One observation we might make in this regard is that it would be useful to add contraceptives and the social marketing of family planning that has often been a key aspect of international family planning programs to the list of factors that have contributed to the globalization of the companionate ideal. We do not mean here that contraceptives have been a sort of technological magic bullet that has inevitably modernized intimate relationships. Instead, we follow the argument of Schneider and Schneider (1995), who have described how class differences in the pace of fertility decline in Sicily led to the rise of reproductive stigma, in which poverty, high fertility, and lack of sexual control became intertwined in the social imaginary for the first time. Kanaaneh (2002), describing the prestige of small companionate families among Palestinians in the Galilee, writes of a similar phenomenon in which women and men draw on values learned through family planning messages to evaluate the relative modernity of their neighbors according to their styles of reproduction. As Thornton (2001) has pointed out, the billboards around the globe that show how "the smaller family lives better" reinforce the idea that marital sexuality and reproductive patterns are a crucial means of demonstrating a modern identity that is both individual and national.

LOVE, MARRIAGE, AND MODERNITY

In very diverse ethnographic contexts, the authors whose work is represented here have found similar transformations in how people construct and represent their intimate relationships. As cultural anthropologists, we have found ourselves simultaneously fascinated and discomfited by the similarities. We are fascinated because there do seem to be real underlying commonalities in how the people with whom we work talk about love and marriage. We are discomfited because focusing on these similarities seems to veer perilously close to putting us in the position of serving up reheated modernization theory, in which inexorable social and economic changes produce progress—progress that can be measured by the degree to which the consumption styles, tastes, and preferences of people around the world come to mimic those of Western societies.

That we are not making a modernization argument is apparent for a number of reasons. First, our emphasis here is as much on the differences in how companionate marriage is interpreted worldwide as it is on similarities, so we make it abundantly clear that this is not a story about some inevitable march toward global cultural homogenization. Second, in several of the chapters, the ideal of companionate marriage is largely experienced through its absence; in other words, the cultural project described by these authors is not how people manage a shift toward a more companionate ideal, but how they negotiate the gulf between an increasingly pervasive ideology and their actual experiences. Third, our focus on individual agency highlights how—far from being the inexorable product of changes in the social and economic environment—the shift toward a more companionate ideal is the product of deliberate strategizing on the part of self-conscious actors. Finally, that this is not a modernist approach to cultural change should be clear from our skepticism about claims that companionate marriage is inherently superior to other forms of intimate relations— that the measure of human progress can be marked by a society's shift from

Figs. Intro.1, Intro.2, Intro.3.   These three images from around the world illustrate the ways in which family planning promotional materials have drawn on and reinforced ideas about the relationship between love and low fertility. In the first one *(above)*, produced by the Secretariat of the Pacific Community's (SPC) Population Project, a couple gazes lovingly at each other under a romantic moon, presumably enjoying the affective fruits of their demographic choices. In the second image *(facing page, top)*, produced by the Institute for Reproductive Health at Georgetown University (which promotes the global use of natural family planning methods), a young woman from Rwanda embraces her partner as they review together the "CycleBead" necklace, in which a string of color-coded beads represents the fertile and "safe" times in a woman's menstrual cycle. Again, as in the poster from SPC, emotional warmth and reproductive control are visually linked. The third illustration *(facing page, bottom)*, borrowed from Kanaaneh's *Birthing the Nation: Strategies of Palestinian Women in Israel*, "the cover of a pamphlet on family planning produced by the Department of Health Promotion and Education, Public Health Department, Ministry of Health, Israel, appeals to Palestinians in its invocation of modernity and middle class status" (2002:79). While Kanaaneh does not call our attention to it, this image shares with the others here the same presentation of the pleasures of togetherness as one of its key visual messages.

משרד הבריאות
המחלקה לחינוך לבריאות

تنظيم الاسرة

حقائق ومعلومات

وزارة الصحة ـ قسم التثقيف والارشاد الصحي ـ اورشليم

תכנון המשפחה

the burka to the bikini (see Stout 2001). Although many of our informants argued to us that this new form of relationship represents real progress for women, we see the shift to a companionate ideal as perhaps more accurately described as bringing a series of gains and losses, both for men and for women.

Rather than linking companionate marriage to the narrative of modernization, we insert it into the analytic of modernity, which refers both to (1) a periodization of "Western" history marked by a belief in progress (although sometimes also by alienation) spurred by a growth of scientific consciousness, an emphasis on autonomous individualism, and the burgeoning of capitalism as an economic order and ideological framework, and (2) "how people in different world areas have been impelled to engage the progressivist project of Western modernity" (Knauft 2002:13), ambivalently embracing, resisting, or reshaping narratives that force people to position themselves (and their cultures or nations) in relation to "tradition" and "the modern." By attending to the intimate, interpersonal, and affective dimensions of modernity, the cases discussed in this volume make an important contribution to this literature. These chapters make clear that modernity can be at once globalized and "vernacular" (Knauft 2002), material and emotional: the idealization of companionate marriage is increasingly pervasive, but also locally variable. It is about interpersonal affect, but affect that is underpinned by certain changes in the organization of production and consumption. We situate love and companionate marriage in three central problematics of modernity: the emergence of the individualized self; the related importance of commodity consumption to practices of self-crafting, as well as the significance of love in the context of commoditized social relations; and the deployment of discourses about progressive gender relations as a means to claim a modern identity, whether this is on the level of interpersonal relations or the nation-state.

LOVE AND INDIVIDUALISM

"i am through you so i"[3]

A number of our contributors observe that when young men and women talk about love, they may be talking about their specific relationships, desires, and practices, but they are also using love as a trope through which to assert a modern identity. This modern identity is very much about the cultivation of a more individualized self—a self who has a particular style, particular tastes, a particular constellation of relationships not necessarily based on kinship, and, finally, a romantic relationship in which each partner recognizes the uniqueness of the other. It is this mutual recognition of individuality, and the intimacy created through it, that is thought to provide the substance that will sustain the romantic relationship as it moves into the stage of companionate marriage.

Holland and Eisenhart (1990) suggest that individualism is at the heart of the cultural model of romantic love, at least in its American college student rendition: "An attractive man ('guy') and an attractive woman ('girl') are attracted to one another. The man learns and appreciates the woman's qualities and uniqueness as a person. Sensitive to her desires . . . he buys things for her, takes her places she likes, and shows that he appreciates her special qualities" (94–95). In this schematic model the central meaning of romantic love is the appreciation of an individual, and the practices that convey romantic love are geared toward expressing this mutual appreciation. While other components of the American model may not correspond to the meanings of romantic love in other world areas, it is true that in many of the settings in which anthropologists have explored local iterations of love, couples speak of courtship as a time to explore each other's personalities and to see how good a fit there is between each person's idiosyncratic desires and the other's ability to fulfill those desires. The idea that, for example, there might be different ways of talking (or of kissing), and that it is the individual's skills in these areas that will make him or her a good partner, seems strikingly different from the idea that one could know enough about one's partner by knowing his or her family reputation.

Discussing these issues in the North American context, Skolnik points to "emotional gentrification" as an important factor in the shift to a more companionate ideal (1991). The phrase, while problematic insofar as it calls to mind a prior mentality urgently in need of a bit of spit and polish, if not major structural repair, is meant to suggest a newly introspective turn in American life. Despite its problematic implications, we find the phrase intriguing in the picture it calls to mind of people purposefully cultivating modern selves. Stone (1977) uses a similar concept, "affective individualism," to convey the increasing glorification of personal emotion in England during the eighteenth century, and he similarly links it to a turn toward companionate marriage during that period. The implication here, of course, is that a companionate marital ideal is actually only one dimension of a much larger cultural transformation: the development of the modern individual self. Giddens addresses this point in his description of the transformation of modern kinship, away from relationships of social obligation and toward "pure relationships" (1992), in which relationships are governed by individual desire, pleasure, choice, and satisfaction. Some ethnographic evidence similarly suggests that the valorization of companionate marriage emerges concurrently with processes that bring about a more individualized sense of self—most notably, wage labor and increased commodity consumption, but also, in some contexts, Christianity (Ahearn 2001; Errington and Gewertz 1993).

However, the individualist characteristics important to romance are expressed not only through innate or cultivated skills, such as kissing and talking, but also through consumption. Quite centrally located in Holland and Eisenhart's model is "buying things"; one shows one's own individualism and recognizes the beloved's individualism through purchased objects that either enhance the self or symbolize one's uniqueness. Thus, in order to trace out the ways in which companionate marriage is tied to modernity, it is important to examine the relationship between love and social relations under capitalism, particularly the central role of commodity consumption.

LOVE AND CAPITALISM

The theorization of the relationship between love and capitalism has a long history and multiple strands. Engels, usually posited as the apical ancestor of such theorizations, argued that in granting people economic independence from parents, wage labor facilitated the possibility of romantic love (1985). Freed from the desire to maintain or augment one's holdings of private property, particularly land, from one generation to the next, the laborer was able to forge relationships based on authentic sentiment rather than on an instrumental logic. Also working within a Marxist framework, but far more skeptical about love, feminist theorists have argued that the conceptual distinction between public and private depends on a capitalist regime in which men subject themselves to the alienating world of work, while the feminized domestic realm is constructed as a safe haven in which social relations are untainted by calculation or interest. Love, then, far from being a human capacity liberated by wage labor (à la Engels), is critiqued as a mystifying ideology that serves to reinforce a particular construction of female gender as selfless, sensitive, and nurturing while also allocating to women the task of reproducing the labor force (Van Every 1996).

Taking the Marxist feminist argument one step further, cultural studies theorist Laura Kipnis draws on Marxist language to argue that companionate marriage not only facilitates the reproduction of labor but in fact has itself become an onerous mode of production, for both men and women. According to Kipnis, modern married couples—indoctrinated by ideologies of intimacy, the value of commitment, and the idea that marriage "takes work"—slog away at the work of conjugality.

> Wage labor, intimacy labor—are you ever not on the clock? . . . When monogamy becomes work, when desire is organized contractually, with accounts kept and fidelity extracted like labor from employees, with marriage a domestic factory policed by means of rigid shop-floor discipline designed to keep the wives and husbands of the world choke-chained to the reproduction machinery . . . It requires a different terminology. This mode of intimacy we will designate . . . *surplus monogamy* . . . (1998:291)

Just who profits from this "surplus monogamy" is unclear in Kipnis's model, making the labor analogy less than satisfying. Nonetheless, Kipnis makes the case—tongue in cheek we think, although we're not sure—that adultery can be considered a kind of workplace protest, "a way of organizing grievances about existing conditions into a collectively imagined form" (294) or, in its more utopian libidinal moments, the attempt to imagine "through sheer will, a different moral and affective universe" (296). While this manifesto is clever and entertaining, it is bound to strike the anthropologist as ethnocentric on multiple levels; for one, it assumes a voluntaristic and implicitly Western actor who can choose to "commit adultery" or not. The anthropologist, on the other hand, might immediately think more situationally of mine workers and sex workers around the world, who are caught in economic contexts in which choice is not so clear-cut (Campbell 1997, 2000).[4] Despite such limitations, Kipnis's piece is valuable as an exercise in thinking about the disjunctures between the ideal of companionate marriage and its lived realities, particularly when companionate marriage—and monogamy, as a key symbol of the trust and intimacy at the center of companionate marriage—are increasingly framed as markers of modern progress.

One final theorization of the relationship between marriage and capitalism—and perhaps the one that is of the most current interest to ethnographers—focuses less on the way love articulates with the organization of labor and more on its articulation with the organization of consumption. Eva Illouz examines the way in which commoditization and romantic experience have been mutually constitutive in North America during the twentieth century (1997). Analyzing advertisements, advice columns, self-help books, as well as interview material, Illouz argues that "commodities have now penetrated the romantic bond so deeply that they have become the invisible and unacknowledged spirit reigning over romantic encounters" (1997:11). For example, she demonstrates that the practice of dating—as opposed to calling on a woman at home—coincided with the rise in real income during the first decades of the twentieth century and quickly "made consumption an inherent element of any romantic encounter" (54). Etiquette books reinforced this pattern by defining consumption as symbolic of the "good treatment" of a woman by her partner. For example, the 1963 *Complete Guide to Dating* provides this little scenario: "There goes the phone and the call's for you: 'Mind if I drop over for the evening?' asks the current man in your life. And what do you say? For a moment you may feel angry: why didn't he ask to take you to a movie, or at least for a soda at the Malt shop? Well, simmer down for a moment before you give him a cold brush off" (in Illouz 1997:69). The marriage education movement, for its part, suggested that a reliable basis for marital success was "sharing common interests," which meant engaging in leisure activities—increasingly conceptualized as consumption activities—together. Commodity consumption was also necessary for the ongoing seduction that was the work of companionate marriage; as one advertisement for deodorant admonished, "Love cools when husband or wife grows careless about B.O." (in Illouz 1997:39). In other words, marital intimacy was framed as a quality that needed to be continuously achieved, and consumerism—particularly of self-enhancement products—was an important tool for this achievement. Illouz's work usefully elucidates a model of companionate marriage in which commodity consumption, individual self-crafting, and romantic love are mutually constitutive and underpinned by economic and demographic changes.

A recent example of this intertwining of love and consumption is a Harry Winston advertisement that ran in the *New York Times* in November 7, 2004; the photo shows a three-stone diamond ring priced at $8,500 and fancy pink diamond band at $15,000, and the tongue-in-cheek caption reads "Monogamy does have its thrills." To be sure, global inequalities shape these intersections between love and commodity consumption, and so it makes a difference whether the commodities in question are diamonds or soap. Without wanting to argue that love is a luxury reserved only for those who have assured themselves of food and shelter, we think the Gregg and Erickson chapters do suggest that it can be particularly challenging to construct love-oriented relationships under circumstances of intense material insecurity.

LOVE, GENDER, AND NARRATIVES OF PROGRESS

While our contributors sometimes diverge in what they think most characterizes companionate marriage in their respective fieldsites, or in the factors that have generated a shift toward companionate marriage, they all foreground gender in their analyses, and all agree that an examination of love and companionate marriage entails a focus on gender. First, marriage in most areas of the world continues to be premised on sexual difference; thus, entrenched notions of biologically-based gender and reproduction still dictate which couples may obtain legal and religious sanction to marry. Reciprocally, the social expectation that young people will ultimately enter a heterosexual and reproductive marriage reinforces gender as both identity category and practice, with young women and men disciplined to behave in certain ways because it is expected that they will someday be wives/mothers and husbands/fathers. As Borneman writes, marriage has conventionally been conceptualized as "establishing and giving gender its fullest meaning in heterosexual union" (1996:220) and thus powerfully fortifies what Butler has called the "illusion of an interior and organizing gender core" (1990:337; see also Rubin 1975). Indeed, marital ideals shape gendered practice even in intimate same-sex relationships, such as those between Hyderabadi men and their hijra "wives," a topic poignantly taken up by Gayatri Reddy in this volume. At the same time, as mentioned earlier, expectations for gender can conflict with expectations for companionate marriage, with potentially dire health consequences when it is assumed that conjugal emotional fidelity will be expressed through mutual sexual fidelity, an assumption that may be incompatible with gendered (usually masculine) prestige structures that reward extramarital sexual conquest or the ability to financially support more than one sexual partner.

One question that can be asked, then, is whether the ideology of companionate marriage has particular implications for gender identities and practices. Is it a potentially emancipatory ideology that can liberate individuals from heteronormativity? Alternatively, is it an increasingly global regulatory ideal that further naturalizes gender categories and "marginalizes, excludes, and abjects that which threatens to disrupt it" (Borneman 1996:227–28)? On the one hand, the logic of companionate marriage—with its privileging of sentiment, choice, and individualism over social obligation and complementary labor—would suggest that gender categories and the importance of gender difference might diminish in importance. If marriage is more about personal fulfillment than social reproduction, then perhaps the anthropologically classic kinship prescriptions concerning affinity and sexual difference matter less. John Borneman, critiquing anthropology's treatment of marriage as "the definitive ritual and universally translatable regulative ideal of human societies" (1996:215), has urged ethnographers to oust the heteronormative family as the basic building block of human sociality and to recognize instead what he calls the "elementary principle of human affiliation: the need to care and be cared for" (2001:37). The ideology of companionate marriage—in some of its versions—seems to embrace this "elementary principle."

Less rosily, on the other hand, companionate marriage is arguably the heteronormative ideology extraordinaire, asserting that women and men belong together not only for the purposes of reproduction and labor, but also for the only real possibility of emotional fulfillment. Certainly most globally-distributed movies and videos depict romantic love and companionate marriage as heterosexual. We argue that the ideology of companionate marriage can be appropriated and deployed for radically different personal and political goals, and that this is one way in which it participates in both a unitary, globalized modernity and its vernaculars. In the Papua New Guinea case, for example, young people employ an ideology of Christian companionate marriage against their elders in order to take the moral (and modern) high ground and thus get their way in choice of spouse. However, when some of these marriages go sour, their elders marshal this same discourse to reject divorce and to demand that young women "work on" their marriages and seek marital counseling from pastors, thus getting out of returning increasingly inflated bridewealth, even in cases where women have suffered extreme physical violence and/or infection with an STD (Wardlow 2006).

Despite the many vernaculars of companionate marriage, one aspect that seems globally shared, and that probably contributes to its global appeal, is its association with modernity—in other words, the discursive intertwining of gender, marriage, and progress, whereby it makes sense to a great number of people in very different places to use gender relations as a means of locating themselves and others along a historical continuum, labeling themselves or others as more or less modern or traditional. How has gender become an idiom of modernization, what sorts of concerns are foregrounded and obscured by using it as a lens through which to consider social change, how do ideologies and practices of love and marriage play a part in this idiom, and to what extent is the equation of companionate marriage with gender equality a discourse deployed by "the West" to measure "the Rest" and find them wanting? Moreover, under what circumstances do women and men around the globe choose to resist or even reject this gendered lens of progress (e.g., Amadiume 1987)?

The idea of a reciprocal relationship between gender equality and other forms of social progress dates back to before the Enlightenment, and traces of it are reflected in the writings of various eighteenth-, nineteenth-, and twentieth-century revolutionary and social reform movements (Kollantai 1978; Dubois 1978; Schneir 1972; Felski 1995) as well as, less stirringly, in the way writings associated with the development of colonialism worldwide use gender to portray the colonized as savages (Lavrin 1989; Stoler 1995; Mohanty 1991). The ugly side of these gendered measures of modernity is the way gender has been deployed discursively as a handy trope to exoticize various peoples who then become urgently in need of outside intervention to save them. It hardly seems possible to think of a more apt example than Laura Bush's radio address, in the days before the U.S. invasion of Afghanistan, deploring the burka as a marker of the oppression faced by women under the Taliban. Ironically, however, the notion of a gendered modernity has also been a crucial tool in the struggle for gender equality worldwide: respecting women's rights (or at least professing to respect them) has become a strategy through which both individuals and nations can demonstrate their modernity (Hirsch 2003; Gutmann 1996; CEDAW 1981).

Love and marriage have been easily elided into such narratives about gender and progress; companionate marriage and gender equality are often assumed to travel hand in hand, the former impossible without the latter (Coontz 2005). On the surface, one might assume that companionate marriage is automatically beneficial for women: most (although certainly not all) contemporary Western conceptualizations of companionate marriage presuppose partners who respect each other as equal individuals. In other words, marital partners may have different salaries or a very gendered division of household labor, but implicit in the ideology of love is the notion that as individuals they have equal value. Moreover, since the relationship is grounded in love, each partner should theoretically be motivated to sus-

Women of Iran

Fig. Intro.4. This drawing by graphic artist Marjane Satrapi, featured in a March 2005 article discussing how Iraq's newly elected government would choose to interpret Islamic law in light of how other Islamic countries have negotiated this complex terrain, used changes in women's head-covering and makeup (note especially the sly grin and the hearts on the headscarf in the last two frames) to make a point about the evolving "middle ground between Islamists, who want to stone adulterers to death, and secularists, who want a pure separation of law and religion." (*The New York Times*, March 13, 2005; used with permission of the artist.)

Fig. Intro.5.   Images such as this one of Afghani women in burkas were frequently seen in major U.S. newspapers in the days following the post–September 11 U.S. invasion of Afghanistan, and on November 17 Laura Bush took over the president's weekly radio address "to urge worldwide condemnation of the treatment of women in Afghanistan." The oppression of women—for which the burka was used as evidence—served in her address to symbolize the barbarity of the Taliban. The original caption to this photo in the *New York Times* (published February 23, 2002), read, in part, "Every catastrophe begets its own linguistic fallout—words and phrases forged by the awful novelty of the moment or catapulted from obscurity into everyday speech." That the burka became a sort of visual shorthand for the Taliban's barbarity indicates how deeply intertwined gender and modernity are in our everyday lives. (Photograph by Ruth Fremson, *The New York Times;* used with permission.)

tain the admiration, attachment, and desire of the other by not dominating or exploiting the other. Finally, implicit in the ideology of companionate marriage is the prioritization of and greater personal investment in the marital bond over other relationships. All this might seem to make for a situation in which wives would have equal authority over household resource allocation, more influence over a man than his natal family, and more control over reproductive strategies.

And while this all seems fairly logical, the empirical story is, of course, more complex, as the cases in this volume aptly demonstrate. Thus, while sustaining a sense of skepticism about narratives that link gender with modern progress, it is important to examine the potential benefits and costs of companionate marriage, particularly since some ethnographic data suggest that women in particular strive for this marital form.[5] In practice there are a number of potential costs to companionate marriage. Holland and Eisenhart (1990) argue, for example, that the American cultural model of equality in romantic love masks a stark gender inequality and that ideologies of romantic love may exacerbate female subordination by persuading women that "staying" in the relationship is the loving thing to do (see also Mahoney 1995). Rebhun suggests that a similar dynamic may be at work in Brazil; as one of her female informants said, "For me, love is the renunciation of I . . . When you like another person, when you love . . . you give yourself totally to that person, you forget yourself and remember to love the other person" (1999a:173). Moreover, in some contexts, companionate heterosexual marriage—however egalitarian—may be more constricting to women than existing alternatives. In her discussion of matrifocal and women-headed households in the Afro-Caribbean and in West Sumatra, Evelyn Blackwood notes that "there is ample evidence of kin practices and intimate relations without marriage or lacking marriage in the normative model" (2005:14) in which women control household production and wealth. Thus, the increasingly globalized images of modern, romantic love may, in some contexts, only serve to "denormalize other forms of relatedness" (15) and thus seal women into heterosexual unions that are disadvantageous.

Moreover, marital ideologies are hardly the only factors that shape gender relations within marriage. Discourses of romantic love and companionate marriage may imply a kind of equality, while at the same time local constructions of gender and economic structures may sustain gender asymmetry. Thus Giddens notes the underlying assumption (more often than not contradicted by reality) that both men and women are equally free to walk away when the magic is gone (1992); the fact that people say they marry for love does not mean that women cease to be economically dependent on men. It is the combination of women's economic dependence on men and ideologies about the importance of love in making a relationship successful, argues Cancian (1986), that has pushed women to specialize in the work of love. Relationships forged by choice, pleasure, and psychological intimacy may be less durable than marriages based on and maintained through economic ties between families, and so it follows that developing an expertise in emotion and the pleasure of others is a critical skill that women need in order to help these fragile relationships survive.

Around the world the popularization of this idea of bonds based on sentiment has coincided with rising rates of marital dissolution. In a sense, in relationships based on choice, the partners must keep choosing each other long after the marriage ceremony; women—and their children—may be put in a vulnerable economic position if men cease to make this choice. Particularly in the United States, some who have noted the trend have tried to stem the tide through interventions such as marriage education programs and welfare reform. The idea behind these efforts seems to be to exalt marriage's ideological status, to provide people with the interpersonal skills to be more successful at the project of intimacy building, and to reduce government support for programs that were seen by those on both the left and the right as having weakened women's dependence on marriage.[6] On the most basic level, this book speaks to the futility of those efforts. The genie is out of the bottle, and there is no going back to a time in which agricultural production, kinship organization, and cultural forces intertwined to make the coffin or the sea the only respectable exit strategies for marriages gone bad, and the priesthood the only route to avoiding it altogether.[7]

Finally, companionate marriage may be hazardous to women's health; for most women around the world, their greatest risk of HIV infection comes from having sex with their husbands (UNAIDS 2000). Increasing attachment to a companionate ideal, with its attendant emphasis on mutual monogamy as proof of love, may actually increase women's risk of marital HIV infection by reinforcing their commitment to HIV risk denial (see Hirsch et al. 2002, reprinted in this volume; Sobo 1995a, Sobo 1995b; Smith, this volume). Other factors (such as labor migration and masculine prestige structures) may continue to create conditions in which it is more likely than not that men will form extramarital partnerships. In rural Mexico, the shift to an ideal of companionate marriage has hardly meant that men have given up their "right" to extramarital sex; rather, they just work harder to be keep these relationships a secret—and their wives, eager to believe that their marriages live up to the modern ideal, are happy to collude in the silence. Thus, increased investment in the ideals of intimacy, devotion, and constancy may create a marital environment of greater disease risk when these ideals are either untenable in practice or no longer as seductive as they once were.

ORGANIZATION OF THE BOOK

The chapters in part 1, "Social Transformations and Marital Ideologies," analyze romantic love both as an ideology spread by globalization and as a practice propelled and constrained by specific economic structures and state policies. The widespread emergence of the idea that marriage should be a partnership entered into by two individuals and sustained by their emotional and sexual attachment suggests that similar kinds of structural and cultural forces may be shaping sexual and marital relationships across a wide range of cultural settings. However, as Maggi's chapter nicely illustrates, it is critical to be ethnographically specific about the source of companionate ideals and the specific local circumstances that make them available and appealing to people as a way of understanding relationships.

The chapters in this first part identify a range of ideological and material forces at work in the emergence of companionate marriage around the world. In Selina Ching Chan's chapter on the changing meanings of jewelry in marital exchange practices in Singapore and Hong Kong, women's increasing financial independence is key to making companionate marriage possible for the younger generation. By comparing women of different generations, Chan shows that as women have entered the work force, they are no longer as dependent on either dowry or approval from their natal families. Thus, they can choose their own partners, and they express this romantic autonomy by talking about jewelry as a sign of status and intimacy rather than a source of financial security and symbol of kinship.

In marked contrast to Singapore and Hong Kong, the Huli household in Papua New Guinea is still very much a unit of production, rather than consumption, and Wardlow finds that discourses linking love with modernity are more influential than economic or demographic shifts. Huli teenagers have adopted romantic practices, such as writing love letters, and they have become astute at marshaling Christian discourse to bolster and legitimate their desires to the older generation. However, there are many forces militating against the project of companionate marriage among Huli youth. Traditional ideology constructs the phenomenological experience of romantic love, particularly by men, as a state of being victimized by love magic. Moreover, a man's female kin often work to undermine his attempts to prioritize the conjugal relationship over kinship ties.

In the last chapter of part 1, Wynne Maggi questions whether romantic love and companionate marriage are necessarily linked to modernity at all. Among the Kalasha of Pakistan, romantic love—being "heart-stuck"— has long been valued, and it is culturally sanctioned (though always a cause of consternation) for women to abandon their arranged marriages and elope with the men they love (Maggi 2001). Thus, the ideology of romantic love and companionate marriage may be associated more with "tradition" than modernity for the Kalasha. Nevertheless, the valorization of women's right to elope is intensified in the contemporary context by ethnic and religious difference. The Kalasha, a small animist group, delineate their difference from neighboring Islamic groups by asserting women's "freedom"—freedom of movement, freedom not to veil, and, perhaps most important, freedom to flee unhappy marriages and to be with the men with whom they are in love. In sum, while the desire for romantic love and companionate marriage may be replacing other forms of union in various locations around the world, the reasons for this change may not be the same everywhere.

A second set of questions addressed by this volume deals with the ways in which local constructions of companionate marriage intersect with sexuality. The ideology of companionate marriage suggests that sexuality can directly generate and sustain attachment between couples, as opposed to indirectly and gradually solidifying bonds via its contribution to reproduction. Thus, the chapters in the second part of the volume, "Changing Sexual Meanings and Practices," examine what sex does (or does not do) to hold together modern marriages.

In the first chapter of this part, Hirsch and her coauthors explore how the shift in marital ideals from *respeto* (respect), in which unions are centered on the mutual fulfillment of a gendered set of obligations, to *confianza* (intimacy), in which trust and emotional closeness are the criteria by which women measure a relationship's success, shapes the social context of married women's HIV risk in a migrant-sending community. For the older generation, sex produced children and kept a man's attention. In unions of *confianza*, mutually pleasurable intimacy is said by women to strengthen the intimacy that is at the heart of the marriage. Thus, sexual intimacy functions as a kind of emotional glue for companionate marriages—making younger women even more committed than were their mothers to ignoring evidence of their husbands' dalliances.

In contrast, Erickson's chapter in this part, as well as Reddy's in the next, suggest that companionship and sexual passion are opposed. Erickson describes how adolescent Latino couples in Los Angeles are sometimes forced, in a context of emotional immaturity and economic insecurity, to respond to pregnancy by making decisions about marriage and parenthood. Thus, in some contexts, sexual intimacy is seen as a crucial building block in creating and sustaining marital emotional intimacy, whereas in others, sexual passion is seen as impeding genuine trust and companionship.

In the Nigerian context, young Igbo men and women equally expect fidelity during premarital romances. However, constructions of masculinity award status and a sense of accomplishment to men who have extramarital partners; thus, once a couple is married, a more hierarchical gender dynamic emerges, and "it is in the expectations about and consequences of marital infidelity that this inequality is most profound." Specifically, a man who cheats on his wife risks little social condemnation, as long as he provides financially for his children. Moreover, within men's peer groups, having female lovers is a sign of continuing masculine prowess and economic success. Igbo wives, however, are expected to be faithful, and many women continue to deploy ideals of intimacy and love to influence their wayward husbands.

Of course it is important to keep in mind that the broad structural transformations that seem to underpin companionate marriage reshape intimacy via their effect on the strategies formed in the hearts and minds of individual men and women. Thus, a third set of questions relates to who, specifically, is pushing for these more companionate relationships, and why. What specific advantages and disadvantages are actually present in this new form of relationship? While people may argue that companionate marriages are more egalitarian, the chapters in part 3, "Gender Politics and Implications," trace out both the costs and the benefits of modern love and examine marriage as an institution through which gender is negotiated and reproduced.

Among poor women living in Brazilian *favela*s (shantytowns) sex is less of an emotional glue for relationships with men and more of a weapon against them. Life is very hard in the *favela*s, and the possibility of an enduring companionate marriage seems remote. As one of Jessica Gregg's informants commented while watching a soap opera, "Do you think there is love like that? There is no such love. It doesn't exist. It's just a thing they put on TV." Gregg argues that while Brazilian women are certainly aware of the idealization of romantic love, structural violence and enduring patriarchal gender ideologies make marriage in any form undesirable. In a cultural context where men are expected to support women financially in exchange for control over female sexuality, virginity is an important means for women to assert their value as wives. However, since few poor men can uphold their role in this implicit bargain, many women assert that their *liberdade*—their independence—is now more important than virginity or marriage.

In contrast to the strategy of *liberdade* pursued by some poor Brazilian women, the "eunuch-transvestite" hijras of India are faithful to their "husbands," often to their detriment. While hijras are ideally men who have renounced sexual desire, symbolized by the ritual physical excision of the penis and testes, many have not renounced their desire for love and intimacy, as expressed in their longing for non-hijra male husbands. (In fact, many have not renounced their sexual desire either, and they seek out sex work clients as both a source of sexual satisfaction and a means to survive.) As one of Reddy's informants put it, "It is a different thing . . . it is not desire. It is a companion through life . . . It is companionship and the hope that the person will be there with you later." Despite the fact that hijras themselves have sexual clients, and their "husbands" often have socially sanctioned female wives, lifelong commitment to one's husband is held up as the ideal. These "bonds of love," as the hijras refer to them, often entail a reinscription of normative heterosexual gender ideologies in which the "female" partner is loyal and long-suffering, often in the face of abuse. Thus, hijras' "bonds of love" with their "husbands" may look more like shackles to the outsider, with many hijra "wives" enduring domestic violence and some attempting suicide on account of abandonment, neglect, or abuse by their husbands. As Reddy concludes, "Although providing powerful egalitarian ideals, clearly not all companionate marriages result in (and from) the empowerment of the 'female' partner in the relationship."

While we have divided this volume into three parts, in fact there is a good deal of overlap between the parts. Indeed, all of the chapters address sexual meanings and practices, social transformations, marital identity, gender politics, and ideologies of love. Essentially, the tripartite division of the volume represents not three separate substantive aspects of companionate marriage, but rather the three overall points of this volume. In the first part, "Social Transformations and Marital Ideologies," we make clear that these changing ideologies of love and marriage exist in some very distinct locations, and we suggest that the factors behind these transformations go further than just the worldwide dissemination of a Western ideology. The second part focuses on the transformation of sexuality in light of these changing practices of intimacy, highlighting the importance of exploring the affective dimensions of sexuality in order to understand physical practices. Given the invisibility of affect in most public health research in sexuality, we highlight this to underline the importance of the connection. Third, having described some of the forms of companionate marriages and provided some ethnographic richness in terms of practices of sexuality, we look at some of the implications of these cultural changes, particularly in terms of HIV risk and the persistence of gender inequality. Overall, our hope is that through this volume we can contribute to a new global approach to kinship studies, as we look both at the microlevel practices that constitute and bind relationships and at the macrolevel forces that shape the landscape of love.

NOTES

1. Giddens calls these relationships bound together by pleasure "pure relationships," but we prefer not to use his term, both because it seems overly evaluative and because it does not quite capture the way in which this shift is, in some places, more symbolic than material.

Nevertheless, we recognize that *companionate marriage* may not be the ideal term either. A central limitation of the phrase is that there are certainly marriages in which one observes a definite form of companionship that is not what we mean by companionate marriage. In Mexico, for example, Dona Catarina cried when talking about how she missed her *viejo* after his death, and the tenderness she felt for him—the product of obligations respectfully fulfilled, of years of careful attention to the minute details of daily life—was definitely palpable. It was not, however, the explicit goal or raison d'être of their marriage. Thus, we differentiate between marriages in which companionship and intimacy developed over the years as a product of living together and those in which companionship and intimacy are the reason for getting and staying married.

2. Recent ethnographic treatments of love and marriage include Rebhun 1999a,b, in rural northeastern Brazil; Kanaaneh 2002, among Palestinians in Israel; Ahearn 2001, in Nepal; Cole 1991, in coastal Portugal; Maggi 2001, in Pakistan; Pashigian 2002, among infertile couples in Vietnam; and Inhorn 1996, in Egypt.

3. e. e. cummings.

4. One also wonders about the advisability of advocating adultery as an emancipatory practice in a world where condom use is impeded for multiple reasons,

where marriage is most women's biggest risk factor for HIV infection (UNAIDS 2000), and where a sexual double standard often means that women are penalized far more than men for their sexual transgressions.

5. For example, in 1968 Caldwell noted that in Nigeria "a surprising proportion of women longed for a non-traditional marriage, one with much more spousal companionship and one where this companionship was reflected in sexual matters" (in Orubuloye et al. 1997:1201).

6. As of 2006, the current U.S. administration is replacing previous welfare programs with experimental marriage promotion programs as a strategy for poverty alleviation. According to this model, low-income heterosexual couples can receive monetary incentives and counseling (often religious in nature) for getting married, but they do not necessarily receive funding for education and job training. Evidence suggests that this plan puts the cart before the horse: the Minnesota Family Investment Program, for example, found that marriage rates among the poor increased *after* welfare funds were used to provide job training, child care, and "earned income disregards" (a policy in which employment income doesn't result in the cancellation of welfare benefits). See also Lane et al. 2004 for a trenchant critique of marriage promotion policies.

7. Those concerned with the extent to which marriage has come to be perceived as a project for personal satisfaction rather than a fundamental building block of social organization, however, have a good point, which is that structurally strong marriages were one way of efficiently managing a number of vital aspects of social reproduction (cooking, the care of the young and the old, etc.).

Part One

SOCIAL TRANSFORMATIONS
& MARITAL IDEOLOGIES

1

LOVE AND JEWELRY

PATRIARCHAL CONTROL, CONJUGAL TIES, & CHANGING IDENTITIES

Selina Ching Chan

According to Saussure, a "sign" has two components, the signifier (sound-image, object) and the signification (concept, cultural system); the relationship between these two are arbitrary (1974:69). Seen in this light, jewelry is perceived as the signifier that carries the meanings and values that are projected by cultural systems. The giving of jewelry is perceived as an embodied activity and one that is embedded within social relations. Like fashionable consumer goods, jewelry is "part of the process through which social groups establish, sustain, and reproduce positions of power, relations of dominance and subservience" (Bocock 1993:40). This chapter analyzes how messages are conveyed with jewelry as a consumer good through buying, giving, and appropriating it. Jewelry as family heirloom or as a consumer good reveals the changing meaning of patriarchal family and marriage. I argue that the appropriation of jewelry reflects how the power relationship between individuals is produced, reproduced, and challenged within the cultural system. The different modes and dynamics of consuming jewelry over time help in understanding how patriarchal control is realized, reinforced, or contested by people from different generations and at different times.

This chapter examines how the different ways of giving and receiving jewelry in two Chinese communities—Singapore and Hong Kong—reveal the meanings of marriage, the emergence of romantic love, and the elevated status of women in the patrilineal family. In Singapore, the Chinese are mainly descendants of migrants who came from China in the late nineteenth century or the early twentieth century. In Hong Kong, the Chinese are mostly migrants from China who arrived in the territory continuously after the 1940s. In traditional Chinese communities, pieces of jewelry were often given to the bride through dowry and bride-price to symbolize her entry into the groom's family. The dowry is received by the bride from her own family, while the bride-price is presented by the groom's family to the bride's. This chapter examines how jewelry in the form of dowry or bride-price symbolized both the love of the natal family as well as patriarchal control.

Nevertheless, the meaning of jewelry given to women has changed drastically over the years as the status of women in Singapore and Hong Kong has improved. This chapter will show that the declining importance of jewelry given by kin at marriage reflects the waning of patriarchal control over women. The giving of "wedding rings" will be examined in detail to understand the triumph of romantic love and conjugal ties. The fact that jewelry has become a popular gift in globally celebrated festivals of Western origin, such as Valentine's Day and Christmas, will shed light on the role of consumerism in the expression of love.

The findings discussed in this chapter reflect the responses of Chinese women from two different generations in Hong Kong and Singapore. The first group, composed of women from the older generation, were all married in the 1960s and are aged sixty-five and above. The younger group consists of women who were married in the 1980s and are around forty-five years old. In-depth interviews were conducted in a nondirective, conversational style with fifteen women from each group, most from middle-class backgrounds. Cases were also selected based on their clarity in illustrating the dynamics involved in their marriage and for the completeness of their information.

JEWELRY AS DOWRY AND BRIDE-PRICE: LOVE, ATTACHMENT, AND PATRIARCHAL ORDER

Weddings are one of the most important and memorable occasions for all women. It is in this event that women in Chinese communities are "overwhelmed" by the gifts of jewelry from their kin. Respondents in the older generation in both Singapore and Hong Kong received their first piece of jewelry at the point of marriage. They went through marriages arranged by their parents in the 1960s on the basis of having matching backgrounds. Romantic love did not exist, and marriage was meant for reproduction and the upbringing of sons. These women did not have a chance to date their husbands for any extended period before getting married. The husband of an old village woman in Hong Kong told me that he only managed to steal a "peep" at her while she was working in the field. The woman was even less fortunate; she did not have a chance to see her husband before they were married. In the case of another respondent in Hong Kong, the bride was from a poor family and had to go through a proxy wedding because the man she was marrying was a sailor out at sea at that time. In place of the groom at this wedding was a rooster, which served as his proxy.

In the old days, jewelry gifts were presented as either dowry or bride-price and were of special importance in a marriage. The dowry was received by the bride from her own family, while the bride-price consisted of various gifts presented by the groom's family to the bride's. The exchange of jewelry, in the forms of dowry and bride-price, was to mark a transfer of rights over a woman from the natal family to her husband's family. It is important to note that women of the older generation had no say over the nature of these gifts from the groom's family or natal family. The jewelry related to the bride-price was a result of negotiation between the bride's family and the groom's family. The jewelry for dowry was at the discretion of the bride's parents.[1] This passiveness and powerlessness reveal the bride's fragile position in the natal family.

The jewelry from dowry and the other miscellaneous items in the bride's trousseau were her only property when she married into her husband's family. Examples of jewelry in the 1960s included gold necklaces, gold earrings, silver earrings, and jade bracelets. Gold was indeed the most popular form of jewelry for the Chinese. This jewelry was combined with other dowry components—such as furniture, blankets, and sewing machines—in the trousseau for open display. Jewelry given by her natal family symbolized the affection and love of the bride's parents. The size of the dowry that the bride brought into her husband's family was very important. A large dowry would help a bride to appear good and decent when entering their husband's family (Chan 1997:153). It was a public display of her standing in the natal family as well as the wealth of her family.

According to my respondents, the more jewelry a bride received from her natal family, the better the treatment and the greater the respect she would obtain from her husband's family (see also Chen 1985; Watson 1985; Freedman 1966). Expensive jewelry was given to solicit respect for the bride in her new home, with the hope that she would be well-treated in her husband's family. Conversely, she would be despised by the groom's family if she did not receive a decent dowry. In other words, the amount of jewelry from dowry that a woman brought into marriage was a symbol that helped to affirm her status in her husband's family (Chen 1985; Watson 1985; Freedman 1966). Jewelry thus revealed the powerful grip of patriarchal control.

Meanwhile, jewelry was also an important part in bride-price, which was given by the groom's family to the bride's family. Unlike the cash and assets that mostly go to the bride's parents, the jewelry would normally go to the bride. In the 1960s, this jewelry included bangles, bracelets, earrings, and rings. Very often, these jewelry items were heirlooms, which were passed down from the mother-in-law to the daughter-in-law. In other words, a woman did not have much control over the ownership of jewelry. One Singapore respondent, who was married in the 1960s, recalled,

> My husband's family was very poor then. My in-laws did not have the money to buy me any jewelry. My mother-in-law gave me her jade hairpin and a gold bangle. In the past, women used to bundle their hair with a hairpin. The jade hairpin was a family heirloom and was therefore valuable.

The gifts of jewelry from the in-laws implied approval of the marriage and recognition of women's status in their husbands' families. They were of particular importance to people in the older generations, who only had their marriages confirmed through customary practices and not solemnized at the Registry of Marriages.[2]

Similar findings were also found among the Hong Kong respondents in the older group. An old village woman in the New Territories of Hong Kong, who was from a middle-class family and was married in 1957, recalled that she received a pair of bangles from her in-laws, as well as two rings from her grandmother-in-law and brother-in-law as part of the bride-price. Her own parents gave her a pair of bangles as part of the dowry. In fact, jewelry in the forms of dowry and bride-price were usually given by parents and in-laws. Only those from better-off families received jewelry from their parents as well as their close kin on the natal side.

In sum, the gifts of jewelry from the natal families displayed love and attachment extended from parents to daughters, while gifts from the grooms' families implied the establishment of a new relationship and the incorporation of the brides into the patriarchal families. However, women had no control over the type or amount of the gift and were merely passive recipients of both the dowry and the bride-price.

CONTESTING PATRIARCHAL CONTROL: CHANGING MEANING OF JEWELRY GIVEN AT MARRIAGE

In both Hong Kong and Singapore, jewelry continues to play an important role in signifying a marriage, but today it carries a different meaning. The wedding jewelry given and received through dowry and bride-price reveals the changing meaning of marriage and patrilineal ideology. This section will examine the decline of patriarchal control by investigating the changing meaning of jewelry gifts at weddings and the different modes of giving jewelry.

Respondents of the younger generation were mostly married in the 1980s. They are witnesses and beneficiaries of industrialization and modernization in Hong Kong and Singapore, where rapid social and economic change began in the late 1960s and 1970s. In these two cities, increasing numbers of women joined the work force as industrialization proceeded. A significant number of them did so with much higher educational qualifications.[3] Women of the younger generation have gradually gained greater financial independence and have increasingly taken the initiative to control their marriages. In 1971 the Marriage Reform Ordinance was implemented in Hong Kong, after which only monogamous marriages were recognized and the traditional concubine status was formally abolished. In Singapore, the Women Charter was implemented in 1961, requiring all marriages to be monogamous. It also safeguarded women's rights by legislation. With the enforcement of monogamous marriage, there was increasing emphasis on affection, companionship, and mutual care between married couples both in Singapore and Hong Kong. Romantic love rather than matchmaking has since become the more common route to marriage in both places. Today, Chinese in both locations get to know their potential spouses fairly well before marriage. The majority of them meet their marriage partners at the workplace or through friends. There is a transition from traditional arranged marriages to companionate marriages in which the meaning of marriage moves away from serving the interests of extended family to serving the interests of the couple. Marriage has today been transformed from an event that was strictly embedded in a large complex family system to an occasion that is largely taken charge of by the couple.[4]

Standards of living have increased tremendously over the past few decades. Upon marriage, women from the younger generations not only obtain jewelry from parents and in-laws; they often receive many jewelry gifts from their kin both in the groom's and bride's families. Although jewelry continues to be the major part of dowry and bride-price, it does not carry the same meaning as in the past.

In both Singapore and Hong Kong, the presentation of jewelry by families is now done at the tea-offering ceremony, where the couple would offer tea to the kin who are more senior than themselves, including of course the parents of the couple. Two such ceremonies are conducted, one at the bride's place when the groom arrives on the morning of the wedding day to fetch the bride, and another at the groom's. Two seats adjacent to each other are prepared for this purpose, which are to be taken consecutively by the respective senior kin in husband-wife pairs (a senior would sit alone if his or her spouse is absent due to death, divorce, or other reasons). The couple either bows or kneels before the parents and seniors while offering tea. After accepting and drinking the tea, each pair of senior kin offers a gift to the couple in return. The possible gifts include jewelry, cash wrapped in red packets, and sometimes watches for the groom. In Hong Kong, the most common practice is to give twenty-four-carat solid gold jewelry, particularly dragon and phoenix bangles. The bangles are usually as wide as 1.5 inches, look fairly heavy, and thus appear expensive. In reality, they are fairly light because they are hollow. The dragon and phoenix carvings on these bangles symbolically represent the bride and groom. Nearly all brides receive two pairs of bangles, one each from her parents and her in-laws. In some wealthy families, close kin also give bangles to the bride. After drinking the tea offered to them, the parents and the kin would present the jewelry to the bride by putting it on her.

Unlike the Chinese in Hong Kong, who treat the dragon and phoenix bangles as an essential piece of wedding jewelry, the Chinese in Singapore do not consider the bangle a staple piece of jewelry for the bride. Instead, it is common for in-laws (i.e., the groom's kin) to give necklaces to the

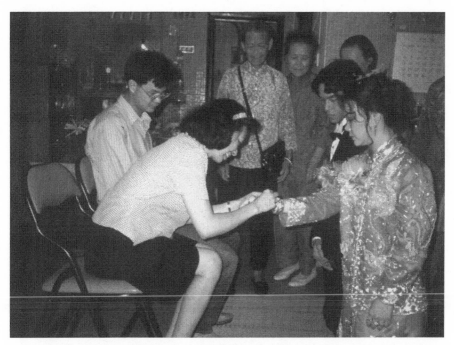

Fig. 1.1.   In this photo, a young Hong Kong bride kneels as she receives a set of bangles from her new mother-in-law. While young couples continue to receive jewelry from their families, they are taking an increasingly active role in selecting the jewelry to reflect their more modern tastes. Some have even gone so far as to sell the jewelry they receive, preferring to use the money in other ways. (Photo provided by Mr. Kenny Wong and Ms. Peggy Lo.)

bride. Since necklaces are worn on the neck, they symbolically tie the bride to the groom's family. Thus, a symbolic aspect of patriarchal control is also evident when the bride is incorporated into the groom's family. Moreover, the Teochew Chinese in Singapore have the custom of giving their daughters-in-law a "four-piece gold set" (*si dian jin*), which includes a pair of earrings, a bangle or bracelet, a necklace, and a ring.[5] Due to the influence of the Teochews, many Chinese of other ethnic groups also follow this practice of giving a four-piece gold set to the daughters-in-law and/or daughters.

In Hong Kong, the bride must wear all this jewelry after the natal-side tea ceremony as she travels to the groom's place. The jewelry that she wears is meant for public view as she enters the groom's house. A Chinese bride in Singapore is also required to bring along whatever jewelry she is

Fig. 1.2. This dragon and phoenix necklace, as its name implies, depicts a dragon and phoenix facing each other. Between them is the Chinese character for "double happiness." This was given to the bride by her paternal grandmother at the wedding. This necklace is considered to be unfashionable for everyday use, and the bride has worn it only once so far, on her wedding day. (Photo provided by Mr. and Mrs. Pang.)

not wearing in a nice box although she does not need to wear all the jewelry given by the natal families to the tea ceremony at the groom's house. This box of jewelry is to be displayed at the groom's house. Everyone else in the groom's family would therefore be able to see "how much" she has brought into the family. In other words, jewelry obtained from the bride's family has to be "on display" in the groom's house. This jewelry is one of the ways for families to show their love to their marrying daughters. However, the amount of jewelry that a wife brings into her husband's family is no longer important in signifying the woman's status in the husband's family. Instead, the educational background and financial independence of the bride play a much more important role in determining her status in the husband's family.

A tea ceremony would subsequently be conducted at the groom's house, similar to that held previously for the bride's parents and senior kin. Jewelry would similarly be given as gifts to the bride by the groom's parents and close kin. Jewelry gifts imply a symbolic acceptance of her into the groom's family. By the time that this second tea ceremony is over, it is not uncommon to see the bride wearing bangles all the way up to her upper arms and rings on all fingers as well as a dozen necklaces around her neck.

Today, in both Singapore and Hong Kong, the gifts of jewelry from both sides of the family imply a symbolic approval of the marriage. However, the gift of jewelry to the bride at her wedding no longer carries the strong connotation of patriarchal control.[6] The extended family no longer has such power over marriages as was the case earlier with the emergence of romantic love. Significantly, the decline in the patriarchal control implicit in the giving of jewelry to the bride is also evident in the new way of choosing the jewelry gifts. In the past, women did not know in advance and could not choose what they would receive from their kin. Today, many in-laws and parents in Hong Kong and Singapore invite the bride to accompany them when they purchase the jewelry. They let the bride have a say in what she wants although the budget is still of course determined by the parents and the in-laws. Brides are treated as respected individuals whose preferences are taken into account. This implies that the bride enjoys greater autonomy and authority than before.

In addition, the way women from the two different generations in both Singapore and Hong Kong handle their jewelry also reveals a weakening in the patriarchal ideology. Most of the women in the older generation mainly store the jewelry given to them, wearing it only rarely. If they do indeed wear it, they would wear the regular piece everyday. Many items are in fact intended to be passed down to daughters or daughters-in-law as family heirlooms. In other words, women do not have complete ownership over this jewelry. Some cases in Singapore reveal that women often pledged these valuables to pawnshops when families were faced with financially difficult times. In other words, a bride would have to sacrifice her personal possessions for the sake of her family when it was needed.

In contrast, women in the younger generation treated the jewelry they had received rather differently. For them, the design of jewelry received at weddings is quite old-fashioned. However, they all claimed that the pieces of jewelry given by parents and in-laws were special objects that bore sentimental value. Many of them did not hold as dearly the gifts given by their husbands' other kin. Some respondents even melted these valuables in exchange for cash. One informant explained while showing me some jewelry,

> These are wedding gifts given by a relative from my husband's side. I don't know them. It is useless to keep them here. I don't like these bracelets and won't ever wear it. I rather have them melted and exchanged for cash, which can be used in a much better way. The cash thus obtained may for instance be used to buy a computer. It is much more useful that way.

Similarly, another informant also melted several pieces of gold given by relatives on her husband's side. The cash thus obtained was used to buy a diamond ring in a design that she wanted. To these women, the paternal kin on the husbands' side are not of special importance, as was evident in this case with the melting of their jewelry gifts. This is however very different with the older women. They would never pawn or melt any of the wedding gifts unless it was absolutely unavoidable. The decline in respect for the more distant kin, particularly those on the paternal side, is therefore observed among the women in the younger generation. In other words, patriarchal ideology had been challenged through the act of melting the jewelry given by kin from the husband's family.

THE CHANGING FORMS AND MEANINGS OF WEDDING RINGS: PATRIARCHAL CONTROL AND ROMANTIC LOVE

Among wedding jewelry, wedding rings are of particular interest because they disclose further meanings of marriage, love, and changing gender roles. In Europe, a new perception of the wedding ring has emerged as a result of religion and the organized feminist movement (Awofeso 2002). Wedding rings in Europe were at first meant for women only when the gender relations were unequal. They were a sign of fidelity and a classification of women as men's property, a marker for discouraging potential mating partners from pursuing a married woman. Only in later periods, after religion reduced spousal inequality with profeminist reforms, did husbands begin to wear wedding rings as well and these rings become symbols of mutual trust and romantic love. In the United States, a comparable change in the meaning of wedding rings and gender roles was also found. Grooms' rings only became traditional in the 1940s, and men only started wearing this marriage token since that time (Howard

2003:837, 844). Wedding rings for men have become a sign of masculine domesticity symbolizing men's increased involvement in domestic responsibilities and embodying companionate marriage with its features of romantic love, companionship, and mutual respect (850). The wearing of the wedding ring by the groom suggests his willingness to participate in the new ideal of companionate marriage (851). Similarly, how wedding rings are acquired in Singapore and Hong Kong has also changed over time. The new implications of wedding rings on marriage and love will be detailed in the following section.

In Hong Kong and Singapore, women from the older generation did not receive any rings from the grooms. Many however received rings from in-laws as part of bride-price, and they referred to them as wedding rings literally. Similar findings are documented in an ethnographic book on Taiwan; it was observed that the groom's mother placed a pair of wedding rings (one brass and one gold ring) on the middle finger of the bride's left hand after the bride-price was settled (Wolf and Huang 1980). The gift of rings symbolizes the incorporation of the bride into the groom's family. After this particular ritual, the bride is considered a full member of her husband's family. Even if she were to die before the actual wedding day, the bride is still considered member of her husband's family. These rings are indeed given by in-laws as a sign of approving and confirming the marriage. In other words, the wedding rings are associated with strong patriarchal control, symbolizing the incorporation of the bride into the husband's family. They are meaningful at marriage in signifying the transformation of women's status from daughters to wives. Upon marriage, the wives are to submit to their husbands and their husbands' families, and wives' labor and reproductive power become the assets of their husbands' families. Thus, the wedding rings acknowledge the transition of women's status as well as patriarchal domination over women.

It is however important to note the wedding rings mentioned earlier were given by in-laws to brides. They neither came in a pair for both the bride and groom, nor were they worn by the men. Wedding rings only started to come in pairs to be commonly exchanged between bride and groom in the 1970s in Hong Kong and slightly earlier in Singapore. A shift from having the wedding rings as a gift that parents-in-law have for the bride to having them in symmetrical exchange between a couple has implications for gender roles and the changing meaning of marriage.

Respondents from the younger generation all had pairs of wedding rings exchanged with their husbands. Without a single exception, couples all have gone through an extended period of romantic love and courtship before marriage. Romantic love is therefore definitely an important ingredient of the marriage decision. Wedding rings are now no longer unilateral gifts given by the groom's parents to the bride. They are gifts chosen by the couple and are commonly worn by both parties in everyday life. Wedding rings are exchanged between the couples at the Registry of Marriages after going through the wedding vows and being proclaimed legally as husband and wife. The exchange of rings and the signing of the marriage certificate symbolize the contractual nature of marriage. This is very different from the vast majority of the people from the older generations, who got to know their spouses through matchmakers and were married according to traditional customs. Indeed, the rising emphasis on conjugal ties and declining influence of senior kin are observed in marriages today.

Women of the younger generation all rank their wedding rings as the most precious item in their collection, although they own many types of jewelry received at weddings.[7] This importance is definitely not based on financial value since the jewelry received from parents or from in-laws at the wedding is often more expensive. It is the symbolic value of the wedding ring that is important. In almost all cases among the younger respondents, both the husband and wife chose their pair of wedding rings together. Most of the couples would decide on either a pair of gold or white gold or platinum rings. Among those couples who are better off financially, it is not uncommon to have a diamond cluster or solitaire on the bride's ring together with a plain ring for the groom. It is also noteworthy that the names of the couples are engraved on their rings, with the bride's ring bearing the name of the groom and vice versa. In addition, the date of marriage and sometimes the word *love* or *promise* are engraved. A young respondent commented, "My wedding ring reminds me of him (my husband) . . . It has actually become part of me . . . I feel very strange if I don't wear it." Through the wedding rings, conjugal ties and romantic love are expressed and celebrated.

Although wedding rings continue to mark the transition in the status of the bride and groom, the implication is now different. Today, wedding rings emphasize the symbolic transition of both bride and groom from single to married. This is different from the past, when wedding rings emphasized the symbolic transfer of the bride from the natal family into her husband's family. Previously, brides and grooms were passive players in the transition process, while parents and parents-in-law took charge. Today, brides and grooms are the ones who decide on when and whom to marry.

Wedding rings are the language through which the active agency of couples is declared and romantic feelings are epitomized.

The emphasis on romantic love and conjugal ties is not only revealed in wedding rings but is also highlighted in the jewelry gifts given by the husband to the wife on other occasions. Unlike the women in the older generation who hardly ever receive any jewelry gifts from their husbands, many of the younger wives get such gifts from their spouses on various occasions, such as their birthday, Valentine's Day, wedding anniversaries, and Christmas. Presenting gifts, especially jewelry, in these festivals is becoming widespread in Singapore and Hong Kong, given the economic booms of the past three decades. These two cities capture the features of late capitalism, with the prominence of mass consumption. Romantic love becomes highly dependent on and easily manufactured by consumption. It is in fact popularized in mass culture, in particular advertising. Through advertisements, jewelry gifts from men to women are portrayed as codified love. Love is easily colonized by the market, is associated with economic practices of consumption, and is subsequently transformed into a structure of feeling (Illouz 1997). The alliance of love and consumption has become the "romanticization of commodities" (25). It is both a "way in which commodities acquired a romantic aura" through advertising imagery and a way "in which romantic practices increasingly interlocked with and became defined as the consumption of leisure goods" (26).

The use of jewelry as a gift for expressing love and celebrating conjugal ties is also observed in many festivals. Many younger respondents actually disclosed that they bought additional pairs of wedding rings a few years after their weddings. Some clarified that the old pairs were unfit because they had put on weight. Some others explained that the original rings were old-fashioned and they had decided to get new ones. The hidden symbolic significance is that love needs to be nourished and should be constantly cultivated through consumption.

As commodities consumed in the market, pieces of jewelry are imaginative tools for dramatizing romantic experiences and structuring feelings. One of my respondents would hunt around for prospective gifts before these occasions and then pass a hint to her husband after she had decided on a particular piece. She even told me that jewelry is the best gift because it is durable and long-lasting, just as a marriage should be. She said, "Food or chocolate are nice, but they would be consumed quickly. They are not long-lasting." Jewelry as gifts from husbands represents love, care, and concern. Jewelry is durable and therefore continues to remind her of romantic love and is thus a special means to consolidate the conjugal ties. As Illouz (1997) pointed out, love and conjugal ties are now emphasized and are often blended within the culture of capitalism.

Women are the recipients of jewelry while men are the givers. The unilateral practice of giving expensive jewelry from the husband to the wife reveals a kind of masculine love in the form that Cancian described (1986). Indeed, men's style of expressing love involves giving women important resources, such as jewelry and protection, that men have and women believe they need. Men become powerful providers through the giving of expensive jewelry and thus receive their wives' submissive love in return. Being a relatively passive recipient of jewelry from men, women have to accept a certain degree of dependency or loss of control. Indeed, jewelry is used to reinforce positions of relative power within the family. Jewelry is also a means to reinforce the patriarchal ideology, in which the relation of active dominance and passive subservience between men and women is reproduced in the process.

The practice of giving jewelry carries with it certain obligations. It is indeed common to observe that the wife has the obligation to wear and display these gifts at parties, dinners, and other social functions. Expensive jewelry worn in the public space also becomes a kind of wealth for display, in particular the wealth of the husband. This is revealed in the comments made by an informant who said that "the jewelry that the woman wears is a showcase of her husband's wealth. A prospective business partner may estimate the depth of your financial resources by looking at what your wife wears." Through the legitimate display of a man's wealth through his wife, she and her jewelry are "objectified." Women have become tools and subjects, to be used by their husbands to display their wealth in public.

CONCLUSION

Jewelry has been examined as an embodied activity that is embedded within social relations. While considering how and why the meaning of jewelry has changed, I have demonstrated how this meaning is tied up with social life and is produced out of socioeconomic and political changes. The different meanings of jewelry show that marriage has now been changed from a relationship that was strictly embedded in a large complex family system to a practice that the couple largely takes charge of. The shift toward conjugalism also shows a transformation from traditional patriarchal authority, with the husband or father in charge, to complementary marriage, with the husband being central and wife supportive (Young 1995:129).

Jewelry is shown to be an important symbol that displays love, status, control, and power in the context of family and marriage. It also provides important insights into changes in women's status and marriage. The different ways of appropriating jewelry reveal how different groups of women express and negotiate their social positions at different points in time. Jewelry constructs and communicates the relationship between individuals within the family, and it may also challenge the relative power held by individuals within the social system. Jewelry is not only a means for one group to express control over another but is also used to express resistance toward the control imposed by another group. In particular, it is a resource that the patriarchy, men, and women use to assert dominance or resist subservience within the extended or nuclear family.

It is clear that women from the older generation do not have much control over economic resources, tend to be more passive, and are submissive to patriarchal control. To a large extent, jewelry serves as a tool of patriarchal control, which is extended from their own natal families as well as their husbands'. Jewelry shows the subservient position of older women, and yet it also provides them a sense of security in the patriarchal family, since it reasserts their legitimate status in their husbands' families.

Nevertheless, jewelry is utilized differently and with new meanings in modern societies with ample economic resources and a dominant ideology of consumerism. Women's position has changed significantly as they acquire more education and financial independence. Today, jewelry given by in-laws, parents, and the husband's kin in the form of dowry and brideprice is no longer as important as in the past. Among all jewelry, the wedding rings exchanged by a couple have become the most important items, symbolizing romantic love and companionate marriage. Subsequent jewelry gifts from the husband to the wife on other occasions further reinforce the loving relationship. Nevertheless, the fact that men continue to offer gifts of jewelry to their wives to express affection demonstrates a symbolic inequality in their relationships. A new kind of gender inequality focusing on the conjugal relationship is evident in the modern companionate marriage. This is very different from the traditional marriage in which women are oppressed by kin in the extended patriarchal family.

In the consumer era, marital intimacy and romantic love are constantly cultivated and enhanced through occasional presents of jewelry from husbands to wives. Modern love is a product of changing gender relations and patriarchal ideology. It has become an ideal emotion between a couple in the modern world, one that is constantly encouraged, assured, and driven by the ideology of consumerism.

NOTES

1. As the status of daughters in natal families is significantly different from that of sons who are permanent members, they have no property rights or claims in natal families (Freedman 1957; Baker 1979).

2. In Hong Kong, marriages before 1970 were not legally registered but were mainly handled in the traditional Chinese way, which only requires the witness of kin as the legitimating authority in the marriage. Similarly, Singaporeans did not use the Registry of Marriage until the mid to late 1950s.

3. Since 1978, compulsory education has been instituted for children up to the age of fifteen in Hong Kong (Young 1995:119).

4. Meanwhile, family size has also changed from an extended to a conjugal model in which a couple and their children live in a nuclear family as in many other industrialized and urbanized societies (Goode 1963).

5. Teochew is one type of ethnic Chinese commonly found in Singapore. Others include Cantonese, Hakka, and Shanghainese.

6. In a multiethnic country like Singapore, the giving of jewelry such as four pieces of gold to bride and groom is a symbolic display of Chinese custom and a means to reassert one's ethnic identity.

7. Many informants own more than one pair of wedding rings, but they still consider all of them to be important jewelry. Some buy another pair many years after marriage for a new design or better fit (see the next section for more details).

2

ALL'S FAIR WHEN LOVE IS WAR

ROMANTIC PASSION & COMPANIONATE MARRIAGE AMONG THE HULI OF PAPUA NEW GUINEA

Holly Wardlow

Yalime, a young Huli woman with an eighth-grade education, had been taking secretarial courses in Port Moresby, the capital city of Papua New Guinea, until some senior members of a women's group used their social connections to have her expelled from the school so that she was forced to return home and agree to an arranged marriage with a prominent Huli politician. The intention was that the women's group, and the vast network of all their extended family members, would vote for the politician in an upcoming election; in return, the politician would channel funds to the women's group for development projects. Yalime's betrothal to the politician both symbolized the loyalty of the women's group constituency to the politician and created a social link between them. In fact, Yalime's bridewealth had already been given while she was absent; by the time she got home, confused and angry, she was already married, and everyone else involved in the transaction wanted her to start acting like it.

Yalime, however, had a Huli boyfriend of her own, a man she had met in Port Moresby who was, she said, a "good Christian" who therefore "knew about love," unlike her kin who were insisting on the arranged marriage. As good Christians, she told me, she and her boyfriend had agreed not to have sex until after they were husband and wife, but they later reconsidered this decision: having premarital sex—and somehow letting it be known or suspected that they had done so—could be used as a strategy to force their kin to accept their own plans for marriage. Premarital sex, either consensual or forced, is a common tactic young people employ to obtain their desired marriage partners, as it is considered a kind of theft of the woman's sexuality from her family and must be redressed, ideally through marriage and the giving of bridewealth. There were rumors that one of the members of the women's group had deployed this strategy herself, locking Yalime in a room with the politician. Most people were appalled by this possibility, and yet some considered it a clever countermove and what Yalime deserved for her display of autonomy and rebellion.

There is much to be made of this incident—not least the grim irony of a women's group derailing a young woman's education, forcing her into an unwanted marriage, and perhaps facilitating a potential rape in order to seal the deal.[1] However, it is Yalime's deployment of a concept of romantic love—romantic love that is discursively embedded in a Christian framework—that interests me here. Increasingly, young Huli people strategically draw on this concept, both to convince others to let them choose their own partners and to work at forging what they see as "modern" marriages—that is, marriages in which husband and wife not only cooperate economically but also enjoy each other's company, spend time with each other and not just with same-sex friends and relatives, and prioritize their emotional attachment over other kinds of social attachments and obligations. "God is love," young people say, and marriage is meant to be the joining of two Christian people united by love and by their mutual desire to obey God's will.[2]

Huli young people are often successful at choosing their own spouses; however, a number of factors militate against their attempts to forge companionate marriages. First, Christian companionate marriage is by no means the only model that informs contemporary notions of love; other, more long-standing discourses construct the phenomenological experience of being in love—particularly for men—as falling victim to deliberate magical assault by one's beloved (Wardlow 2006). In this model, the symptoms of romantic passion—dreaming about the beloved, obsessively thinking about her, feeling nervous and weak-kneed in her presence—are interpreted as resulting from spells meant to undermine a man's autonomy and self-determination. Perhaps more important is the competition that emerges between a man's wife and his mother and sisters, which also works to undermine the trust and affection that newly married couples are striving to sustain. Antagonism between affinally-related female kin is not a new phenomenon among the Huli, but it is exacerbated in the contemporary context in which men have more access to cash and women depend on their ties to men to acquire it.

ETHNOGRAPHIC BACKGROUND

Most of the research for this chapter was carried out from 1995 through 1997. It consisted of participant observation while living in four different Huli households, semistructured life-history interviews with fifty women, analysis of village court cases (most of which concerned domestic conflicts of one sort or another), and analysis of hospital records. Additional research in 2004 helped me to confirm and refine the arguments made here and to follow up some of the marital relationships described.

With a population of approximately ninety thousand, the Huli are one of the largest cultural groups in Papua New Guinea. Most Huli subsist primarily through horticulture; however, the economy is sufficiently monetized that cash is needed for transportation, school fees, clothes, pots and pans, blankets and towels, and some foodstuffs such as rice and canned mackerel. In the ethnographic literature, the Huli are known for extremely rigid gender pollution beliefs and codes of heterosexual avoidance (Glasse 1968, 1974; Goldman 1983, 1986; Frankel 1986). In the past, the health of Huli society and land was thought to be intimately tied to individuals' adherence to the rules governing proper heterosocial and sexual relations. Huli women did not cook for men, they slept in separate houses, they maintained separate gardens, and a range of taboos protected men from even the most indirect or metonymic contact with women's sexual substances. Thus, for example, some men will not eat sweet potato cooked on a fire made from wood that a woman has stepped over for fear that the smoke might carry her substances into his nose and thereby damage his health, beauty, and social efficacy. Such taboos were particularly rigid for newly married women: when menstruating they were not supposed to sleep, drink fluids, or have the slightest contact with others—male or female—through handing them things, looking at them, or talking to them. Accompanying these practices was a system of beliefs that characterized women as *ngubi* (smelly), impulsive, oppositional, and without *mana*— that is, without cultural knowledge or the capacity to internalize social rules. Moreover, it is often said that women "do not know how to speak,"

Fig. 2.1. Warfare, these days involving guns as well as bows and arrows, continues to be important to Huli masculinity. (Photo by Holly Wardlow.)

meaning both that they are not as articulate as men, and that as speaking subjects they are unreliable and often inscrutable (Goldman 1983, 1986). Such time-honored aphorisms are often deployed to discredit women as public speakers, as witnesses in the ubiquitous village court cases among the Huli, and as wives with opinions about and strategies for their marital partnerships.

In the contemporary context, it is still widely accepted by men and women alike that the health and beauty of never- and newly married young men are easily compromised by inappropriate contact with women. Nevertheless, some of the more arduous practices have been abandoned, and, largely because there is no longer consensus about whether menstruating women are "really" dangerous or not, it is considered the right and duty of each individual husband (usually influenced by his mother and older male kin) to determine which practices his wife will follow. Not only do individual men vary in the kinds of gender avoidance practices they undertake and the rigor with which they adhere to various taboos, but it is also the case that the same embodied practices can be interpreted and experienced differently. Thus, some men profess a strong need to monitor their wives for

Fig. 2.2.   Huli society is largely heterosocial. At this marketplace, for example, women sell produce in one area and men play darts in another. (Photo by Holly Wardlow.)

fear that women's innate carelessness and impulsiveness will have dire consequences, while other men, such as Igibe (discussed at the end of this chapter), view adherence to menstrual taboos as a health project jointly undertaken by the couple and, in fact, a way of fostering intimacy from afar.

DISCOURSE ABOUT COMPANIONATE MARRIAGE

It is primarily young people who are asserting desires for marriages in which psychological companionship and emotional attachment are the requisite antecedents and (ideally) the sustaining bases of the relationship. However, lest one assume that it is only young people who yearn for companionate marriage, it is important to note that a number of times when I was interviewing older women in the privacy of my flat, they would suddenly look around and then meditatively state something like, "This—what we are doing right now—this is what marriage should be like. Married couples should sit out on the veranda together and smoke and drink tea and talk." Or, as other women put it, they should "*wok wok, helpim helpim, story story, bung wantaim na lotu*"; that is, they should "work together, help each other, have nice conversations together, and go to church and worship together." Thus, older women too expressed desires for greater spousal emotional intimacy and amiability.

That smoking together is an important component of women's visions of companionate marriage might strike some readers as curious; however, this very concrete image is far from trivial. The rate of smoking among Huli adults is quite high; indeed, many people would agree that only the very old and the keenly Christian do not smoke. At the same time, smoking is primarily a homosocial activity, and many men assert that women should not smoke. Smoking in homosocial contexts (among women at market, among men in the clan men's house) symbolizes trust and congeniality, while heterosocial smoking on the part of women suggests a whiff of inappropriate sexuality, as well as a transgressive lack of deference to understood rules about proper femininity. Thus, when women say that a companionate marriage should include smoking together, they attempt to reframe the meaning of heterosocial smoking, at least in the marital context, and they signify a desire for trust, companionability, and perhaps most important, equality between spouses. The repeated image of intimate marital conversation in women's discourse about companionate marriage similarly signifies a desire for both an equal voice and a sensibility of mutual trust in the marital relationship.

This exegesis of women's discourse about companionate marriage is not meant to imply that marriages characterized by mutual warmth and companionability did not traditionally exist among the Huli. Many old women whose marriages had been arranged said that they eventually achieved an affectionate companionship with husbands, and the way in which they talked about their husbands showed warmth and tenderness. However, these women were careful to explain that this affectionate companionship had developed gradually over the course of the marriage, usually after their children had been raised, they had strategized together about how to participate in various bridewealth and compensation payments, and, importantly, sometimes only after the wife had moved back to her own natal land, a common pattern when the reproductive phase of a marriage is over. Thus, it was working, planning, and strategizing together over the course of a lifetime that built trust and affection—and these qualities were sometimes most enjoyable and rewarding only after a woman had gained some autonomy and had a house of her own back at what she still considered home. Moreover, some older women—and even some younger married women who had children—expressed wariness about the increasing idealization of marital intimacy and companionship (in sermons, in videos, in young women's talk), declaring, for example, that the marital exchange of confidences potentially undermined a woman's power; if a man really knew and understood his wife, they said, he could more easily manipulate, dominate, and take advantage of her (in interviews conducted in 2004 married men articulated these same misgivings about marital intimacy). Trust and candor, women cautioned, were best saved for conversations with one's sisters or mother. These comments suggest that intellectual and emotional companionship are traditionally thought of as achieved qualities in a marriage—not preconditions for a marriage—and while appealing to many, they also are viewed with ambivalence and not necessarily seen as the most important marital goals.

It is also important to note that women's pensive and sometimes wistful remarks about spousal companionship express far more than a desire for a different kind of marriage. Many of the preceding remarks suggest that companionate marriage is always about more than the marriage itself; it is also about certain lifestyles, certain practices, and a certain kind of personhood. For example, partners in a companionate marriage should have nice conversations, but the kind of relationship in which such conversation is possible is that between two individuals who have been properly shaped into Christian persons through worship together: to "*story story*" (happily converse) is not possible without also "*bung wantaim na lotu*" (joining together for Christian worship). Similarly, when women imagine the kinds of conversations that might take place between partners in a companionate marriage, they also imagine a house made from permanent, store-bought materials complete with a veranda, table and chairs, and an ashtray—spaces and objects associated with modernity (Wardlow 2001a, 2002a). Women imply that such modern possessions and practices automatically accompany or are necessary props for companionate marriage. Moreover, the kind of housing women describe is generally only available to married public servants; thus, when women imagine companionate marriage, they are also imagining a move away from subsistence agriculture and into the world of the salaried. Thus, for many women, both old and young, companionate marriage is as much about desired objects, spaces, and kinds of personhood as it is about a certain kind of relationship.

LOVE AND MARRIAGE, PAST AND PRESENT

The Huli have a long tradition of romantic love, or at least a long-standing poetic genre in which a female beloved is idealized, eroticized, and yearned for. *Dawe* (courtship) songs employ poignant tropes to evoke feelings of desire, attachment, and loss, particularly in relation to a man's first true love. However, these songs are performed solely by men, with a primarily male audience in mind, as a form of competition between male singing teams; they were not and are not used by individual men to woo individual women, and, in fact, virtuous women are not supposed to know about *dawe* songs, let alone sing them or compose them (Wardlow 2001b, 2006). Moreover, they are only performed in the ritual space of the *dawe anda*, a term that literally means "courtship house" but in the present context means something more like "brothel." As in the past, only already married men whose wives have had children (ideally two or more) are allowed to attend *dawe anda*, indicating that acute feelings of romantic and sexual longing are appropriately invoked only in a very specific ritual context and only by older men who have fulfilled the more important duties of starting families and contributing to social projects, such as bridewealth and homicide compensation payments.

Women who attend *dawe anda* are stigmatized; often they have fled unhappy marriages, and people assume that they have abandoned their families in order to sell sex. Nevertheless, some of them are eventually taken as third or fourth wives by men they meet at *dawe anda*. (No man would take a *dawe anda* woman as a first or even a second wife: his kin would refuse to contribute to bridewealth payments for such an ignominious match, and in any case *dawe anda* women are disparaged as lazy and infertile—not qualities men are willing to risk as they embark on building pig herds and families.) These marriages are thought of as "love matches," and the women are conceptualized more as emotional and erotic companions than as economic or reproductive partners. Such marriages suggest that romantic love need not always be kept safely sequestered in ritual space and can, in fact, be embodied in a wife. However, the practice of taking a *dawe anda* woman as a wife is highly stigmatized, and many men deride such marriages, sneering, "What would a man eat if he married a *dawe anda* woman, her vagina?" Comments such as these clearly vilify women who attend *dawe anda* for their illicit sexuality, but they also reveal that the dominant notion of wife is that of a productive partner, not a romantic or erotic partner. Moreover, similar comments—though usually not with the same graphic imagery—are used by the older generation to ridicule the love matches of the young today. It is scornfully said, for example, that young people who marry for love—"good Christians" or not—will gradually starve to death, unable to create a workable partnership for the necessary tasks of food production (and, it is implied, having too much sex, which is thought to overheat, drain, and prematurely age both men and women).

The way love is constructed in the space of the *dawe anda* contrasts significantly with the way love is constructed by Huli young people. In the former, love is always positioned as an object of nostalgia. *Dawe* songs are about the loss of a man's first true love, but they are only sung by men who are already long married, and the assumption is that one never marries one's first true love. Love is never what one has—except in the rare case of men who marry *dawe anda* women—and always what one has had to give up. Moreover, *dawe* songs are composed by and sung with other men, perhaps enabling a construction of masculinity in which feelings of longing and attachment are ritually eroticized, often trivialized and made light of, and ultimately consigned to the safe space of the *dawe anda*. In contrast, for young people love is the desired and moral basis for a modern marriage.

According to Robert Glasse, the first ethnographer of the Huli, most marriages at the time of his fieldwork were arranged (45%) or formed through what he called "betrothal" (45%). The latter category he explains as beginning with "a chance meeting in a garden or on a path" (1968:52) that eventually develops into mutual attraction and ends with the young man approaching the woman's family through an intermediary to request the marriage and negotiate the gift of bridewealth. It would seem, then, that the Huli have a somewhat long tradition of choosing their own spouses, presumably based on mutual attraction. However, what Glasse describes as "chance meetings" were, I suspect, more likely encounters masterfully engineered by the grooms-to-be. According to older men and women I interviewed about their first marriages, in the past young men "spied on" young women while they worked in their fields; gathered evidence that they were hardworking, generous, and good-natured; and then—knowing the habits and character of the desired young woman—planned a "chance" meeting.

A fair amount of erotic energy was attached to such stories: older women gleefully recounted the moment when their husbands confessed that they had watched and waited from afar, and women took pleasure in the thought that they had long been objects of surveillance and strategy, when all along they thought that first meeting had been one of innocent serendipity. Older men I spoke with confirmed that they had engaged in such crafty strategies and noted that although they had certainly chosen their spouses, they were usually pushed in the direction of certain young women by kin, and they made their choices based primarily not on attraction but rather on a young woman's reputation, the reputed strength of her clan, and the land that the marriage might give them access to. Thus, although Glasse's category of "betrothal" does suggest elements of free choice and romance, it does not convey the same meanings or motivations that young people articulate today when they discuss marital unions—actual or desired—as properly based on mutual attraction, shared experiences, and a sense of emotional intimacy.

Of the fifty women in my life-history sample, only a few entered arranged marriages in which they had no prior knowledge of the groom, and in this way Yalime's arranged marriage was quite atypical. Twenty women knew their spouses only vaguely before their marriages, and their unions were "arranged" in the sense that they were usually facilitated by the women's older brothers; nevertheless, most women took pains to emphasize that they had consented to these marriages after a brief acquaintance with the groom and were not forced into them. Ten women—the younger women for the most part—had become *lawini* (girl/boyfriends), often through school or church, and both families had eventually approved of the marriage, suggesting that the new heterosocial spaces of modernity are places where young people can learn about the desirability of companionate marriage and can meet potential partners. Sixteen of the remaining women were made to marry because of premarital sexual activity, or at least the suspicion of illicit sexual activity.

This method of obtaining a spouse—marriage because of premarital sexual activity—appears to be relatively new. In such cases, the requirement that the man compensate the woman's family for "stealing" her—that is, appropriating the sexual/reproductive resource embodied by her—overrides other potentially competing desires, such as her family's desire (and occasionally her own desire) that she marry someone else. Thus, although premarital sex is stigmatizing, particularly for young women, it is often a successful means for young people to foist their own wishes on their kin. From women's narratives it is difficult to ascertain to what extent these premarital trysts are consensual or not. Three women in my sample stated quite forthrightly that they had been raped and then forced to marry their rapists. In contrast, six women acknowledged that they had deliberately conspired with their beloveds in order to force their marriages upon the older generation. The remaining seven women, however, articulated narratives in which they were "sort of raped": they knew their assailants and wanted to marry them, but had not expected and were ambivalent about the sexual assault that had ensured that the marriage would go forward.

Young men, for their part, express much anxiety about their ability to assemble the necessary cash and pigs for bridewealth payments, and they worry that the women they have chosen will be married to other young men who are able to mobilize these payments first. Regardless of all machinations prior to marriage, time is often of the essence in Huli marriages. He who arrives with the bridewealth first gets the girl. In women's life histories there were often stories of expecting to marry one man, but then on the fateful day being married to another simply because he was able to assemble the necessary pigs more quickly. Conversely, I also heard of incidents in which a woman's family changed their minds about a marriage at the very last moment, and the groom, because his pigs were already in limbo—retrieved from various relatives and assembled on public grounds with no one assigned to feed them—quickly had to choose another spouse simply so the pigs could be distributed and put into the care of their new owners. Sexual assault of one's beloved, however, was usually a reliable means of preventing other possible marriages. Thus, if a young man believes that another suitor will be able to assemble the necessary bridewealth more quickly, then he may feel that his only guaranteed recourse is premarital sex. Most women, for their part, appreciate the desperate desire implied by such assaults, and yet many asserted that they had been afraid during the assault and ashamed afterward at having to confess the incident to the community.

Many Huli marriages, as is probably clear, pivot around the issue of bridewealth (Wardlow 2006). A father often needs his daughter's bridewealth to repay debts he incurred through marrying his own wife in the previous generation (see also Sturzenhofecker 1998), and his distributions of bridewealth ensure others' future economic support when his sons decide to marry. Moreover, the importance of bridewealth is woven into ideologies about biological reproduction: if a couple has difficulties getting pregnant, people will first wonder who was slighted during a bridewealth distribution and who might therefore be "blocking" the woman's womb. Similarly, when "promiscuous" women are diagnosed with a sexually transmitted disease, this is often attributed to the fact that they had sex without bridewealth being given (Wardlow 2002b). It is the giving and receiving of bridewealth that binds people together, both horizontally between clans and vertically between generations. Sexuality outside of the bridewealth system results in unmanaged and thus dangerous social relations and substances. And Christian missions, while attempting to discourage the exchange of bridewealth, have intensified the moral value placed on female virginity at marriage, the stigma attached to women who engage in premarital sex, and thus the importance of insisting on marriages between young people caught behaving improperly. Thus, while young people may attempt to make a case for love marriages by invoking Christian moral authority, as Yalime did, if this fails they—or at least the young men—may find themselves considering sexual strategies that undermine their self-presentations as righteous, moral persons.

WHY ROMANTIC LOVE AND COMPANIONATE MARRIAGE?

A number of factors have produced young people's desires for romantic love and companionate marriage. Most important, as other ethnographers have pointed out, these experiences and social forms are associated with being a modern person (Ahearn 2001; Collier 1997; Rebhun 1999a). A variety of imported mass media represent love both as a necessary precursor to marriage and as an attribute of modern persons. For example, in an earlier article I discussed the huge popularity of the Turkish movie/video *Teardrops* in Papua New Guinea (Wardlow 1996). The movie tells the story of a young woman who is cast out on the street by her husband because he falsely believes she's been adulterous, his realization—after she kills herself to prove her innocence—that he is the father of her child, and his eventually successful search for his son. In that article I asserted that Papua New Guinea women were drawn to the film because they felt that the unwarranted distrust of the female protagonist by her husband resonated with their own experiences. Equally important, however, is that the film's two romantic protagonists are represented as modern—they wear modern clothes and live in a modern house—and that they marry for love: they are shown talking intimately, eating together, walking hand in hand, laughing at each other's jokes, and even swimming together. Moreover, almost no kin from either side are depicted in the film; the viewer assumes that they are in the background somewhere, but they seemingly have no role to play when it comes to marriage. This is a union clearly founded on the mutual attraction, affection, psychological intimacy, and (initially) trust between two individuals.

In such films, to be modern is, among other things, to be an individual who recognizes certain traits in another individual, cultivates an affinity for that other individual because of his or her unique character traits, and becomes a more fulfilled individual through choosing the other. Thus, romantic love implies individualism, as well as taste, discernment, and choice (all also aspects of individualism). Even the martial arts and action videos that are more common in Papua New Guinea typically contain some sort of romance as a subtheme, and these romances are based on emotional and sexual attraction rather than social obligation and economic interdependency.

Imported Hollywood videos are not the only public representations of "modern love," however. Equally important are the Christian ideologies and practices that, albeit in a different way, also portray love-based unions as an essential aspect of modern personhood. Many young Huli women asserted to me that "God is Love," and they drew my attention to a verse in the Bible, Matthew 19:4–7, in which Jesus says, "Have you not read that he who made them from the beginning made them male and female, and said, 'for this reason a man shall leave his father and mother and be joined to his wife, and the two shall become one flesh.' So they are no longer two but one flesh. What therefore God has joined together, let not man put asunder." These few sentences are loaded with meaning for young Huli women. Most important, this text emphasizes the primacy, according to God, of the marital unit over bonds of kinship, and it discursively positions wives as equivalent and equal to a man's mother and father, certainly not a status new wives generally have in Huli society. Second, the text states that men should leave their parents to be joined with their wives. The Huli are virilocal, and this phrase has not been interpreted as asserting that marriage should be uxorilocal. Rather, young Huli women interpret this verse as a metaphorical reminder to married couples that men should work at psychologically detaching themselves from their natal families in order to emotionally invest in their marriages.

Thus, as Yalime asserted earlier, it was love between two Christian people that joined them together, and it was both un-Christian and "*bush kanaka*" (unsophisticated, too traditional) for the older generation either to force marriages that were not based on love or to prevent marriages that were based on love. The epithets "un-Christian" and "*bush kanaka*" are, of course, bases for two very different kinds of appeal. The older generation cares little if they are derided for being "too traditional" since many aspects of modernity—individualism, urbanism, increased mobility and autonomy—are frowned upon. To be deemed un-Christian, on the other hand, is far more problematic. Because Christianity is an important doctrine through which people now frame morality (Robbins 1998; Tuzin 1997), to be un-Christian is to be immoral. Since young people embed their desires for romance and love marriages within the discourse of Christianity, and thereby invoke Christianity as a moral authority for their desires, older people are forced into the position of being "bad Christians" or "skin Christians" (superficially or hypocritically Christian) if they obstruct such marriages. While young people's desires for romantic love and companionate marriage may be motivated more by the desire to be modern and less by the desire to be "good Christians," it is the appeal to Christian moral authority that lends persuasive force to their arguments.

Moreover, the church has promoted a range of practices that emphasize conjugality and the importance of the marital bond, and most of these practices have effectively changed the gendered nature of Huli space (see also Sturzenhofecker 1998). For example, most of the Christian missions among the Huli have urged people to live in "family houses"—rather than separate men's, women's, and bachelors' houses—in which persons of all ages and sexes eat and socialize together, a dramatic departure from the domestic arrangements of the past. Thus, two-thirds of the approximately thirty households that I surveyed lived in "family houses," and of the three families I knew who were in the process of building new houses, all had decided to abandon their gender-segregated housing and build family houses. Similarly, the Catholic Church, which with the Seventh-Day Adventist church draws the most followers among the Huli, demands that couples undergo Christian training and counseling for marriage before it will allow them to be married inside a church building. And Christian missions have been very successful at creating structural spaces that enable heterosociality among nonrelated young people. Thus, for example, many of the churches sponsor coed youth groups and coed volleyball teams that regularly throw young men and women into a kind of contact that would have been unthinkable in the past—again, contact that the older generation is uncomfortable with but feel they can do little about since these activities are strongly encouraged by churches.

Even the space of the typical Christian church itself facilitates romance between young people. Lucy was a young woman whose brother kept her strictly isolated in the home. She was not allowed to go to town, to play volleyball, or to meander from tradestore to tradestore, a common pastime on Sunday afternoons after church. However, since contemporary female virtue depends on church attendance, Lucy's brother could not stop her from gazing at young Thomas Terepa, who was up in front playing guitar every Sunday and who happily directed all his hymns to her. Neither family was in favor of the marriage, but since both Lucy and Thomas were active participants in church activities, had come to know each other through these activities, and had proclaimed their Christian love for each other, the families were at a loss. Lucy's brother, in particular, wanted a more economically strategic match than Thomas, who didn't work and who was known as a charming but lazy and unambitious young man. Thomas's own father, doubtful of his son's ability to maintain his own household, warned Lucy on her marriage day that she had better be prepared to do all the work. As he put it, "Now you have said, 'I am coming to join your family,' so what on earth are you going to eat . . . He doesn't have a garden of his own. He doesn't have a house. He doesn't work. He just sits around playing guitar [for church services, youth groups, etc.] . . . In the future your father and I will end up throwing blows at each other [i.e., the marriage will fail, and this will result in bridewealth disputes], so just forget about this."

In his quite public cautionary lecture to Lucy was an implicit critique of the church and the changes it has wrought—namely, participation in church activities is seen by some in the older generation as more of a leisure activity than a spiritual pursuit, and they believe that overzealous participation results in the neglect of everyday economic necessities. Moreover, Thomas's father expressed a common concern about the community-wide repercussions—namely, bridewealth disputes—that can result when young people choose each other without a thought for the economic interdependence that should be the bedrock of marriage. Nevertheless, Lucy and Thomas were successful in their bid for marriage, largely because of their invocation of Christian moral authority.

While volleyball teams and Bible-study groups have been successful in promoting a particular vision of marriage among young people, less successful have been missionaries' attempts to convince people to abandon long-standing practices designed to circumscribe the powers of female sexuality—such as the strict avoidance by men of their wives during their menses. Although most couples practice some sort of menstrual and sexual taboos, they are quite cognizant that the churches disapprove, and they are familiar with pastors' and priests' standard rationale that such practices denigrate women and erode the trust and respect that should be the foundation of a Christian marriage. The Seventh-Day Adventist (SDA) church, for its part, has condemned the exchange of bridewealth, arguing that it commoditizes women and thus weakens the proper bonds of marriage. This attempt to eradicate bridewealth has had mixed results: some SDA families I knew exchanged bridewealth anyway, or, if they were uncomfortable with flagrant violation of SDA rules, they distributed bridewealth pigs and cash to non-SDA kin. Some even converted to another Christian faith that was not so rigid about this particular issue. Nevertheless, even where Christian missions have failed in eradicating particular practices, they have successfully put the marital bond in the spotlight, emphasized its primacy among various kinds of relationships, and made people aware that Christian churches believe that marriage should be characterized by certain moral and emotional qualities.

LOVE AS COMBAT AND ASSAULT

Even as young people may be successful at bolstering their claims to romantic love through appeals to Christian discourse, there are ideological and structural factors that militate against the success of these love marriages. The first of these is an alternative cultural model that characterizes love and desire as a kind of combat between the genders in which men in particular need to be cautious and wary. The following popular myth well illustrates this construction of love.

Once there was a woman named Bebego Wane Pandime. There was also a man whose name was Gambe Kogo Ralu. Bebego Wane Pandime lived alone on her land and Gambe Kogo Ralu lived alone on his land. One day Gambe Kogo Ralu was out walking during the dry season and he became very thirsty. He spied two *keromi* fruit (red fruit the size of papayas which grow on vines that coil around trees). He was extremely happy. He climbed up the tree and grabbed the two *keromi* fruits and held one in each hand. Suddenly he heard a voice say, "Gambe Kogo Ralu, it's the dry season, and you must be thirsty. What kind of fruit are you trying to pick? Those are my breasts you've got in your hands, and I want them back." Bebego Wane Pandime then yanked her breasts out of his grasp. Gambe Kogo Ralu was very angry and embarrassed, and as he climbed down the tree he muttered to himself, "How can I get even?"

One day Bebego Wane Pandime went to her garden. Her house

was on one side of a river and her garden was on the other side. A huge rainstorm came, flooded the river, and swept the bridge away, leaving her stranded. She followed the river downstream looking for a place to cross and finally found a beautifully constructed bridge—not just a footbridge, but one with handrails as well. She had one hand on each handrail as she made her way across the river. Then she heard a voice yell out, "Bebego Wane Pandime, you think you're crossing a bridge, but now I'm taking my arms back!" The handrails suddenly disappeared, leaving her balancing precariously on the bridge. "This bridge is my cock, and I'm taking it back," Gambe Kogo Ralu yelled out again. Bebego Wane Pandime plunged down into the middle of the river. The flooded river swept her away and threw her onto the shore far downstream. Feeling cold and ill she shivered miserably as she made her way home.

One day Gambe Kogo Ralu went on a journey. He walked on and on, and on the way a huge rainstorm came. The rain soaked him to the skin, but there was nowhere for him to get out of the rain. Then he came upon a beautiful house with tall house posts. So he went inside and made a huge fire. He fed it with sticks until it was blazing, and then he fell asleep. As he was dozing off, he heard the voice of Bebego Wane Pandime jeering, "So now you think you're cozy and falling fast asleep," and then she removed her two legs. Suddenly the house vanished! The house posts had been her legs, and the nice dry roof had been her grass skirt. Gambe Kogo Ralu was left to be drenched in the pouring rain. He was furious and shouted, "Bebego Wane Pandime, you've really treated me badly now!" Then he thought to himself, "But what can I do in revenge? We've both tricked each other and treated each other badly, and neither of us has won, so what should we do? Let us forget all this and get married." And so they did.

This story never fails to elicit gales of mirth at the moments of salacious revelation. However, what is also interesting is that sexual desire, while metaphorically concealed, is depicted as something that feels like excruciating need: her breasts are fruit when he is most thirsty, his penis is a bridge when she is desperately stranded on the wrong side of the river. Heterosexuality here can be characterized as an escalation of trickery, a kind of combat that is fought through the manipulation of desire. Whoever wants the other more (i.e., must have the fruit, must use the footbridge) is the more vulnerable, and thus the loser. This notion of love as a kind of war, and desire as dangerous weakness, is quite powerful and pervasive among the Huli, and while this myth is intended to be funny, such feelings of vulnerability are often not a source of humor, particularly to Huli men.

Among the Huli, it is men who are the epitome of beauty and that which is desirable (Glasse 1974; Goldman 1983). During ritual celebrations, it is men who slick down their bodies with oil; paint their faces with bold yellow, black, and red paint; and don the long woven aprons that cover them in the front, but provocatively provide glimpses of their thigh and gluteal muscles from the side. And women? Well, "it is a shame," older men would sigh, but in order to attract men, mere physical beautification is often not enough. Women are not thought to be "naturally" beautiful and pure in the way that men are. Thus, women must resort to *hubi bi* (love magic)—spells that can be put into cigarettes, Coca-Cola, or betel nut, and then given to the male beloved so as to coerce his affections and attachment.

It is acknowledged by men and women alike that in the game of love it is not a level playing field and that women must sometimes resort to duplicitous means; nevertheless, the use of love magic is feared and frowned upon. Love magic is seen as an aggressive act: its intention is to undermine the autonomy and to appropriate the self-determination of the so-called beloved. And while most women talk about love magic as a means to secure the affections of a man whom they proclaim to love, some women talk about love magic as a way of "*daunim man*"—that is, a way of subordinating men—and they liken it to men's violence against women and to ideologies about women as dirty and untrustworthy, both of which they claim "*daunim meri*"—that is, subordinate women. Thus, it is not surprising that young men are fearful that love magic will be performed on them and that they will be assaulted and permeated by words and substances that will sabotage the inner sense of self-determination that makes them human (see also Johnson 1981).

And many men do subjectively experience the feeling of being in love as a frightening loss of autonomy that suggests the possibility of spiritual assault. My male field assistant, for example, fell in love with a woman during the gold rush at nearby Mt. Kare (Ryan 1991). They worked happily together as a team, he digging through the cold, rocky terrain, and she carefully inspecting each pile of earth for nuggets or flecks of gold. However, when he realized that he was taking far too many suggestions from her, following her advice, coming when she called, wanting to spend as much time with her as possible, even having the occasional dream about her, he immediately broke off the relationship in fear and anger that he might be the victim of her love magic and agreed to an arranged marriage. He confided that he still thought about this woman, and he agreed with my pronouncement that he had been "in love," but his interpretation and experience of being in love was far from benign.

STRUCTURAL IMPEDIMENTS TO COMPANIONATE MARRIAGE

Not all young men internalize such ideologies about women's innate duplicity and the dangerous nature of love. Indeed, some self-assured young men embrace the notion that love is a kind of combat, confident that they have the strength to withstand any love magic, and the charms and attractions to win any battle. Other young men deride such ideologies, labeling them "*bush kanaka*," and reject practices such as menstrual taboos as part of a self-conscious quest to be modern. Such young men are more likely to proceed forward at the point where my field assistant fled the field of love. Yet this does not mean that they and their female beloveds will be successful in establishing and maintaining "companionate marriages." Powerful structural impediments militate against the ability of young people to forge the kinds of marriages they envision for themselves.

Most important is the isolation of the newly married woman in her husband's parents' household and the attempt by a man's mother and sisters to undermine the trust and emotional attachment fostered through romantic love. The following case studies illustrate the power that a man's female kin can exert in eroding the psychological intimacy that characterizes companionate marriage.

Case 1

Kelapi and Hiwi, active members in the Catholic Church, fell in love and managed to force their relationship on their parents by engaging in premarital sex. Although bridewealth had already been given and Kelapi had already moved in, Hiwi's mother and sisters were determined to sabotage the marriage. They took advantage of Hiwi's absences to shove chewing gum in the lock to Kelapi's house so that she couldn't get in, and they threw her bedding down the family pit latrine. When this failed to drive Kelapi away, they physically assaulted her and told Hiwi that she had cheated on him while he was away. Ultimately, Kelapi's father was so enraged by how she was being treated that he ordered her to come home and refused to return any of the bridewealth, a result that was quite satisfactory to Kelapi by that point. Hiwi, for his part, though amorous and charming before the marriage, seemed to turn mute after Kelapi moved in. I never interviewed him, so I do not know what he felt or wanted during this period, but Kelapi stated that she was shocked by how easily and quickly he succumbed to his sisters' attempts to malign her.

Case 2

Malena had completed grade ten and had worked as a secretary, and Igibe had a grade eight education and engaged sporadically in a range of wage labor jobs. Igibe had "spied" on Malena as she worked in her garden and when she walked around Tari town, and eventually he struck up a conversation with her and the two of them fell in love. Malena was cheerful, hardworking, and generous, and Igibe's family was happy about the marriage. Both of them confided in me separately that they loved the other's company and felt that they learned from and were entertained by the other's conversation. Malena was happy and proud that she had a husband who would walk with her side by side through town and even hold her hand on occasion, practices that Igibe said he deliberately modeled in public in order to show Huli people how to be modern couples. Malena became tearful when she told me how Igibe requested that she come with him to the garden when she was pregnant, not to work, but to talk to him while he worked because her conversation made the day go by quickly.

Although they liked Malena and had happily agreed to the marriage, Igibe's family was not comfortable with this degree of affection and attachment. Igibe's female kin took him aside and told him Malena must be using some sort of love magic on him; they were unhappy with how much time he spent with her, that he no longer helped them with their own gardens, and that he shared his money with her and not them. They claimed that Malena had boasted about how she had him under her thumb and that she made fun of him behind his back. Eventually Igibe could not help being influenced by this campaign. Once while working in a hillside garden Igibe heard Malena and some other women laughing on the road above. He immediately assumed that she was laughing at his expense, and he ran up to the road and knocked her down. Shocked and humiliated, Malena ran to their household, got a rope, and attempted to hang herself from a tree, an acceptable recourse for women who feel falsely accused and publicly shamed by their husbands (Frankel 1986). Other incidents of a similar nature occurred until Malena and Igibe decided that there was no way they could make their marriage work unless they moved away from the influence of his family, an option that is not possible for most newly married Huli couples but was for Malena and Igibe.

It is clear from these cases that a man's female kin can exert a powerful and damaging influence on a couple's attempts to forge a companionate marriage. Struggles between a woman and her female affines is not new among the Huli, but love marriages potentially shift the traditional balance of power in ways that threaten a man's mother and sisters. In the past, a newly married woman had little power in her new household. She lived with her husband's mother during the first six months of the marriage, learning what was expected of her and working hard to win the respect of her new family. Only after she had planted and harvested a sweet potato garden did a husband and wife begin sexual relations, and usually they lived, slept, and ate separately. A man's primary emotional attachment was to his sisters, who could continue to depend on him emotionally and economically after his marriage. Indeed, when I happened to mention to some elderly Huli men that in America widowers tend to die earlier than men who are married, they responded that among the Huli there was a similar pattern, but it differed in that men whose sisters were deceased tended to die at younger ages than men whose sisters were still alive. In companionate marriage, the primacy of the conjugal union above other relationships, the emotional intimacy, and the material practices that stem from this intimacy all threaten the brother-sister relationship.

These tensions are exacerbated in the contemporary context in which men have greater access than women to cash through wage labor, and women's ties to men are an important means of obtaining cash. While a very few Huli women manage to make their way through the educational system and acquire jobs as nurses, teachers, and clerks, most rely on selling extra produce at market to make their own money. Aside from that they are dependent on gifts from husbands and male kin who have jobs, own trade stores, win money gambling, receive gifts of cash from bridewealth or homicide compensation payments, or receive lump sums of money from the local mining companies that compensate people for the use of their land. Just who is supposed to pay for things like store-bought foods and children's clothing and school fees is the source of much conflict between spouses. On the one hand, children are traditionally part of women's households and should be cared for by them; on the other hand, women

Fig. 2.3. A Huli family photo, with a man and his mother up front, while his wife sits in back. (Photo by Holly Wardlow.)

state that men are the ones with more access to cash and should therefore pay for such things. Men, for their part, assert that women unrealistically overestimate how much money men actually make and do not understand the multiplicity and complexity of economic demands made on men by friends and kin. In such a context it is easy to see why new wives might attempt to use the emotional attachments of companionate marriage to justify claims on men's money, and it is also easy to see why a man's female kin might be angered and threatened by romantic attachment and take steps to disrupt it.

"FOLLOWING RULES":
FORGING A COMPANIONATE MARRIAGE

Malena and Igibe's marriage was one of the few I observed that I would call companionate. By this I mean that they were one of the few couples I knew who married for love, who stated that they preferred each other's company over the company of other people, who asserted that talking to each other was one of their favorite activities, whose relationship seemed to be held together primarily by mutual affection and psychological intimacy, and who self-consciously reflected on ways to shore up this intimacy. This by no means signifies that their relationship was free of conflict. Like many Huli wives, Malena had threatened to kill herself a number of times and halfheartedly gave it a try once. Like many Huli husbands, Igibe had lost his temper and beaten Malena a few times, and indeed I got to know Malena well because whenever she fought with Igibe she would come stay with my neighbors.

And yet, Malena and Igibe themselves knew that they were different from other Huli married couples, and they cultivated this difference. Igibe told me that he sometimes held Malena's hand as they walked in public not only because he liked her but, more importantly, to demonstrate to other people that good Christian men did not shun their wives, and modern couples were supposed to display affection for each other. Thus, to my eyes, Igibe and Malena both were psychologically more intimate than other couples I knew, and they deliberately cultivated and performed this intimacy as an important marker of their Christian, modern personhood.

Interestingly, when asked what they thought made their marriage work, both of them elaborated on two deliberate steps they had taken. First, they had moved off of Igibe's clan territory and onto church grounds, which they said had reduced the potential for their kin to promote conflicts between them. Equally important was "following rules" (*bihainim lo* in Tok Pisin), by which they meant imposing on themselves strict bodily and spiritual practices that they believed would shape them into moral and pure persons, and thus would allow their marriage to flourish. To this end, they rigorously followed both a modified version of traditional menstrual taboos and a rigorous adherence to Christian practice, which entailed going to prayer groups and enrolling in a training course for lay pastors. In this model, abiding by menstrual taboos was no longer an expression of anxiety about "pollution," but rather a kind of Foucauldian work on the self through bodily practice and the regulation of desire (1990). Menstrual taboos and other sexual avoidance practices became for Igibe and Malena a joint, companionate, moral project. At the same time these practices were also an expression of care and intimacy from a distance: Malena confided that Igibe had fondly said he could tell when she started her period because he could feel a change in his own body, which she interpreted as an indication of the degree to which they were joined spiritually. She added that she liked it when Igibe moved out of their house for the duration of her period because she knew that he was washing his body at least three times a day, trimming his fingernails, and engaging in all the same cleansing practices that she was. For her it was a paradoxical time when they were distant spatially, but intensely intimate, both bodily and spiritually, because they were engaging in similar practices and devoting themselves to the same project of moral and bodily cleanliness. While Malena and Igibe were fairly unique in my experience, I did know a few other young couples who deliberately undertook this same amalgamation of Christian and bodily practices when their marriages appeared to be failing due to anxieties about love magic, suspicions of infidelity, conflicts over power inequalities in the marriage, and divisive pressures from kin. It was by recovering and creatively resignifying the traditional definition of marriage as moral, bodily work in the service of social reproduction that they were able to cultivate a kind of conjugality that was affectionate, emotionally intimate, and modern. According to Malena and Igibe, Huli companionate marriage required a specific kind of personhood, and this personhood, as they described it, was an amalgamation of the moral Christian individual and the Huli healthy and pure body. Both of these things could only be achieved through adherence to the rules that those theologies demanded.

CONCLUSION: THE FEMINIZATION OF LOVE?

A number of ethnographers have stressed the structural, and particularly the economic, changes that enable romantic love and companionate marriage to thrive as ideologies about modernity. Thus, some argue that women's participation in wage labor and their increasing economic independence mean that women have more freedom to choose their own partners and to conceptualize relationships as about emotion, not economics (see Chan, this volume). Others argue that as households become sites of consumption rather than sites of production couples are no longer as economically interdependent and that romantic love itself becomes an important site of consumption and a means to perform one's individualism, one's taste, and one's self-work. Still others note that in the context of capitalism, the home becomes ideologically demarcated as the safe haven of emotional intimacy, a place where one recovers from the alienation of the marketplace. Romantic love is idealized as a domain free from the values of capitalism, and habitation within this domain rejuvenates the worker enough to face the onslaughts of capitalism once again.

Among the Huli, households are still primarily sites of cooperative production, women are not economically independent, and the home is not a site of emotional respite from wage labor. If anything, structural factors—primarily kin relations—significantly constrain companionate marriage, if not romantic love. The idealization of romantic love and companionate marriage infuses itself into the Huli cultural repertoire through mass media, Christian sermons, and the exegesis of Christian text. This idealization is mobilized, particularly by young people, as a means to forge themselves as modern persons and to resist those structures that would seal them into the sociopolitical webs of power created and sustained by practices like bridewealth.

A number of ethnographers have observed that romantic love, and especially companionate marriage, are desired and valued more by women than men in many areas of the world, perhaps because of the apparent (and perhaps misleading) promise that companionate marriage entails less hierarchical gender relations. Rebhun, for example, notes that in the Brazilian context romantic courtship leads women to expect a companionate marriage, and they assume that egalitarian gender relations established during courtship will endure into marriage. However, "when a man courts a woman, his actions are influenced by his desire to prove his sincerity to her . . . But once a couple marries . . . his actions are directed toward another audience, his . . . male buddies, to whom he must prove he is not controlled by his wife" (1999a:176). Daniel Smith (this volume) similarly notes that while gender relations are typically egalitarian during courtship, "a more patriarchal gender dynamic emerges after marriage. It is in the expectations about and consequences of marital infidelity that this inequality is most profound."

Like their Nigerian and Brazilian counterparts, young Huli women are also more outspoken than Huli men about their desires and hopes for romantic love and companionate marriage. There are a number of reasons why this would be the case. First, romantic love and its accompanying practices are one of the few means that women have to enact modern personhood. Young men may attend school, travel to cities, wear jeans and Blundstone boots, become part of a politician's entourage, and buy radios and cultivate a knowledge of various bands. Women's resources for cultivating and displaying a modern sensibility are far fewer (Wardlow 2002c). Being in love, however, opens up the possibility of publicly sharing a Coke with or writing letters to one's beloved (Ahearn 2001), behaviors that are considered modern and for which young women are castigated but that they engage in anyway. Love letters in particular are important ways in which young women broadcast that they are literate, know about love, and are familiar with modern teenage conventions for expressing love, such as writing HOLLAND at the end of a letter (an acronym for "hope our love lasts and never dies").

Many women also assert that bridewealth and marriage are becoming more commoditized—that while women used to be the desired items of value for which men gave pigs, now cash is the desired item for which men give women (Wardlow 2004). In the past, they say, the emotional benefits of marriage came from natal kin; that is, women were valued by their kin for the wealth that they brought in to their clans upon marriage and for the political and economic ties they helped to create between brothers-in-law. Now, they assert, although women's bridewealth is valued, the women themselves are not, and women lament that they feel abandoned by their kin after marriage. Thus, women may be seeking more emotional benefits from marriage itself, and marriage may not seem "worth it" unless love can be privileged as a criterion in the selection of spouse.

Finally, perhaps like their counterparts in Nigeria and Brazil, young Huli women do hope that romantic love will bloom into companionate marriage, which will entail more and different kinds of power than was exercised by women of previous generations. Women hope that if they develop a relationship characterized by *"wok wok, helpim helpim, story story, bung wantaim na lotu,"* they and their husbands will peaceably decide together how to pay for children's school fees, how to manage kin relations, whether to use birth control, how much a husband should spend gambling on darts and billiards, and whether a man should take additional wives—all decisions that most women feel are made unilaterally (and not to their liking) by a husband, or together, but only after expressions of resentment, self-righteous anger, and fragile negotiations on both sides. In other words, women hope to reframe these issues as jointly shared problems and projects instead of sites where gendered power must be exerted and resisted time and again. Thus, romantic love and companionate marriage are polysemous ideologies that encompass and signify a range of things: the delights of emotional passion, a means to enact and display a modern individualism as well as an upright Christian identity, a means to resist or redress the commoditization of bridewealth, and the hope for a psychological attachment that will readjust the political landscape of Huli gender relations.

NOTES

1. When I pointed out to a few members of this women's group that their behavior toward Yalime might appear to contradict their stated goals of empowerment and development for women, they flatly replied that "development" meant income generation, which required the political connections that the politician could provide. Other issues, such as combating violence against women or increasing their autonomy, came second after economic power. Individual women had to be prepared to make sacrifices for this larger goal of strengthening the women's group economically and politically.

2. The conflict between Yalime and her kin had not been resolved when I completed my doctoral fieldwork in 1997: the politician was getting increasingly annoyed about the failure of the women's group to coerce Yalime into cooperating, and Yalime was trying to find work as a secretary, hoping that a salary would enable her to avoid coercion from all parties, including her boyfriend, who was becoming increasingly insistent that they flee back to Port Moresby, but who was not very forthcoming about when and how he would pay Yalime's bridewealth. I returned to Papua New Guinea in 2004 and learned that Yalime had eventually succeeded in marrying her boyfriend, to the annoyance of the women's group, but to the relief of the politician who was happy to escape a situation that had become awkward and embarrassing. Interestingly, the women's group seemed to have adopted a different strategy of empowerment: it was using some of its funds to pay for the tertiary education of a few young women, particularly those who showed loyalty to the group and who were willing to go into fields chosen by the women's group: rural agricultural economics (to come back and help the group develop coffee and other cash crops), anything to do with the mining industry (Porgera Joint Venture, a gold mine, was the area's most important source of jobs at that time), and architecture and urban planning (the group optimistically hoped that economic development would come to the area, and when it did they wanted one of their own ready to take any job available for designing new government buildings).

To many people's surprise (although not all), it turned out that Yalime's boyfriend (now husband) already had a wife that he had not told Yalime about. In his mind, polygyny was compatible with the Christian companionate marriage he intended to forge with Yalime. She did not see it that way but had failed to find work, was economically dependent on her husband, and thus found herself trapped in a marriage that was not what she had expected or fought for. This story and others I heard in 2004 suggest that while young women may set their hearts on companionate, monogamous marriage (and assume that their partners share their vision), polygamy can provide men with the possibility of trying different kinds of marriage simultaneously ("traditional" with one wife, companionate with another, and so on). As polygamy becomes more and more frowned upon (because it is seen as un-Christian and too traditional) and less and less affordable for most men (because of a deterioration in the economy, loss of jobs in the area, and devaluation of the national currency), I suspect this emotional/economic strategy will diminish.

3

———

"HEART-STUCK"

LOVE MARRIAGE AS A MARKER OF ETHNIC IDENTITY AMONG THE KALASHA OF NORTHWEST PAKISTAN

Wynne Maggi

Zailun first saw Miramin at a funeral in Rumbur valley. Zailun was only twelve, not even menstruating yet. She had made the long trek over the rocky pass from her natal home in Bumboret Valley with her parents. Almost everyone from Bumboret had come, including Zailun's husband, a good man chosen by her father several years earlier. "Good," says Zailun, "Yes, he was good. He tried to be kind. He never forced himself on me. But I thought he was awful." At the funeral, a major event involving three days of nonstop singing, dancing, and feasting, Zailun and Miramin didn't talk to one another. They didn't dance near one another. But they both knew: They were "heart-stuck," *hardi satik,* which literally means that their hearts had joined, connected. Miramin's mother told me that her son had pulled her aside and pointed out Zailun. "I'll make that girl my wife," he proclaimed. "You must allow it this time, Mother. You never like the girls I choose. You always find something wrong. But this time, please, she is the one I want."

After that first meeting, Miramin would come to Bumboret valley and camp out along the river for days, just to get a glimpse of Zailun sitting on the high porch at her parents' summerhouse. Remembering their

Fig. 3.1. Miramin and Zailun first became "heart-stuck" at a funeral like this one. Kalasha people from all three valleys have come together to celebrate and mourn and dance—and court. (Photo by Wynne Maggi.)

courtship, Zailun says, "From the time I was small I was so in love . . . He came all the time to Bumboret, we saw one another and fell in love[1]—just like you say—love at first sight. For three or four years we made love—not bad works [they were not sexually involved], no, only with words. We would look at one another and get happy. He'd bring me little gifts. In love. So, if I saw him far away, I would get so happy. My heart would bloom like a flower—I've seen my friend! He never asked to sleep [have sex] with me. He said to other people, 'I'll lead that girl [elope with her]'."

Miramin's friends started approaching Zailun, telling her that he was talking of eloping with her. She would say, "Well, good. Later I'll see." Every twenty days or so, his friends would come back, urging her to "give straight words," telling her that Miramin liked her so much that he was becoming crazy, urging her to agree to elope with him. She also liked him, but she would say, "I'll see later. Now I can't come. I am a man's wife. One year later, two years later, three years later, we'll see." They were in love for four years. Then during a harvest night dance, when everyone thought she was sleeping, Zailun evaded her husband's friends who were standing guard outside her parents' house, scrambled over the steep scree slopes, and descended into a high pasture where Miramin was waiting for her.

The price for her elopement was steep. Zailun's father and grandfather and uncles had formed a strong and deep *khaltabar* (in-law) relationship with her former husband. They felt Zailun had betrayed her natal family. For two years, Zailun could not visit her home, even to attend her beloved grandfather's funeral. Miramin did not dare go into Bumboret for fear of being beaten by his wife's former husband and his friends. Finally, Zailun's former husband accepted the customary double bridewealth payment. Zailun says that these words convinced him to overcome his violent animosity: "Are you Muslims that you fight like this? No, we're Kalasha! When love 'sticks,' we exchange bridewealth and resolve our differences."

Before I mine Zailun and Miramin's story for the Kalasha contribution to our collective knowledge about how love works and what it does (and Kalasha people would tell you that they know a lot about love's power), let me tell you something about where they live and who they are. The Kalasha are a tiny community of about three thousand people who live in three small finger valleys of the Hindukush, near the town of Chitral in Pakistan's Northwest Frontier Province. Kalasha speak Kalashamun, an Indo-Aryan language similar to Khowar, the language of Chitral. While all neighboring peoples in this region celebrate a common faith in Islam (though there is, of course, great sectarian, cultural, and linguistic diversity), the Kalasha still actively practice their indigenous religion. A hundred years ago, communities with similar, though distinct, religious practices populated the nooks and crannies of Afghanistan's Hindukush mountains to the west of Kalashadesh in what is now known as Nuristan. In 1895, when Pakistan's Northwest Frontier Province was separated from Afghanistan, the Kalasha fell under British protection. They were thus spared the just-appointed emir of Afghanistan's brutally successful campaign to convert to Islam all the "Kafirs" on his side of the newly drawn border.

Because the Kalasha are the only remaining practitioners of their religion (and perhaps because the valleys themselves are such a nice place to be), Kalasha culture has received more than its share of ethnographic attention (Jettmar 1986; Parkes 1983, 1994, 1997; Loude and Lievre 1988; Cacopardo and Cacopardo 2001; Maggi 2001, 2003). Kalasha people, like most people carving their lives in narrow valleys throughout the Hindukush, practice a mixed economy that combines transhumant pastoralism (mostly goats, but also a few sheep and cattle) with small-scale agriculture. They also share with Muslim neighbors a cultural ideal of warmth and generosity; a belief in fairies; a love of good cheese, walnuts, grapes, and mulberries; and an appreciation for the beauty of their landscape.

And like their Muslim neighbors, Kalasha people also celebrate romantic love. People from both communities tell and retell love stories, practice love magic, send tokens of affection to their lovers, and sing sentimental—some might even say sappy—love songs. Yet for all this, among neighboring Muslims—Chitrali, Pukhtun, Kohistani, and Gugar—"love marriages," marriages in which young people fall in love and then marry their beloved, are exceedingly rare, potentially deadly, and usually bound up with young people's assertions of *modern* identity (cf. Lindholm 1982; Grima 1992; Keiser 1986; Tapper 1990). In this way, romantic love in most of northern Pakistan has much in common with romantic love in some of the communities explored in this book: passionate, romantic love—while a powerful and present force in people's lives throughout history and cross-culturally—is not traditionally the genesis of marriage. So "love marriages," marriages in which young people assert their right to choose their own partner and expect that their passionate courtships will mature into intimate sexual, emotional, and social relationships, feel "new," "modern."

Laura Ahearn, for example, vividly describes the increasing emphasis young Magars in Nepal place on romantic passion as a prerequisite for marriage. For them, love, in both courtship and marriage, is increasingly associated with being "developed" and successful, and is more and more associated with independence and the ability to overcome all obstacles in life (2001). Indeed, in almost every corner of the globe, anthropologists have revealed the ideals of romantic love and companionate marriage as a core ideology of modernity, from Nigeria (Smith, this volume), to Mexico (Hirsch, this volume), to the Huli in Papua New Guinea (Wardlow, this volume), to Spain (Collier 1997), to Korea (Kendall 1996), to Egypt (Inhorn 1996; Hoodfar 1997). As Wardlow and Hirsch explain in the introduction to this collection, "Around the world, young people are talking about the importance of affective bonds in creating marital ties, deliberately positioning themselves in contrast to their parents and grandparents."

It's not surprising that love is at the heart (so to speak) of identity politics. Who one loves and how and what one hopes that love will bring is an integral part of every person's identity. And in turn, what people in a culture are expected or allowed to do with love is an integral part of every group's cultural identity. Communities decide whether to allow the desires people feel for one another to produce kinship—the larger foundation upon which most culture is elaborated. Will love, whatever it means, be allowed to become marriage, whatever that means? Will the desires of individuals be encouraged to shape the larger connections between people in the community, or will individuals expect themselves to put aside their personal desires and agendas and yield to someone else's decisions? Romantic love is important to both Kalasha and surrounding Muslim groups. What each community expects individuals to do with these feelings is entirely different. For Muslims, the feeling of being intensely in love but not being able to act on it is an expression of religious piety, brings honor to family and community, and is an expression of moral selfhood. For Kalasha, the fact that they claim a cultural right to act on their romantic passions is an important ethnic marker.

So in contrast to much of the rest of the world, the love marriages of the Kalasha—marriages that begin in dramatic elopements—are a long-standing cultural tradition, linked to ethnic heritage rather than modernity. The cultural right that young Kalasha people claim to translate love and longing into marriage, unique in this very conservative region, is a central marker of Kalasha ethnicity. In particular, the freedom exercised by young women—in many respects the least powerful people in the community—to choose whom they will marry, often against the best laid plans of irate parents, village elders, and ex-husbands, is a lived metaphor for the passionate tenacity all Kalasha need to practice their traditional religion and culture in a region where Kalasha are an oppressed and despised minority.

LOVE AND MARRIAGE GO TOGETHER. SOMETIMES.

Kalasha marriages are interesting, both to them and to me, because there are so many variations. Some people get married quite young, some late, some only once, and a rare few change partners four or five times. A very few men, men who are relatively wealthy and have great social and political finesse, have two wives. And, importantly, some marriages are arranged, and some are elopements.

Among the Kalasha there are two ways of marrying. Like Zailun, whose story began this chapter, two-thirds of all Kalasha women were "given" by their parents to a husband when they were still children, between six and twelve years old, before they were old enough to "know their own choice."

Often girls are given to men much older than they are, men whose previous wives had eloped with other men. But sometimes the husbands are also children—in a few cases the children had been promised to each other as infants. In every case, the boy's relatives "search" for the girl, never the reverse. Male representatives from his family ask male members of hers to "give" them the girl. The girl's family usually represent themselves as having been coerced into whichever decision is made. If they agree to give their daughter—and all uncles and aunts and grandparents, not just the biological parents, are involved—they say it was because the boy's family asked them and—"what could they do?"—to refuse would be an insult. If they refuse the offer, they almost always assert that although they would certainly like to give their daughter, they fear that when she is older she would rebel and make her own "choice" anyway, by eloping with another man. Zailun explains:

> First they say, "Will you give your daughter to me? I'll give her to my son." Then, if he [the father] likes the idea, he'll say, like, "I'll give her. What can I do? You've asked me, you've gotten under me (*may noa ata*). I've given you my daughter." If [the father] doesn't like it, he says, "It's her own choice, when she's big she'll go *alaSing* (elope). It's her mood. I can't give her to someone who is looking for a girl. If I give her, then she'll say later, 'you gave me forcefully, you ripped my heart out.'"

Of course this script, which everyone knows, has endless convolutions. It is also highly political, since it is not just the future of the girl but the future relations between families on which each potential match pivots. In fact, neighboring Muslim families, who always arrange matches for their children and for whom divorce or future elopement is nearly unthinkable, seem to think far more about the compatibility of the couple, while Kalasha "wife-making" negotiations often seem to have little to do with the future husband and wife.[2] I don't mean to imply that parents don't love their daughters or think about their happiness and welfare when agreeing to arranged marriages for them. But because every girl will have the chance to elope later if she is unhappy with her marital situation or in love with someone else, her parents, and especially the men in her family, are able to put the particularities of this important political, social, and economic alliance ahead of thinking about the sort of life their daughter will have with this husband and his family.

On the other hand, the idea that the girl could—indeed very well might—elope causes her new husband's family to treat her with special consideration. A mother-in-law often slips the choicest treats—a ripe tomato, a peach, the best piece of meat—to their little daughter-in-law. Romantic passion—or even lukewarm affection—between a husband and his "little wife" is not expected. (In fact, in little girl culture it is a scandal to show any interest whatsoever. I saw one little girl, Rosh Begim, suffer merciless jeering by her little girlfriends when she was seen braiding her hair before her bridewealth ceremony—tacit acknowledgment that she cared how she looked). On the other hand, husbands are well aware that they have a few short years to win their "little wife's" affection and loyalty. They court her with gifts of store-bought cookies and the hippest and most extravagant plastic sandals. In the few years before she begins to menstruate, she'll move back and forth between her husband's house and her father's house.

After the marriage proposal is accepted by the girl's family, the husband's paternal lineage members as well as close maternal relatives bring bridewealth to the girl's family, and the parents of the young couple begin establishing a close *kaltabar* relationship. This relationship is central to Kalasha political life and economic exchanges, but *khaltabars* also expect to establish or solidify warm, enduring friendships. *Khal* means "to taste," and *khaltabars* are thought to bring sweetness to life.

However sweet, this alliance is fragile because it lasts only as long as the marriage itself, and so it depends on the future cooperation of a female child who is likely to grow up and sever this relationship by eloping with another man. As Zailun's sister-in-law, who also eloped from her former husband, claims to have said to her father: "I was little when you gave me away, and so you didn't ask my opinion. Now I am grown up and I am telling you that I have different ideas about what I want." And in fact, 43% of Kalasha women who had been "given" as girls did have different ideas and eloped with another man when they reached adolescence (Maggi 2001).

Every Kalasha woman has a poignant and dramatic story about how she got married and how she decided to "sit" with her first husband or to elope with another man. Some elopements are first marriages. If parents decide not to "give" their daughter, she will "elope" on her own when she is a bit older, usually at seventeen or so. The songs little girls love to sing best are some variation of "my father loved me so much he couldn't give me away."

Elopements, though they by definition involve being "in love" (whether for four years like Zailun and Miramin, or about four hours like another couple in the family I lived with, whether deeply or fleetingly), are also highly political. Beyond the immediacy of desire, rejection, anger, action, and intrigue felt by the young people themselves is a realm of politics and power in which elopements like Zailun and Miramin's, and indeed all Kalasha elopements, are embedded. Peter Parkes (1983), who lived and worked in the valleys in the late 1970s and since, argues convincingly that orchestrating elopements is the primary way in which important lineage elders garner power and prestige for themselves. From the perspective of male political leaders, the politics of elopement serve as public contests in which lineage elders demonstrate their relative power and influence through dishonoring political rivals and finessing the wealth and support needed to settle bridewealth compensation. (The new husband's extended family must pay double the bridewealth her first husband gave to her natal family, and counting *mal* is a contentious process that can take continuous days or even weeks.) Further, mediating or arbitrating elopement conflicts is the main occasion for elders to act as political leaders. It took Miramin's uncle two years to organize the material and social resources that allowed Zailun and Miramin's elopement to take place. And it took two more years of long, hard, intervalley mediating by elders from both valleys before the compensating double bridewealth was accepted. "Indeed," Parkes notes, "without such hostilities to resolve, it is difficult to imagine what political leadership might entail in Kalasha society" (1983:591).

For the women, it's not just hostility that's political, but love itself. Love is more than a feeling, it's an attitude that predisposes one to act in a certain way. Kalasha women know, and will tell you, that if you are too in love with your husband, he has it "over" you, while if you're not in love with him, and stay with him anyway, he has to (1) be grateful and (2) work harder to see that you don't leave him. Also, if you marry a man you don't want to marry because your family wants a relationship with his, you also have it "over" your natal family, and they are obligated to help you financially, emotionally, and socially.

Needless to say, in Kalashadesh, these two ways of marrying, elopements and arranged marriages, crash into one another. Love stirs things up. Romantic passion is unpredictable and puts people together in unpredictable ways. Dramatic love marriages put gashes in the carefully woven social fabric and (albeit temporarily) sever the webs that bind people together in this small community. Of course the Kalasha are not unique in having to deal with such disruptions. But while anthropologists agree that all humans have the capacity to experience romantic passion (Ahearn 1998; Buss 1988; Chisholm 1995; Fisher 1995; Jankowiak 1995; Lindholm 1995), in many cultures, until recently, it was more or less effectively driven underground—or at least it was private and certainly not encouraged to make kinship. As we see in this collection, conflicts that arise when young people assert their desire to marry for love, rather than accept a more pragmatic match made by their parents, swell with the growing tide of modernity, which Scott Lash and Jonathan Friedman describe as characterized by movement, flux, change, and unpredictability (1991:1). So in this discussion of "modern love" it is interesting that for the Kalasha such marriage conflicts are *not* a response to modernity, but an institutionalized cultural tradition and an important marker of who they are as a people.

The movement, flux, change, and unpredictability of Kalasha people's lives have little to do with the encroachment of "modernity," but rather with the continual and sometimes violent tension of being a tiny enclave community whose most cherished religious and cultural practices many of their devout Muslim neighbors find appalling (Parkes 2000). Their project is not trying to link themselves with conceptions of progress but to maintain the boundaries of their world against intense, sustained, and often-forceful pressures to convert to Islam. Conversion is a one-way process. Once a Kalasha person has said the *khalima*—there is no god but Allah and Muhammad is his prophet—he or she *is* a Muslim, and there is no way to return. It is inconceivable that a Muslim would convert to Kalasha.

Kalasha commitment to making room for romantic love allows them to sustain their community in two important ways. First, sexual and marital freedom for women (at least in comparison to neighboring communities) is an important incentive not to convert. Also, peacefully managing the inevitable conflicts romantic passion brings to their social world allows them to maintain solidarity and prevents the escalating blood feuds for which this region of the world is known.

Kalasha are strikingly different from the peoples around them. Women wear elaborate dresses, headdresses, and pounds of colorful, expensive glass beads, and they do not veil their faces. They make and drink wine. Both men and women dance and sing publicly. They worship a pantheon of lesser gods and goddesses, though they also agree that there is only one God. Yet when asked what differentiates them from their Muslim neighbors, Kalasha people almost always remark that "our women are free (*homa istrizia azat asan*)."[3] The right to elope with a man other than the one your parents have "given" you to, to go *aLaSing* (or to choose not to), is the prototypic act that defines Kalasha women's "freedom"—a freedom that is always configured against the ground of an equally compelling discourse about respect for and devotion to one's family and patriline. This freedom is clearly limited. The Kalasha word *azat* means "released from restriction" (as when we say a person was freed from prison). Although Zailun found her first husband detestable, she couldn't leave him except to become another man's wife. Further, "good" Kalasha women don't "chase" men— like Zailun, the men come to them and then they *choose* whether to love them or not. Still, the ability to leave an unhappy marriage for a man you love makes Kalasha women's lives strikingly different from the lives of women in surrounding communities. My Muslim friends also told love stories, but they always ended in the death and disgrace of both lovers. I often heard Kalasha men lament the fact that their young brides could leave them. "But what can we do? We're Kalasha," they would inevitably conclude.

In addition to being a core symbol of ethnicity, the concept of women's freedom serves as an important incentive for Kalasha women not to defect from the community by marrying into one of the wealthier and more prestigious Muslim groups that surround them. There are interesting parallels between Kalasha and Maya of Guatemala. Maya culture, of course, is surrounded by politically and numerically dominant Ladino culture. Like Kalasha women, Maya women wear distinctive, elaborate clothing, while Maya men are difficult to distinguish from Ladino men. Carol Smith argues that Maya women also have greater latitude to make decisions about their sexual and marital lives than do Ladino women—as long as they remain within the Maya community (Smith 1995). Kalasha women value and cultivate their sexual and marital freedom, and explicitly cite it (well, and the fact that they would have to give up their beautiful beads) as the most important reason not to convert.

In turn, this "custom" is backed up by the very real threat that young people could (and do) convert to Islam if their parents and lineage members don't acquiesce to their demands. (And since no young man would have the resources by himself to come up with the double brideweath he would need to elope with a married woman, he'd *have* to have the cooperation of his family.) The neighboring Muslim community is eager to embrace—at least initially—converted Kalasha. By converting, the couple would escape the authority of their parents and of Kalasha traditions. They would be married by a mullah and bound in a new moral community. Converting to Islam is a desperate act, because it is irrevocable—but for this

very reason it is an effective threat that gives young lovers powerful leverage in these emotionally charged situations. It is also Kalasha custom that
disputes over marriage are settled through the exchange of bridewealth
rather than deadly violence. When Kalasha women elope they risk the dis-
appointment and disapproval of their families (which by itself is consider-
able), but they know that they are not risking their own lives or endanger-
ing the lives of people they love. Zailun's male relatives, furious over
Zailun's elopement with Miramin, were finally convinced to accept the
double bridewealth payment customary after elopement after hearing,
"Are you Muslims that you fight like this? No, we're Kalasha, when love
sticks, we exchange bridewealth and resolve our differences." It is a point
of pride, an aspect of Kalasha-ness, that elopements do not develop into
the deadly blood feuds characteristic of this region. As Lincoln Keiser
notes, among the nearby Kohistani communities, "accepting such indem-
nity would be unthinkable . . . Incidents like these require an instant
exchange of gunfire. The passion for revenge aroused in the cuckolded
husband demands that he at least attempt to kill his wife's lover"
(1986:494–95; cf. Lindholm 1981). Kalasha women (and the young men
who elope with them) can more boldly exercise their agency in regard to
marriage decisions because the consequences, while certainly serious, are
not lethal. And importantly, the tiny community of Kalasha is not perma-
nently fractured by the blood feuds, which sometimes last for generations,
so common in this region.

BUT DOES LOVE MARRIAGE LEAD
TO COMPANIONATE MARRIAGE?

Finally, Kalasha marriages are interesting to our current discussion for
what they tell us about companionate marriage: almost nothing. It's our
ethnocentric assumption that love marriages lead to loving marriages, so
one might think that Kalasha people who elope are more likely to expect or
desire or try to make a companionate marriage than people in arranged
marriages (cf. De Munck 1998). Yet, despite the intensity of romantic love
and the cultural identity Kalasha invest in allowing love to evolve into marriage, I heard no one—not man nor woman, dreamy adolescent nor
reflective widow—talk about companionate marriage. Indeed, I heard
almost no one talk about marriage at all—getting married, yes, but not
about *being* married.[4] The quality of Kalasha marriages seemed to me to be
a very private and individual spot in what is generally a very public and
community-oriented culture.

It's not that marriages are not companionable. There is clearly an expectation that husbands and wives respect one another, work together, and share a bed. Wives do their husbands' laundry. Husbands build a little storehouse for their wives, carving out a small space for their nuclear family within the joint household economy many young couples live in. There is very little marital violence. Kalasha people are polite in general, and that extends into their most intimate relationships. But there is certainly no expectation that the love that drives love marriage will sustain the marriage itself, or that it will continue, or that it will dwindle. The qualities of marriages people had, whatever route they took to get there, were wildly variable.

Indeed, for Zailun, what sustains her life now and makes her feel at home is not the companionship of the husband for whom she once felt such passion, but the companionable relationships she has built with other members of his family. When Miramin, fifteen years after their elopement, asked her if she would like to move back to her natal valley (a very unconventional proposal), she refused: Her home, family, future, and children's future were in Rumbur with her in-laws.

This isn't to say that romantic love never lasts, just that it is not part of the marital script that it must. Most women laughed when I asked them if they were still in love with their husbands. Some readily agreed that they were. Some said they have become more in love over the years, while for others, the passion has waned. One woman, a man's second wife, told me that even after thirty years, her heart still leaps when she sees him coming up the cliff to their house. Romantic loves that burned the longest seemed to me to be those that did not end in marriage. Lovers sometimes meet secretly over decades, or pine for one another their whole lives though they are never together again.

CONCLUSION

I worry that in this short chapter I have overplayed the extent to which the Kalasha are, to use Jan Collins and Thomas Gregor's term, a "love-facilitating culture" (1995:88). To portray the valleys as a place where "free love" reigns would be to do a great disservice to the Kalasha, as this reputation is precisely the false promise that brings horny young Pakistani college boys to the valleys as tourists—where they are a menace, and sometimes physically dangerous, to Kalasha women. Even in Kalashadesh, romantic love conflicts directly with the structure of ordered society (Person 1988), so love is hard-won and always sacrificed for. But perhaps, the

Fig. 3.2.   A woman and her aunt reunite at a festival. They are almost certainly discussing the intrigue and politics of recent marriages and elopements. The woman's six-year-old daughter listens intently. (Photo by Wynne Maggi.)

very difficulty of love is what makes it a meaningful ethnic marker. "Love," say Collins and Gregor, "is intrinsically related to personal freedom and respect for the individual" (1995:91). Kalasha commitment to allowing— even embracing—love's certain disruptions of social life is an ideal metaphor for their commitment to remain autonomous and maintain their religion. If young Kalasha women—the people with the least material and political power—hold fast to what they want, are patient and clever, and can endure intense social pressure, they know they will be allowed to choose the husband who makes their "heart bloom like a flower." So for the Kalasha, a people who have little material and political power, love is a lived metaphor for the passionate tenacity all Kalasha need to practice their traditional religion and culture in a region where they are an oppressed and despised minority.

NOTES

I am grateful to many institutions and the people behind them for the financial support that made this project possible. My research in the Kalasha valleys was assisted by a grant from the Joint Committee on South Asia of the Social Science Research Council and the American Council of Learned Societies with funds provided by the Andrew W. Mellon Foundation and the Ford Foundation. Additional support was provided by the American Institute of Pakistan Studies, the National Science Foundation, the Wenner-Gren Foundation, the Louis Dupree Prize, a P.E.O. Scholar Award, a Fulbright student grant, and an Emory University Graduate Fellowship.

1. *Ogoek pashi ashek howimi*—We saw one another and were *ashek* (romantic love). Kalasha language distinguishes between many types of love that English lumps together. *Ashek*—romantic love—derives from the Persian *ashiq*. Also commonly used is the phrase *hardi Sati shio*, which translates as "to be heart stuck," from the verb *SaTek* that is used in cases of active joining together.

2. De Munck wisely cautions that when we dichotomize between "love marriages" and "arranged marriages" we may not realize that "things are not so simple" (1998:291). Often, the couple's romantic love or potential for romantic love is an important aspect of arranged marriages, though love is not discursively foregrounded. And economic and political interests are not absent from love marriages, just backgrounded (see also Trawick 1990).

3. The Kalasha conception of freedom is quite different from American ideas that tend toward dreams of freedom *from* restriction or constraint. *Azat* carries the meaning of our word *free* as in "released from restriction"—but always within it is the assumption that those restrictions are there, and are real.

4. Well, that's not quite true: Young men who spoke some English and had had extensive exposure to tourists as guides or guards at the checkpost sometimes talked of taking their new brides on a "honeymoon," and the dream of how they would travel together, just the two of them, did seem to be tethered to modernity's star.

Part Two

CHANGING SEXUAL
MEANINGS & PRACTICES

4
———

THE SOCIAL CONSTRUCTIONS OF SEXUALITY

COMPANIONATE MARRIAGE & STD/HIV RISK
IN A MEXICAN MIGRANT COMMUNITY

Jennifer S. Hirsch, Jennifer Higgins,
Margaret E. Bentley, & Constance A. Nathanson

The night before her wedding, a girl kneels down to pray. She prays
for three things:
> Dear God, please make my husband faithful to me.
> Dear God, please keep me from finding out when he is
> unfaithful to me.
> Dear God, please keep me from caring when I find out
> he is unfaithful to me.
> —Joke told in Degollado, Mexico, summer of 1996[1]

This chapter describes the social context of the migration-related HIV
epidemic in western Mexico, highlighting the ways in which ideologies
of companionate marriage may, ironically, increase women's risk for marital HIV infection. In recent years, epidemiologic and ethnographic
research has suggested that an increasing proportion of AIDS cases in
Mexico are related to Mexican men becoming infected in the United States
and then returning home to infect their wives (Bronfman, Sejenovich, and

Uribe 1998; Gayet, Magis, and Bronfman 2000; Magis-Rodríguez et al. 2004). In this chapter we apply recent thinking about cross-cultural variation in people's ideas and emotions about desire, partner choice, and sexual behaviors—in short, the social constructions of sexuality (Weeks 1981; Nathanson 1991; Parker 1993; Vance 1991; Dixon-Mueller 1993; Hirsch and Nathanson 2001)—to the question of how social context shapes women's risk of migration-related HIV and STD infection. Specifically, we show how a shift toward a more companionate marital ideal among women from two migrant-sending communities in Mexico has created generational differences in women's attitudes toward men's sexual infidelity, and we argue that a growing emphasis on sexual intimacy within marriage may make young Mexican women particularly invested in ignoring evidence of infidelity. Our discussion of how access to resources shapes the ways that women use companionate ideologies underlines the malleability of shared ideals for marital companionship, and it points to the value of a strategic—rather than static—approach to thinking about culture. A central theme of this volume is the cross-cultural variability of these ideals for marital companionship, but here we push that point further, calling attention to intracultural variability as well.

For most women around the world, their biggest risk of HIV infection comes from having sex with their husbands (UNAIDS 2000). Previous studies of AIDS risk denial have demonstrated how women's commitment to the illusion of fidelity can increase the risk of infection with HIV (e.g., Sobo 1995a,b). Here we document AIDS risk denial in a context in which it has not previously been noted, and we show how it may potentially be exacerbated by changing notions about marital intimacy. We also suggest that the same ideas that hinder women's recognition of their risk may contain possibilities for culturally relevant prevention messages targeted to men.

As we trace the contours of sexuality in these migrant-sending communities, we discuss differences between older and younger women in terms of how they talk about sexuality, marriage, and infidelity. These generational differences call attention both to the importance of studying how sexuality changes across time and to the ironic possibility that increased communication between married couples about some aspects of sexuality (such as mutual pleasure) does not necessarily imply a greater likelihood of communicating about the risk of infection and the need for prevention. We also describe differences among women in how they interpret this discourse about marital intimacy and the meaning of infidelity, pointing out that changes in the social constructions of sexuality are not uniform across society. In the conclusion, we critique programs that aim to prevent heterosexual HIV transmission by working with married women and make some concrete suggestions for how these findings about sexuality and marriage could be used to shape culturally relevant prevention campaigns for Mexican migrants.

METHODS

The data come from a comparative ethnographic study of gender, sexuality, and reproductive health among Mexicans from a migrant-exporting community in rural western Mexico (Hirsch 1998, 2003; Hirsch and Nathanson 1998). The broader study explored the effect of generational and migration-related change on gender and sexuality and the way these changes in gender and sexuality shape reproductive health practices. The primary method of data collection was life histories interviews, conducted with thirteen women in Atlanta and thirteen in the Mexican communities.[2]

The women in Atlanta were systematically selected to represent the range of diversity in Atlanta's migrant community in terms of social class and resources in their families of origin in Mexico, as well as factors such as age, legal status, English skills, and reproductive and labor force experience. The life history informants in Atlanta were recruited from an initial set of research contacts from El Fuerte, Michoacan, and Degollado, Jalisco, who lived in the Atlanta metropolitan area. The informants in the Mexican fieldsites were the sisters or sisters-in-law of the life history informants in Atlanta. Of the twenty-six life history informants, fourteen had experienced migration-related spousal separations of at least three months, and for ten of those fourteen couples the periods of separation stretched anywhere from a year to two years. Furthermore, four of the fourteen had spent most of their married lives living apart, with the men making annual or biannual visits to Mexico. Interviews were also conducted with eight of the life history informants' mothers and eight of their husbands.[3]

With the life history informants, the six interviews explored childhood and family life, social networks and U.S.-Mexico migration, gender and the domestic division of labor, menstruation, reproduction, and fertility control, health, reproductive health, sexually transmitted diseases, and courtship and marital sexuality. With the older women (the life history informants' mothers) and the men, the interviews covered U.S.-Mexico migration, courtship and marriage, infidelity, and fertility regulation.

These interviews were complemented by participant observation, which took place over the course of fifteen months split between the Mexico and U.S. fieldsites. Key sites for participant observation included private homes, a yarn store, doctor's offices, and religious, social, and life-cycle events (see Hirsch 2003:28–49).

The Mexican fieldsites consisted of the town of Degollado, Jalisco, and a rural community, El Fuerte, in the state of Michoacan. Migration represents a primary source of income in both of these fieldsites, although there are still a few in both Degollado and El Fuerte who try to eke out a living from the land or from raising pigs. As the county seat, Degollado also has a small professional class and a slightly larger commercial class, as well as some artisans who carve the local sandstone. In Atlanta, the Census Bureau estimated the metro area Latino population at over 175,000 at the time the fieldwork was conducted, and other estimates placed the number closer to 250,000 (CARA 1998; U.S. Census Bureau 2000).

The data for this study consist of the transcribed interviews and field notes. The analysis involved multiple readings of the text. A first reading generated topical themes (e.g., infidelity) and sorted sections of narrative into separate topical files for each code. A second reading looked at the variability within topics (e.g., differences in what women said about infidelity) to establish subcodes. A third level of analysis explored differences between the subcodes (e.g., looking at the differences between women who said they would never confront their husband when faced with evidence of infidelity and those who said that they might). (For a more detailed discussion of analytic methods, see Hirsch 1998, 2003; Miles and Huberman 1994.)

THE SOCIAL CONTEXT OF U.S.-MEXICO MIGRATION AND THE MIGRATION-HIV NEXUS

There is a long history of labor migration to the United States from western Mexico; some of those interviewed for this study had fathers and grandfathers who traveled to the United States as temporary labor migrants (Hirsch 1998; see also Durand 1994; Hondagneu-Sotelo 1994; Massey et al. 1987). The female proportion of Mexican migrants to the United States has increased in the past decade (Cornelius 1991; Cerrutti and Massey 2001), but significant numbers of married and unmarried men still travel north for nine or ten months every year from towns throughout Mexico, leaving their wives or girlfriends behind. As noted previously, fourteen of the twenty-six life history informants had experienced these extended marital separations.

Mexican migrants' relative youth, their loneliness and social isolation, and the fact that many are single or traveling without their spouses place migrants at risk of engaging in sexual behavior, and low levels of education and limited English may make it harder to reach these migrants with messages about HIV prevention (Bletzer 1995; Gayet, Magis, and Bronfman 2000:134–38; Cardenas-Elizalde 1998).[4] Social factors such as more permissive sexual norms, the higher incidence of HIV/AIDS (especially in the states that have been the destinations for great numbers of Mexican migrants), more widespread use of injected drugs (Weatherby et al. 1999), the lack of Spanish-language prevention campaigns, and migrants' limited access to health services can also increase migrants' vulnerability to HIV (Gayet, Magis, and Bronfman 2000; McCoy et al. 1996; Bletzer 1995; Magaña, de la Rocha, and Ansel 1996; Weeks et al. 1995; Singer and Marx-uach-Rodríguez 1996).[5] In addition, the very fact of migration—which is itself a product of the political and economic relationships between the United States and Mexico (Massey et al. 1993)—may put Mexicans at risk because men who experience extended separations from their primary partners may be at increased risk of having extramarital sex[6] (Cardenas-Elizalde 1998).

Migration has emerged as a risk factor for AIDS in rural Mexico, as figure 4.1 suggests. Its data draw on a variety of sources, all of which indicate that an increasing proportion of total AIDS cases in Mexico are to be found in rural communities—measured as those in which the population is less than 2,500. Many of these rural cases have been linked to travel to the United States. In 1995, 25% of rural Mexican AIDS cases were among men who had been in the United States, while only 6% of urban cases reported travel to the United States (Magis-Rodríguez et al. 1995). In Jalisco (where Degollado is located), early studies found that half of the reported AIDS cases had traveled to foreign countries (Diaz-Santana and Celis 1989; see also Bronfman, Camposortega, and Izazola 1989), and in neighboring Michoacan, where El Fuerte is located, 39% of those with AIDS had traveled to the United States (Pineda et al. 1992, cited in Bronfman, Sejenovich, and Uribe 1998). More recent studies have found that in both Michoacan and Jalisco more than 20% of AIDS cases in rural areas report having been in the United States (Magis-Rodríguez et al. 2004:S219). Because women account for 20% of rural cases but only 14% of urban ones, it seems especially urgent to explore how life in rural Mex-

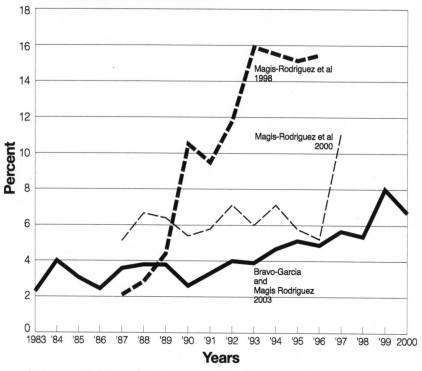

The Proportion of Total AIDS Cases in Mexico Occurring in Rural Areas: An Increase over Time

Fig. 4.1.   AIDS cases occurring in locations with populations of less than 2,500 are thought to be strongly linked to circular labor migration between Mexico and the United States. While the percentage of overall cases that are rural varies across these data sources, all three agree that the proportion of total AIDS cases occurring in rural areas is increasing over time. (Data from Bravo-Garcia and Magis-Rodríguez 2003; Magis-Rodríguez et al. 1998; Magis-Rodríguez et al. 2000.)

ico puts women at increased risk (Bravo-Garcia and Magis-Rodríguez 2003:15; Magis-Rodríguez et al. 1995; Magis-Rodríguez et al. 1998; del Rio-Zolezzi et al. 1995). Many have argued that seasonal labor migration to the United States is responsible for these urban/rural differences in sex ratios (Santarriaga et al. 1996; Mishra, Connor, and Magaña 1996; Bronfman and Minello 1995; Bronfman, Sejenovich, and Uribe 1998). In order to prevent migration-related heterosexual transmission of HIV, it is important to know more about marital sexuality in rural Mexico.

FINDINGS: HIV/AIDS-RISK DENIAL AND
HIV PREVENTION STRATEGIES

J: So how can you prevent AIDS?

E: Well, mostly by just having sex with your husband, and if they are running around, then using a condom, but it's not very trustworthy because sometimes they break, or they come off, or things like that, and then you are at risk.

J: You say that by just having sex with your husband, but what if he is running around on you?

E: Well, it's supposed to be both of you—"I just do it with you and you just do it with me"—but that's where you have to really trust your partner, because it's possible that he says to you, "no, you are the only one," and if you trust him but after all he is going around behind your back, what can you do? It's not as if—you're not going to—he'll just say, "don't you trust me?" That is, you really can't prevent it—you just have to believe in him.

—Esperanza,[7] married, age nineteen, interviewed in Degollado

Women saw a clear association between men's temporary labor migration to the United States and HIV risk.[8] As one woman in Atlanta recounted, "AIDS is really spreading in Mexico because many men whose wives are in Mexico come here and get involved with someone, and they don't know if she has AIDS. Then they get it, and they go back to Mexico." Women said that men who spend long periods of time away from home are likely to develop some kind of sexual relationship, but most claimed that their own husbands were an exception to this rule, making comments such as "I don't worry about that because he seems like a good guy." Women identified men's extramarital relationships in the United States as a source of risk for those men, and even connected that to the possibility of transmission to Mexican women in general, but they did not translate the scenario into one in which women like themselves—married women who "behave themselves"—are at risk. These women have embraced the message that monogamy is an effective HIV risk reduction strategy (e.g., as advocated in Wasonga 1996; Weiss, Gupta, and Whelan 1995; Cohen 1995, cited in Soler et al. 2000; Weiss and Rao 1994). During interviews and in casual conversation, women frequently said that the best way to prevent HIV and other STDs was to have sex only with one's husband; some even quoted directly from health education lectures, saying that the only kind of *sexo seguro*, safe sex, is *con tu pareja*, with your partner.

Although the Mexican National AIDS Council (CONASIDA 1997) data had two recorded AIDS cases for the county in which Degollado is located at the time this study was conducted, informants mentioned several cases of people living with AIDS in Degollado and El Fuerte and other instances in which men from the community had reportedly died of AIDS in the United States. Almost all of the life history informants recounted having heard about other women who had gotten an STD other than HIV from their husbands; many of these stories (with no prompting about connections to migration) were about men returning from stints in the north.[9] All of the women knew that illnesses can be transmitted through genital contact during sex, but they all denied having had personal experience with sexually transmitted infections.[10]

Almost all of the life history informants had heard that condoms prevent the transmission of AIDS and other sexually transmitted diseases, but women's ideas about the technical, sensory, and symbolic aspects of condoms make it unlikely that they would push for condom use. About half of the women had tried condoms as a method of pregnancy prevention, but none favored them, and only a few used them occasionally in combination with rhythm (see Hirsch and Nathanson 2001). One reason for preferring other methods, these women said, is their belief that condoms are ineffective. Both those who had used them and those who had not made comments such as "*no es tan seguro*" (it's not so safe/effective) and "*a veces salen medio defectuosos*" (sometimes they are defective). Women also talked about how condoms are a barrier to intimacy.[11] One woman who had tried using condoms said, "I told him, to have sex every now and then and to do it with a cover, all covered up, no way." Women spoke of not wanting to be "*tapado*" (covered up) and said that sex with a condom is less natural and less pleasurable (for both women and men). Women saw unprotected sex as the most intimate kind of sex, and thus argued that if a man were going to use a condom, he should use it with his other partners. One migrant's wife said she'd tried to get her husband to use condoms as a method of pregnancy prevention during a surprise homecoming, only to be told by him, "No, then what the hell kind of pleasure would that be? In that case it would be better to go with another damn woman." Men and women reunited after a migrant separation are jokingly said to be *de luna de miel*, on honeymoon; the romance of this honeymoon period would be considerably dampened by the implication that condoms were necessary because either partner had strayed.

Given the risk posed by a strategy of unilateral monogamy, one approach might be to educate these women about their HIV risk and develop interventions to encourage them to negotiate with their husbands for condom use. Indeed, many of the articles cited in Gayet, Bronfman, and Magis's review article on HIV and migration suggest that prevention programs should focus on increasing women's condom negotiation skills. In the remainder of this chapter, we will argue against this seemingly obvious response. It is not just that women do not like condoms (though they may not), or that they may not have the power to insist on their use (though they also may not). Rather, negotiating for condom use is unthinkable to these women, because they see requesting condom use as tantamount to acknowledging or even giving permission for a husband's infidelity.

GENERATIONAL CHANGES IN MARRIAGE AND SEXUALITY

The marital ideal has changed over the course of a generation from one of *respeto*, respect, to one of *confianza*, intimacy. The marital goals of the older generation (as described by the mothers of the life history informants and the older informants [those in their late thirties and above]) centered on mutual fulfillment of a gendered set of obligations (Hirsch 1998, 1999b, 2003). Husbands and wives certainly may have felt love and tenderness for one another in the past, but marital success and stability depended on the way the union fulfilled the basic needs of the couple and the wider kin group: production of food, shelter, heirs, and social status, not on emotional closeness.

Within the new ideal of the Mexican companionate marriage, young couples spend more time together, enjoy a somewhat less strongly gendered division of labor, and claim joint decision making (though frequently with ultimate masculine authority) in many areas of domestic and economic issues. These companionate marriages are not necessarily egalitarian; in fact, the emphasis on the importance of marital ties above all other social connections may make women more isolated and dependent on their husbands. Young women also speak differently than their mothers did about the nature and role of sexuality within marriage. For the older women, marital sex produced children and held a man's attention, and thus served to direct his resources toward a woman and her children rather than outside the family. The younger women, in contrast, claim that mutually pleasurable sexual intimacy strengthens the *confianza* that is at the heart of these modern marriages (see Hirsch and Nathanson 2001; Hirsch 1998, 2003). They see sex as a sort of "marital glue," helping a couple's affective relationship survive through good times and bad (see Giddens 1992).

The younger Mexican women in Atlanta shared values about relationships, sexual intimacy, and gender with women in the sending communities, but women in the Atlanta fieldsites live in very different social circumstances than do their sisters and sisters-in-law in Mexico, and so some women in Atlanta had a great deal more domestic power than did their sisters or sisters-in-law in Mexico (Hirsch 1999b). The contrast between the shared culture and the distinct social settings of this type of migrant community provides a unique opportunity to explore the way that social and cultural factors shape sexuality, and the way that women strategically interpret companionate ideologies.

INFIDELITY AND COMPANIONATE MARRIAGE

Women's attitudes toward male infidelity reflect these broad changes in marital sexuality.[12] The older women valued a pretense of ignorance about a man's extramarital relationships. As one woman said, for a man to "keep some respect for you" would mean that "you don't know what they are doing, . . . that is, that they act as they wish but do it so that you don't know." Since a man owed his wife first and foremost financial support and secondarily some measure of respect, his sexual behavior was largely his own concern except to the extent that he publicly embarrassed his wife. Older women said that drinking, violence, or laziness were significant problems in a marriage, and there was little dissent that the worst quality a man could display was to be *desobligado* (being unwilling or unable to support his family), but none suggested that infidelity might be a reason to leave one's husband. Blatant male infidelity may certainly have wounded women—as one said, "you don't say anything to them, but you still feel kind of bad, in your heart"[13]—but infidelity did not terminate the underlying contract. Furthermore, older women suggested that men physically need to have sex on a regular basis, that this need for sexual release cannot be satisfied by masturbation, and that a man's sexual involvement with another woman need not threaten a marriage. As one of the older women said in an interview, discussing her husband's long absences while working

Fig. 4.2. Mariachi singers, which are de rigueur at elegant weddings in Degollado, can easily cost hundreds of dollars. The growing splendor of local weddings is just one aspect of the political economy of migrant love, in which young men go north to earn the money necessary to return in splendor and secure a local bride. As we argue here, however, some labor migrants bring back more than dollars when they return from the long cold months in the north. (Photo by Jennifer Hirsch.)

in the United States, "I have said to my husband, 'I can't say that you did not use (*que tu no usaste*) some woman, but if you did it, it was because you needed to (*porque se te baria necesario*).'"

Younger women, in contrast, see men's sexual behavior as inseparable from marital intimacy. If sex is the language of love, then to be sure of their husband's love they must believe that he is faithful while away. As one young woman in the rancho said, "I wouldn't feel comfortable with him, knowing he'd been going around with another woman." A man's sexual infidelity, these younger women said, would weaken or destroy the *confianza* they have with their husbands. One younger woman told a story about calling her husband in Atlanta from Mexico. The phone rang all night, but he never answered. When she accused him the next day of having been out with another woman, he said he had been home and just not heard the phone. She reflected on this incident with some general comments about infidelity.

When the man doesn't want to lose you, he tries to fix things, to make it [better]—and I prefer this, to him saying to me, "Well yes, I did go around [with another woman]." ... For me, *I prefer that he lie*, that it was a slipup, that he went out, that he just stepped out and came right back, but that he doesn't admit it like that. ... Though maybe it's bad, I prefer the lie, if it's going to be just a dalliance (*un pasatiempo*) or a thing that just happened, that he drank a lot of beer, and got drunk and all that, *better for him to hide it from me, so that he doesn't hurt me.* (Emphasis added)

Women's commitment to the image of their husbands as sexually faithful, even when confronted by compelling evidence to the contrary, draws on the idea that sexual betrayal indicates a lack of love (see Sobo 1995b). The new cultural ideal of marital companionship and shared sexual pleasure gives younger women yet another reason not to raise issues of infection and infidelity. The younger couples prided themselves on their communication about sexuality, emotions, and pleasure, in contrast to the older women, for whom open discussions about sexual matters indicated a lack of respect. However, the value these younger couples place on communication about some aspects of sexuality does not mean that these younger women are any more likely than were their mothers to suggest that a man use a condom for disease prevention purposes.

SOCIAL CLASS, SOCIAL CONTEXT, AND CONSTRUCTIONS OF SEXUALITY

Within this broad pattern of generational change in sexuality lies a second kind of diversity. The life history informants fell into four groups when asked how they might respond, hypothetically, if confronted by evidence of infidelity: those who would leave him, those who would talk it out, those who would go out of their way to make him feel special, and those who would do nothing at all. The different ways that women interpret the ideology suggests that the type of "modern" sexual relationship a woman builds may depend on where she lives and the resources on which she can draw.

Six of the twenty-six life history informants said that infidelity was grounds for leaving one's husband.[14] Only the women who could support themselves adopted this rights-based language to talk about infidelity (see Petchesky and Judd 1998); they all had an independent income, and five had at least a high school diploma as well. When asked about men who said that extramarital sex was their right, one woman who lived in Atlanta and contributed as much as her husband to their joint budget said,

> Just like he could go out [with someone], I could too. How would it seem to him if the tables were turned and if I did that to him? He wouldn't forgive me, right? We are human beings just like them . . . neither he nor I is made of stone or straw . . . We both have hearts, we both feel the same.

She argued that in the emotional contract of marriage, both partners have essentially the same set of rights. When asked why women do not put up with infidelity now, she continued, "Before, women did what their husbands said when they got married. The rule was that here the man was boss. . . . Now we both are the boss." These Mexican women have woven together ideas about sexual intimacy as the foundation of marriage with their personal histories and their self-image as modern women to produce a distinct set of attitudes about where to set the limits on men's sexual freedom.

Others said that they might address the issue by trying to discuss it with their husbands. (The "talk it out" group presented a strategy for dealing with infidelity when forced to do so, not for raising the issue in a preventive health context.) Talking about how she would counsel a friend to act, one said, "the thing is to make him understand, communicate well with her, so that he realizes that his wife is worthwhile." These women share with their sisters the idea that infidelity is a fundamental violation of the marital bargain, but these women seemed particularly skilled at talking about their feelings, and they prized the open communication they have achieved in their marriages. Moreover, they all resided in Mexico. The fact that women in Atlanta and wealthier women in Mexico are so forthright in saying that they would leave their husbands, while their matches in Mexico say that they would do their best to talk things through, shows how emotional closeness can be a strategic resource for a woman who is socially and economically dependent upon her husband. Women in Degollado or El Fuerte may have some resources that their peers in Atlanta lack (e.g., broader social networks, a mastery of the language), but these resources do not enable women to live without a man's economic support. Furthermore, women in Mexico continue to face the issue that *el hombre es el respeto de la casa*, that a woman needs a man to be respected (see Hirsch 1999b, 2003), as well as the stigma of divorce, still strong in rural Mexico.

The idea that these women in Mexico would try to talk it out implies ultimately accepting a man's infidelity (just as their mothers might have), but saying that they would at least confront the issue allows them to assert that they are women who deal actively with problems and who are free to speak their minds. For both groups of women, infidelity represents a betrayal of the special sexual relationship that married people should share, but the two groups use the ideology differently, based on their social and economic circumstances.

Not all women, of course, were so thoroughly invested in these modern strategies for building relationships. The idea that a successful relationship depends on a woman's ability to keep her man happy, to work through his good side (*manejarlo por las buenas*), was alive and well among Mexican women in both U.S. and Mexican fieldsites. The four women in this third group focused much more on their feminine ability to satisfy and hold on to a man. A satisfying sex life, they all said, was one of the keys to a good marriage. One responded to the question, "If a couple does not get along well in bed, how will they do in the rest of their marriage?" by saying, "Badly, I think, because I have heard that for the man [you need to] have his food ready, his clothes ready, and the bed ready, and he will be all content, and if not, then [he'll be] a real devil." In the event of actual or suspected infidelity, these women said that they would use their feminine wiles to make themselves irresistible. All of them mention the important of being more *cariñosa*, sweeter or more loving. The women in this group are young (under twenty) and recently married. Though they lived in both the U.S. and Mexican fieldsites, none worked outside the home, and the ones in Atlanta were there without any of their own blood relations to count on in an emergency. Their support for this strategy is most likely a product of many factors: age, family histories, their personality and their husband's, the sort of marriage they have, and their lack of other resources.

Finally, six of the life history informants said that they would do nothing in reaction to suspected or confirmed infidelity. None relished the thought, but neither did they argue that it would be grounds for separation. Though this group included women interviewed both in Atlanta and the Mexican fieldsites, those in Atlanta had spent some if not all of the years of their marriage in Mexico; all of the women in this group were older, less educated, with less work experience and fewer possibilities of economic independence. In other words, the women whose material circumstances were most similar to women of the older generation were least likely to embrace this new ideology of sexuality.

DISCUSSION

The younger generation's new ideas about sexual intimacy transform men's infidelity from a painful reminder of gender inequity—but not necessarily an indication that a marriage is a failure—to a betrayal of the *confianza* that young women hope lies at the core of their marriage. If infidelity represents a breach of trust, and an STD or HIV is the ultimate evidence of that breach, then every act of sex without a condom is a mutual performance of trust. The *confianza* of which younger men and women speak implies a shared commitment to pleasure and emotional intimacy, predicated upon the unquestioned and unquestionable assumption of mutual monogamy. It does *not* mean that they are open to discussing issues of risk and infidelity or negotiating condom use. In a marriage with *plena confianza* (complete trust), a woman might feel freer to initiate sex, to have oral sex, or to don some racy lingerie, but she is no more likely than her mother was to ask spontaneously about her husband's adventures in *el norte*.

Whether in Atlanta or in the Mexican fieldsites, women expressed this commitment to marriages of *confianza*; younger women in Mexico were more similar to younger women in Atlanta than they were to older women in Mexico. The greater a woman's social and economic resources, however, the less likely she is to say that she would try to work it out if confronted with hard evidence of infidelity. Women's imagined responses show that social stratification has an important effect on the options that women see as available to them.

Developing effective strategies for HIV and STD prevention among married women whose husbands are seasonal migrants will mean finding a way to work around women's HIV risk denial. Asking a man to use a condom implies mistrust and, as one young woman in Atlanta (who gossip suggests has good reason to worry about her own risk of contracting an STD) said, "mistrust is a lack of love (*la desconfianza ya es falta de amor*)." Sobo (1995b) found that African-American women in the United States held similar views, and she argues that women's commitment to the ideal of monogamy contributes to their risk of HIV infection.[15]

Our data here support Sobo's conclusion, but we also extend her work by placing married women's AIDS risk denial within the context of broader global changes in the meaning of marriage. Ethnographic research from across the developing world has described the development of similar ideals about marital companionship and sexual intimacy (see other chapters in this volume, as well as Inhorn 1996; Yan 1997, 2003; Hollos and Larsen 1997; Ahearn 1998; Hirsch 1998, 2003; Rebhun 1999; Smith 2001). The similarity of these ideals does not mean that marriage in El Fuerte is exactly the same as marriage in Egypt, but the widespread link between marital sex and emotional intimacy suggests that married women's AIDS risk denial, combined with persistent gender inequality, may have greater implications for the spread of marital HIV transmission than has previously been acknowledged.

The continuing focus, however, on why women will or will not negotiate for condom use represents an astonishing failure on the part of the global HIV prevention community to confront how gender shapes—*and constrains*—our imagination. The focus on women may be in part a product of scientific knowledge about women's greater biological risk of sexual infection with HIV (Farmer, Connor, and Simmons 1996), but this does not explain why we have assumed that women can modify their sexual behavior to press for condom use but men cannot[16]—nor does it justify the fact that we have continued to push the message that monogamy is an effective HIV-risk reduction strategy (e.g., Abdool, Mantell, and Scheepers 1996; Obwogo 1996, 1998; Wasonga 1996; Weiss, Gupta, and Whelan 1995; Weiss and Rao 1994) when we know that the assumption that marriage equals monogamy may be costing women their lives (Bolton 1992). Men's sexual behavior presents a public health problem, and thus these men's behavior is the proper object of our attention. To suggest that we can help married women protect themselves by "empowering" them to negotiate for condom use is to suggest that we can change the outcome of gendered inequalities in power without doing anything about the actual inequality.[17]

Given all that a woman in this community might feel she stands to gain by ignoring her risk of contracting an STD from her husband, small wonder that women do so little to protect themselves. These women would not benefit from programs to help them with condom negotiation; in many areas of their domestic and wider social lives they are already expert negotiators. Women in this community do not want to use condoms for disease prevention because the emotional cost of acknowledging that sex with their husbands is not safe sex is simply too high. As Karen Mason has

Fig. 4.3. As this poster indicates, Mexican AIDS prevention programming is increasingly trying to engage with the ways that shared ideas about masculinity form the social context of HIV risk. (Poster produced by CONASIDA; used with permission.)

pointed out, the idea that women's empowerment would increase condom use "is plausible only if there is reason to think that women are more motivated than men to use condoms, but are unable to enforce their use in the face of male opposition" (1994:224).[18] In this particular Mexican case, the cultural logics of marital sexuality suggest that public health efforts to stem a rising tide of migration-related heterosexual transmission of HIV in Mexico should instead concentrate on two fronts: on the behavior and social circumstances of migrants while they are in the United States and on the wider sources of gender inequality that structure women's lives.[19]

CONCLUSIONS

The research presented here could serve as the basis for a prevention program that builds on the ideas of respect and trust (*respeto* and *confianza*) to shape health education messages targeted toward men to promote extramarital condom use. Men and women may not agree on whether men who profess to believe in companionate marriage should ever have outside partners, but they do agree that for a woman to find out about her husband's infidelity represents both a betrayal of trust and a lack of respect on his part. Health education messages could use these terms to emphasize a man's responsibility to protect his family from disease and hurt feelings. Telling men that if they have outside partners they should use a condom to protect the *confianza* they have with a spouse and to avoid showing her a *falta de respeto*, a lack of respect, may be one way to frame this important health education message in culturally meaningful terms (see Weeks et al. 1995). This would essentially mean taking a sort of harm-reduction approach to marital HIV transmission; in a parallel to the successful HIV prevention efforts with injecting drug users, the policy response would be to make a particular behavior (in this case, extramarital sex) less dangerous from a public health point of view, rather than trying to discourage people from engaging in it.

Our call for prevention programs addressing health issues of HIV among Mexican migrants, however, needs to be considered in the context of Mexican migrants' generally limited access to health services. In Atlanta, the only way a Mexican migrant is likely to get attention from the Fulton County Health Department is if he has active tuberculosis (see Institute of Medicine 2000). Nationally, Latino immigrants' limited access to quality U.S. health care services has been well documented (Chavez 1984; Chavez,

Cornelius, and Williams 1985; Chavez, Flores, and Lopez-Garza 1992; Evans 1995; Flaskerud and Kim 1999; Rumbaut et al. 1986). At the time of the writing of this chapter, most of the men who were laying bricks and hanging sheetrock in the ever-larger suburban minimansions that ring Atlanta, along with their *paisanos* mowing lawns and planting seasonal flowers, had very limited access to primary health care. These men who spend long months in the cold north may be powerful in relation to their wives, but we should remember that they are not just men—they are poor, dark-skinned, primarily non–English speaking, frequently undocumented men. Addressing migration-related HIV in anything other than a superficial way will mean facilitating access to health care in a more general fashion.

It will also mean reframing migration-related HIV in relation to American consumption patterns; American consumers benefit from the cheap labor that buses tables, mows lawns, plucks chickens, and delivers take-out, but part of the reason that this labor is so cheap is that employers can (and do) pay undocumented workers less, passing the "savings" along to us, the consumer, in the form of lower prices for food and housing. But the real cost of this is borne by the workers. This is the classic externality, in which a cost of producing a good or set of goods is borne neither by the producer nor by the consumer, and so goes unmeasured in the price. If the jobs at which Mexican immigrants labor provided health insurance, or if state and local governments made publicly funded primary care available to undocumented residents, affordable clinics with translators and evening hours could create a wide range of opportunities for primary and secondary prevention of sexually transmitted diseases and for HIV prevention (e.g., Santelli et al. 2000).

AIDS *is* an emergency, and the sort of research presented here takes a long time (though partnering with local social scientists and beginning research projects with a firm grounding in the vast ethnographic record can certainly speed this up). However, it is precisely *because* of the pressing nature of the global pandemic that we must take the time to do careful ethnographic research. In particular, the data presented here speak to the value of anthropological research for drawing connections between culture and changing patterns of social inequality. As we enter the third decade of the epidemic, we must use all the tools within our grasp, including the full range of anthropology's explanatory power, to address the global challenge of AIDS.

NOTES

This chapter is a reprint of an article first published in the *American Journal of Public Health* in 2002, "The Social Constructions of Sexuality: Marital Infidelity and Sexually Transmitted Disease/HIV Risk in a Mexican Migrant Community." August 2002, 92 (8): 1227–37. We gratefully acknowledge having been granted permission to reprint this piece. The first author would also like to note having received fieldwork support from the Andrew Mellon Foundation through a grant to the Department of Population Dynamics at Johns Hopkins University, from the National Science Foundation Program in Cultural Anthropology (SBR-9510069), the International Migration Program at the Social Science Research Council, as well as other forms of material support from the Emory AIDS International Training and Research Program, which is funded by a grant from the Fogarty International Center at the National Institutes of Health (1 D43 TW01042–02), and the Department of International Health at the Rollins School of Public Health. Thanks also to Claire Sterk and Carlos del Río and to three anonymous *APJH* reviewers for comments, and to Carlos Magis Rodriguez of the Consejo Nacional de SIDA for generously sharing surveillance data on rural AIDS in Mexico. The second author gratefully acknowledges financial support from the program in Women's Studies at Emory University.

The study described here received approval from the Institutional Review Board at Johns Hopkins School of Hygiene and Public Health, and all subjects provided informed consent before participating in interviews.

Our deepest debt is to the women and men who opened their homes and their hearts throughout the course of this study; we cannot acknowledge them by name, but we hope at least to have been true to their stories.

　　1. This joke was told by a middle-aged woman during a Sunday outing in the car; her husband, sister- and brother-in-law, and teenaged niece all thought it was very funny.

　　2. In a systematic ethnographic sample, the goal is a sample that includes the variety of types of people, not one that is statistically representative (which would be impossible due to the lack of sampling frame). Barbara Katz Rothman has a useful metaphor for explaining the difference: the goal is not to determine that percentage of marbles of each color that are in a jar, but rather to learn what are the colors of marbles in the jar, and to explore the key ways in which they differ (1986:18–19). In this study, for example, we were interested in seeing if access to resources, social class, or social context affected women's reproductive health practices, given a set of shared, culturally constructed ideas about gender and sexuality. It was important, therefore, to construct a sample with variety along these three axes. By selecting a group of women who varied in terms of their current resources (measured in Atlanta by English skills and driver's licenses and in both places by current employment), as well as their social class of origin and the context in which they lived (i.e., Atlanta or Mexico), we were able to evaluate the effect of all three sets of factors. For a more extensive discussion of methods and findings, including a description of how participant observation contributed to the study findings, see Hirsch and Nathanson 1998, 2001; Hirsch 2003. For a general discussion of the techniques involved in participant observation, see Bernard 1994.

3. A number of the matched pairs of women were sisters, and one of the life history informants' mothers was deceased, so the eight mothers interviewed represented more than half of the fourteen mothers who could possibly have been interviewed. In terms of the husbands, there were only twenty-two husbands who could possibly have been interviewed because two of the life history informants were not married and the husbands of two others worked as migrant laborers in the United States but not in Atlanta. None of the men from the small farming community, El Fuerte, were willing to be interviewed formally, although several did engage in casual conversation with the lead author over the course of the fieldwork.

4. Many have noted low rates of condom use and limited perceptions of personal risk among migrant men (Bronfman and Minello 1995; Bronfman and Lopez-Moreno 1996; Hirsch, Albalak, and Nyhus 2000; Magaña, de la Rocha, and Ansel 1996; Pérez and Fennelly 1996; Muñiz-Martelon et al. 1996).

5. In comparison with more long-standing migrant-receiving communities, relatively new ones such as those in Georgia may face a particular dearth of second-generation Latinos available to work as translators and advocates (Georgia Department of Human Resources 1994). As migrants continue to travel to more diverse destinations in the United States (Massey and Durand 1998), this issue of regional variation in culturally-competent public health infrastructure is likely to grow in importance.

6. The fact that men remain in Mexico is of course no guarantee that they will not seek out other partners; one recent analysis of a household survey in Mexico City reported that 15% of men interviewed had had extrarelational sex during the past year (Pulerwitz, Izazola-Licea, and Gortmaker 2001). Furthermore, not all men who spend time in the United States as temporary labor migrants have sex while away from home; preliminary analysis of data from a pilot study with a community-based convenience sample of Mexican migrants in Atlanta reveal that slightly over half of the men (53%) had not had sex (Hirsch, Yount, Chakraborty, and Nyhus n.d.). We focus here on migration, infidelity, and HIV risk because those migrants who do seek out extramarital sex while in the United States are generally at greater risk of HIV infection than are men who remain in Mexico.

7. All the quotations presented here use pseudonyms.

8. All of the women interviewed for this study knew that SIDA (the Spanish word for AIDS) is transmitted sexually. Most knew that it was not curable, and several noted that someone could be infected with AIDS but look apparently healthy. All the women stated that a woman is safe as long as she only has sex with her spouse. There were no striking generational differences in women's levels of knowledge, nor did what women know vary much with migration experience.

9. There is nothing particularly new about the link between migration and infection; one woman recounted how her husband's grandmother had been infected by her grandfather. Nor is the relationship between sexually transmitted diseases and increasing economic and social ties to the world beyond the *pueblo* an entirely new phenomenon: Luis Gonzalez, in *San José de Gracia*, describes how the first cases of gonorrhea were diagnosed in San Jose in the late 1940s, shortly after the highway was completed that connected San Jose to larger towns and cities in Michoacan and beyond (1974). Degollado's highway to Guadalajara was completed around the same time.

10. Women discussed sexually transmitted diseases as the focal point of the shame associated with men's infidelity to their wives. In the words of one woman, "They are shameful [or embarrassing] things (*cosas penosas*) . . . For example, if my husband . . . gave me a disease, well I wouldn't tell anybody. . . . People just keep it to themselves."

11. MacCormack and Draper describe people in Jamaica (1987; see also Sobo 1993) as having similar ideas about condoms as interfering with the social effects of sexual relations.

12. In the fifth interview, the life history informants were asked a number of questions about infidelity, including how they would react if confronted with evidence of their husband's infidelity and how they would deal with a friend whose husband they knew had another partner. Their mothers were prompted to speak about infidelity through questions about how a man might show respect or disrespect to his wife and about whether there were situations that justified a woman leaving her husband.

13. Our discussion of infidelity focuses on men's extramarital relationships. Attitudes toward female infidelity seem to have changed very little. Men and women regarded it as grounds for divorce, as a terrible thing both in and of itself and because it tarnishes the reputation (and thus the marriageability) of one's children. Women's sexuality had a very different value than men's in the traditional Mexican marital bargain: by committing to support them, men earned unlimited exclusive sexual access to their wives, the positive assurance that all children within the union would be fathered only by them, and the woman's best efforts at the manifold tasks of social reproduction. A woman's infidelity meant something different than a man's because her sexuality, unlike her husband's, was family rather than individual property; by sharing her body with someone other than her husband, she violated her part of the bargain. Even in the more modern marriages, no one suggested that a husband's extended absence might justify sexual transgression on the part of his wife, though several women did say that if a woman has a strong sexual appetite her husband should bring her to live with him in the United States so that she is not subject to constant temptation. The unacceptability of female infidelity does not mean, of course, that it never happens—just that women stand to lose more when they are discovered. Furthermore, because married women almost never migrate without a spouse, women's infidelity occurs in situations in which a woman who has remained in Mexico selects a partner from among the population of nonmigrant men remaining in the village. In these cases, her infidelity is unlikely to carry a great risk for HIV infection. Women's infidelity is not without sociological interest, but it is unlikely to make a significant contribution to the epidemic of migration-related HIV in rural Mexico.

14. For the older women, leaving one's husband *under any circumstances* meant that one's reputation—and thus one's daughter's marriageability—would be irreparably damaged.

15. Sobo's work is part of a growing body of literature that looks at the relative importance of economic, social, and psychological factors in shaping women's desire and ability to use condoms with different kinds of partners. Some have argued for the primacy of economic factors while others have shown that a

woman's reluctance to ask for condom use stems from her unwillingness to acknowledge that her relationship falls short of her ideals for monogamous intimacy (Hinkle et al. 1992; Kline, Kline, and Oken 1992; Sobo 1995a,b; Zierler and Krieger 1997; Morril et al. 1996; Santelli et al. 1996; Hetherington et al. 1996; Miller et al. 1993; Farmer, Connors, and Simmons 1996). Both are important in this particular context, as Mexican women's attachment to the fiction of mutual monogamy is a cultural manifestation of their social and economic dependence on men.

16. The majority of programs targeting men's behavior change have been directed at gay men. There have been several intervention research programs that have either targeted heterosexual and homosexual men together or else have focused primarily on heterosexual men (Caceres and Rosasco 1993; Celentano et al. 1998; Mishra, Connor, and Magaña 1996; O'Leary et al. 1996; William and Britton 1999). In general, however, heterosexual men have been relatively neglected as targets of condom promotion programs.

17. More than ten years ago Fullilove and Fullilove argued that the debate about which particular social or economic factor is key in helping women negotiate for condom use misses the point that women often do not have the power to negotiate with men how and under what circumstances sexual activity (and relationships) will be conducted (Fullilove et al. 1990:62), and in 1995 Amaro wrote, "Risk of HIV infection in women cannot be separated from the unequal status of women in American society and the resulting differences in power between men and women" (1995:445; see also Farmer 1999). These arguments seem to have had limited impact on public health thinking about women and AIDS.

18. In fact, at least one study among women and men in the United States has shown that in some circumstances women are quite resistant to the idea of condom use—not just because of the emotional implications of condom use, but also because many of the women interviewed reported not liking how condoms feel (Higgins 2005).

19. By arguing that women in this community and others like it in Mexico are not appropriate targets for campaigns promoting condom use to stem the tide of heterosexual marital transmission, we do not mean to suggest that the same is true for married women everywhere around the world. Data presented by Susser and Stein (2000) show that married women in South Africa feel differently about the trade-offs between the emotional risk of acknowledging infidelity and the health risks of not doing so. Across the globe, there may be cultural and social circumstances in which women feel that it is appropriate to take action to protect themselves, and in these settings it certainly makes sense to proceed with intervention research on how to improve women's condom negotiation skills and with basic research to develop and make available effective microbicides.

5

THE ROLE OF ROMANTIC LOVE IN SEXUAL INITIATION AND THE TRANSITION TO PARENTHOOD AMONG IMMIGRANT AND U.S.-BORN LATINO YOUTH IN EAST LOS ANGELES

Pamela I. Erickson

Most academic disciplines either ignore love or treat it in accordance with the rationalist tradition . . . In essence they downgrade romantic love and endorse some version of nonpassionate 'love' which is based on a rational decision to commit oneself to a person or situation . . . mature, as it were—and based on mutual respect, shared values, and common interests. Duty and responsibility are valued above emotional pleasure and romantic passion . . . Passionate love, on the other hand, is seen as dangerous and destructive . . . foolish at best . . . a temporary giddiness, an affliction, or even a kind of illness or madness. (Person 1988:16–17)

The role of romantic love as the social and emotional context of sexual behavior is largely absent from the public health and clinical discourse on adolescent sexual behavior, pregnancy, and childbearing. This is a rather astounding fact, considering that most people have had personal experience with romantic, passionate love and the powerful feelings it can evoke. It is even more astounding because of the preoccupation with passionate love in popular culture and our expectation that the companionate love favored by middle-class Americans for marriage and child rearing should ideally be a transformation of the passionate love that brings the couple together in the first place (Hatfield and Rapson 1996; Person 1988).

Among unmarried adolescents, pregnancy, whether intended or not, forces young couples to decide a number of very important things about their future in a relatively short period of time. They must decide whether or not to have the baby, the implications of this decision for their own relationship, and if they have the child, they must make plans for taking care of it physically, economically, and emotionally.

Most studies analyzing paths to adolescent childbearing treat the phenomenon as a product of rational decision making—a kind of cost-benefit analysis of steps made by young women and, to a lesser extent, young men (i.e., whether to have sex, whether to use contraception, and if pregnant, whether to have an abortion; Michael and Joyner 2000). Qualitative studies of adolescent sexual behavior and childbearing, however, rarely document this form of conscious decision making about sexual behavior on the part of adolescent research participants (Thompson 1995; Erickson 1998–99). Although there are many paths to adolescent pregnancy (e.g., accident, conscious choice, coerced sex), the primary factor among the Latino youth in voluntary romantic relationships with whom I worked in East Los Angeles was the experience of falling in love and the decidedly unplanned nature of the course of subsequent events (Erickson 1998, 1998–99). When the young women in the study were asked about the development of the relationship with their partner, all of them described the experience of falling in love, experiencing what has been characterized as passionate love, "a 'hot,' intense emotion, sometimes called a crush, obsessive love, lovesickness, head-over-heels in love, infatuation, or being in love" (Hatfield and Rapson 1996:3) and having unprotected sex with the loved one.

In normative American scripts for love and marriage, prospective spouses should first fall in love. During this phase of "limerence," which can last between eighteen and thirty-six months, they should get to know each other well, have sexual intercourse, and perhaps live together (Lauman and Michael 2000; Tennov 1979). If they are compatible, if love persists, and if they choose to have children, they should then marry or live together in union and their passionate love should transform to companionate love, which is more compatible with child-rearing and family responsibilities. "When people are young, it is appropriate to be casual about love" (Hatfield and Rapson 1996:86). In adult life, however, it is committed, permanent relationship that should underlie child rearing units (Lauman and Michael 2000).

The young people in my study who chose to become parents were suddenly forced out of the first stage of this normative script—they needed to become adults, willing and able to put the needs of their child above their own. They had to make plans to feed, house, and raise their child. If they were to remain together as a family, they needed to transform their relationship from one of passionate love to one of companionate love, "(sometimes called true love or marital love) . . . a 'warm,' far less intense emotion . . . [which] combines feelings of deep attachment, commitment, and intimacy . . . the affection and tenderness we feel for those with whom our lives are deeply entwined" (Hatfield and Rapson 1996:3).

A decision to have the baby thrust these young women prematurely into a situation in which the self-absorption of the shorter, passionate love phase had to give way to the much longer companionate love phase more appropriate for raising a family, or the couples split up.

The chapters in this book focus on the variety of ways that Western notions of romantic love are shaping marriage and union worldwide. In this chapter, I focus on the impact of romantic love on Latina adolescent childbearing. I describe how the dangers of passionate love draw teenage Latina women into sexual relationships and how being blinded by love justifies premarital sex. In a culture that tends to value premarital virginity and nonaggressive, modest, sexually ignorant, and sexually passive young women (Flores 1990; Pavich 1986; Scrimshaw 1978; Williams 1990), being in love can change the rules. When pregnancy occurs, these young women must find a way to transform relationships begun in passion to relationships founded on commitment and affection. The social, developmental, and economic barriers to such transformation are enormous but not always insurmountable.

METHODS

The data are from interviews with 96 young Latino women and men who participated in a study of the social and cultural context of Latina adolescent childbearing in East Los Angeles in 1994 through 1999.[1] Participants were recruited using adolescent mothers as index cases, then recruiting their sexual partners and a female nonmother control. The index teen mothers were recruited in the Family Planning Outpatient Clinic at the

Los Angeles County—University of Southern California Medical Center (LAC-USC MC), a large public hospital providing care to a low-income, primarily Latino population. Clinic clients who had been under twenty years of age when they delivered their first child were approached to participate in the study and, if interested, they provided informed consent.[2]

The index cases were selected to be representative of teen mothers of different Latino background, age at delivery, and acculturation level who delivered at LAC-USC MC (see Erickson 1998). They were all 19 years of age or younger when they became pregnant (mean, 15.3) and were between 14 and 21 years old at the time of the interviews (mean, 17.7). The young mothers included U.S.-born Latinas (31%), Mexican-born immigrants, including both long-term residents and recent arrivals (47%), and Central American immigrants (22%), of whom 34% were English-speaking, 25% were bilingual, and 41% were Spanish-speaking. The final sample included 46 index teen mothers, 18 of their male partners, and 32 female nonmother controls (see table 5.1).[3]

At the first interview session, each study participant completed a survey eliciting basic demographic information for self and partner, pregnancy and delivery information, level of acculturation, and gender role orientation. Life histories of participants were collected during one to five infor-

TABLE 5.1. Characteristics of Study Participants (N = 96)

Characteristic	Teen Mothers N = 46	Partners N = 18	Controls N = 32
Country of birth			
USA	31%	67%	61%
Mexico	47%	22%	32%
Central America	22%	11%	7%
Language			
English	34%	71%	64%
Bilingual	25%	7%	22%
Spanish	41%	24%	14%
Age range	14–21	17–30	14–21
Mean, standard deviation	17.7, s = 1.4	22.5, s = 5.0	16.6, s = 1.9
Age at first sex	11–18	12–18	12–21
Mean, standard deviation	14.4, s = 2.4	14.4, s = 1.9	14.9, s = 1.3
Age at pregnancy	13–19	15–30	13–20*
Mean, standard deviation	15.3, s = 1.5	not asked	16.6, s = 1.9
Married or living together	66%	63%	28%
Trying to get pregnant	46%	29%	3%*
Partner wanted pregnancy	56%	54%	57%*

*7 of the controls had been pregnant.

mal interview sessions of one to two hours in length. Participants were simply asked to tell us the story of their lives. Topics probed included neighborhood, family, religion, sex and romantic relationships, pregnancy and delivery, being a parent, school and work, migration history, acculturation, health care, and future life plans and goals. Interviews were tape-recorded and transcribed in the language of the interview. The final interview session consisted of systematic data collection techniques to investigate life course, sexual behavior, and contraceptive methods (Weller and Romney 1988). Completion of the project required between three and five sessions, and participants were paid $25 per session. The interviews were conducted by bilingual, bicultural female interviewers in a private room in the outpatient building of the hospital.

RESULTS

Three things impressed me in the stories that young women told about how they met their boyfriends and how their relationships evolved. The first was the centrality of the concept of passionate love in the formative stages of the relationship. Indeed, many of the young women behaved as though possessed or in a trance, throwing caution to the winds, ignoring advice and counsel of parents and friends, doing things they would never consider had they not been under the spell of love. The second was the pervasiveness of the idea that the woman's first love (i.e., first sexual partner) should be her lifetime partner and mate. The third was how similar the courtship stories were to each other, following a set script with only minor variations. These three themes are discussed in the context of attitudes about love, romance, sex, and gender and how they foster adolescent childbearing among low-income Latinas in East Los Angeles.

Gender, Sex, and Romantic Love

The cultural ideal of sexual naïveté and virginity before marriage for young Latinas described by numerous authors (Alarcón, Castillo, and Moraga 1993; Pavich 1986; Scrimshaw 1978; Williams 1990; Zavella 1997) was widely held in this population, as this comment from Eva, a bilingual, U.S.-born teen mother shows.

> Eva: I really did love him a lot and I really did care for him, but it
>   was just the fact that I was gonna lose my virginity. I mean, that
>   was like . . . for a Hispanic girl, you know, that's like, God, that's

a big thing. That's like something precious. And, you know, like, you just have to wait 'til you're married and stuff, you know?

In fact, most of the young women interviewed were quite naive about sex and sexuality when they first became sexually involved. For the most part, they were not taught about their bodies or about reproduction, contraception, or sex in the home, and many (68%) had already left school and, thus, were not exposed to sex education in school. Very few thought they knew enough about sex when they became sexually active, as the following quotes from Eva who was fifteen the first time she had sex, and Silvia, an immigrant teen from El Salvador who was sixteen when she first had sex, show.

Eva: The first time [we had sex], I was living with him, he just came outside, but I still got pregnant. [Sex] scared me at first because I was never introduced to my body or even a male's body. I didn't even know how my body worked, you know? . . . To me, in my head it [premarital sex] was wrong. . . . I knew Rudy had sex before. Because I knew he was always in the streets and stuff, you know? But I didn't even know about protection or stuff.

and

Silvia: Nobody educated me, nobody taught me [about sex]. I think that's why I got pregnant so young . . . Because for me, they never told me anything. I never knew anything and because of that, I think, things happen.

Most of the young women were also quite young when they began having sex—the mean age was 14.8 years—and they entered into relationships with young men on average five years their senior (range 1 to 16 years difference) knowing virtually nothing about sex and contraception. Eva's boyfriend was only two years older than she, but Silvia's was 15 years older. As Sandi, one of the U.S.-born control teens, notes, there is a lot of pressure on young women with older partners to have sex to show their love.

Sandi: I think when you are going out with an older guy [sex is] just to please the older guy. Mostly when younger girls go out with older guys, it's the pressure and the pleasing him and the "I want to show him I love him." . . . I think when you are at thirteen and fourteen you are naive, and if a guy tells you he loves you, I mean, you do almost anything. [When I was fourteen] I thought that stuff [sex] was, you know, couples do it. That is what I thought then, but now I have more conservative thinking than when I was younger.

For most participants, sex was only considered appropriate within a committed, husband-wife relationship or its equivalent—living together as though married—and strong cultural norms reinforced the ideal that for a woman sex, love, marriage, and motherhood should be fused into lifetime partnership with only one man (Alarcón, Castillo, and Moraga 1993; Thompson 1995). Many of the young women were certain that their first love was "the one" almost from the moment they met their partners. Take Julia, for example, a Spanish-speaking immigrant from Mexico who at age fourteen knew that seventeen-year-old Juan, a U.S.-born Latino, was her soul mate, and he knew she was his. Here Julia talks about her first sexual experience with Juan.

> Julia: Yes, I knew what I was doing [having unprotected sex]. He gives me everything. He excites me, makes me happy. This is a love that is beautiful. I wanted to be his wife and have his children.

Juan met Julia in Mexico where he was visiting his grandparents. She was twelve years old when they first met, but told him she was fifteen. He was sixteen. For two years, he visited whenever he could. He wrote her poems and called her on the phone. He moped around the house and neglected his studies. He was in love. Here Juan talks about his feelings for Julia.

> Juan: It was more, uh, spiritual, you know, than just wanting to kiss her. No, it was true love. So I didn't want to have sex with her. I got tempted sometimes—when we were kissing so passionately—but I respected her. She was the first girl I respected.

They had their first child when she was fifteen, another two years later, and they married when she turned eighteen.

Some of the young women seemed almost possessed by love, like Silvia who met Luís when he was visiting relatives in El Salvador.

> Silvia: When I was fifteen years old, I fell in love with him, but he didn't know. And two years later, he came back.
> Interviewer: And you were still in love with him? In those two years there was no one else?
> Silvia: Well, I was never interested. In my mind there was only him.

And the second time he came back to visit after two years, they had sex, she got pregnant, and he took her to live with him in the United States.

Other young women did extraordinary things to be with the man they loved. Jessica met Lalo, ten years her senior, while he was visiting family in Nayarít. He came to her home several times, played soccer with her and her brothers, and visited with her parents. She fell in love with him. A few months after he went back to the United States, she set out on her own, at age fourteen, to track him down in Fresno. She left home, telling no one but a cousin where she was going, took a bus to Tijuana, engaged a *coyote* to take her across the border to San Diego, and enlisted the aid of her aunt who lived in Los Angeles to pay the *coyote* and take her to Fresno. Jessica didn't even know exactly where Lalo lived, and he didn't know she was coming. When she found him a few weeks after arriving in Fresno, Lalo's wife, about whom she hadn't known, had just left him for another man, taking their two children with her. Lalo was in a terrible state—depressed, drinking heavily—and Jessica took care of him and helped him through this time during which she got pregnant and got what she wanted—him. They now have a child and live with his mother in Los Angeles.

Although not all of the love stories told by these young people were as dramatic as these three, the message was clear that for these young couples, being in love legitimated the loss of the young woman's virginity, as these quotes show.

> Silvia: When I gave in and got pregnant I was head over heels in love with him.
> Juan: No, we just felt so free that it just happened. When you're in love, it's like a sense of freedom—like you could do anything. You feel real positive about things. I couldn't believe it that she was there with me . . . and I was thinking, well, if I'm gonna

marry her it might be OK. So, then, it just happened and it was like we didn't—it wasn't even planned.

Julia: It's because I loved him very much. I love Juan a lot. That's why. It's like I've always loved him. Even now I can't be separated from him.

Many young women, particularly the more acculturated teens, were more "in like" than "in love" with their boyfriends, but that "like" was reevaluated as love once they had sex—even under extraordinary circumstances as Cori's case shows.

Cori: I didn't really want to [have sex]. It just happened, because I left my house. My mom threw me out. I didn't have anywhere to go, and so I stayed [at his house]. I felt like I was trapped, and I am not going to say that he forced me, but I was trapped. . . . I don't know, we did it for the wrong reasons. I felt like I was so desperate, I had nothing else to live for. [I thought] "I don't care about anything else, you know? Forget it, it's just you [her boyfriend, Carlos] now."

Romantic Scripts

With the stage set by sexual naïveté, female purity, and the one-man-for-life ideal, young Latinas are not well prepared for entry into dating relationships. Moreover, there are two decidedly different "dating games" or scripts to which young Latinas in the United States are exposed (see Gagnon 1990 for a discussion of scripting theory in sex research). One exists among more acculturated Latinos and American youth. In this script, dating relationships that are usually initiated between the ages of twelve and sixteen are a time for experimentation with different partners and different roles as a prelude to later marriage in the mid to late twenties. Although the sexual double standard is in full play and much attention is devoted to maintaining a good reputation among young women—that is, not being perceived as promiscuous—the majority do not expect to be virgins when they marry, nor is this any longer a dominant cultural ideal (Thompson 1995; Lauman and Michael 2000). Teen dating norms emphasize love and romance within heterosexual relationships with no expectation of marriage, and the time frame between dating and marriage can be as much as ten or more years. In the Latino community from which these teens come, traditional dating patterns have the more serious purpose of finding one's mate to allow for the fusion of love, sex, marriage, and pregnancy within a one- or two-year time frame (Alarcón, Castillo, and Moraga 1993).

The courtship stories told by these young women were highly scripted. First, the girl meets and is pursued by a young man. Here, Erika describes Junior's wooing strategy.

> Erika: In the beginning I didn't really care for him, to tell you the truth. When I first started seeing him, I was like, ay, go away, you know, go somewhere else. He kept coming and coming and coming, so I guess that is what made me like him because he kept on coming.

After several weeks of clandestine meetings, the suitor must ask the girl's parents for formal permission to date her. After approval from the family, the couple officially become *novios* (literally, fiancés, although the term is also used for less serious dating relationships) and are eventually expected to marry if all goes well between them. The period of courtship should ideally last one to two years, by which time the girl is considered old enough (i.e., fifteen to eighteen) to marry.

If the family does not approve of the relationship, the couple has three choices: stop seeing each other, continue seeing each other in hiding, or run away together (the term actually used is *robarselo*, to steal her from the family). None of the young women stopped seeing their boyfriends due to their parents' objections. Rather, they continued seeing each other on the sly or ran away together. For example, Silvia's parents objected to her relationship with Luís and tried to put an end to it because she was so much younger than he. They even threatened to call the police and have him put in jail, but Silvia and Luís kept seeing each other secretly for about three months until she got pregnant and he took her to the United States with her parents' blessing now that a child was on the way.

The other alternative is for the couple to run away and live together. This is what Juan and Julia did. Juan was seventeen years old when Julia came to live with him at his mother's house. Here Juan describes his anguish at having to resort to "stealing" fourteen-year-old Julia from Mexico.

> Juan: I decided to steal her with her permission. And everybody was trying to talk me out of it because I was too young, but I was really in love with her . . . So, when she was here [in the United States visiting aunts], I stole her. That's when I got on the bad side of her parents. And they really got upset with me and I understood, because that made me feel like less of a man. So, I decided to go ahead and live with her. I didn't want to 'cause I wanted to get married first instead of taking her, 'cause I knew that once she was there, where was she gonna sleep? So, I just thought I might as well sleep with her, but I swear I wasn't thinking about the physical—the sexual part didn't hit me until a day before [she moved in].

More acculturated teens—primarily those who had been to school in the United States and immersed in American teen culture—tended to adhere more to the middle-class dating pattern and often held less traditional values about sex and gender than less acculturated teens. But they also knew that Latino culture had its own more conservative dating rules, and they were confronted by strong pressure to conform to community norms. Thus, they were often torn between competing worldviews, and their more liberal behavior frequently caused intergenerational conflicts since most of their parents were themselves immigrants from Mexico or Central America. They protected their image by appearing to conform to the "good girl" role and by hiding their sexual relationships, pregnancy scares, and abortions from their families. Sandi, a control teen, expresses it this way.

> Sandi: I knew about things [contraception]. I didn't know who to go talk to [where to get it]. My mom told me about sex and protection, but I never did it [got birth control] because—that's my mom, and I am the baby and I don't feel, you know, she doesn't know anything about, you know [that I have sex].

For most of the young mothers, the father of their baby was their first sexual partner. Love, passionate love, caught them off guard and led to sex, pregnancy, and parenthood (see Erickson 1998–99). Once a sexual relationship was established between the couple, most of the young women became pregnant within one year of initiation of intercourse (average 1.1 years, range 0–4) because most of them did not use contraception or used it sporadically, and almost half (46%) were trying to get pregnant. If they chose to have the baby, they moved in together—usually in one of their parental households—but official marriage was often delayed until the young woman came of age (at 18) or until the couple could afford a church wedding. From their point of view, however, they were husband and wife, and the child solidified this status in the community. Even if their own parents were initially opposed, once there was a grandchild the couple was welcomed back into the family, or at least tolerated. If the young man left his partner in the lurch, she was almost always taken back into her own family—if not by her parents, then by other relatives. If there were serious family problems, the Department of Children's Services (DCS) stepped in, and/or young mothers were referred to privately funded residential programs for teen mothers with nowhere else to go. In fact, two participants were lost to follow-up after being removed from their homes by DCS during the study, and several participants lived in residential programs for teen mothers run by nonprofit groups.

It is important to note here that the control teens told the same kind of love stories as the young mothers, but they avoided parenthood through abortion, contraception, or miscarriage. Some, like Sandi, "woke up" after a pregnancy scare or an abortion and began using contraception.

> Interviewer: So, did you plan to have that pregnancy or was it an accident?
>
> Sandi: Uhmm, I didn't plan it, but it was . . . I mean it was kinda stupid, you know. I wasn't really using anything. I tried to avoid it [thinking I might be pregnant] and then finally one of my girlfriends said, "Why don't you just go get tested?" And finally I did, and it came out positive and I was like in shock. And they wanted me to go talk to a social worker right away and they were like . . . prescribing me iron and just like rushing me into like having the baby. But I didn't want to continue with it. It was like right after my sixteenth birthday. It was scary. It wasn't a joke any more. And then I thought "God! I need to go to school. I want to do all these things." I was thinking, "No, I am not ready for this. I don't want to be a housewife."

And Sandi decided to have an abortion.

Others, like Manuela, a Spanish-speaking control teen from Mexico, had miscarriages and would very much like to become pregnant again.

Manuela had a miscarriage after becoming pregnant at age seventeen. She would like to try again, but her partner—ten years her senior—wants to wait until he finds work. Until then, Manuela is just marking time. When asked what would make her happy in her life she responded: "I would like to be a mother, I'd like to have a child."

Prospects for Companionate Love among Adolescent Parents

As time passed, the young women described the waning of the passionate love phase especially when they were faced with the demands of parenting. Most of the young women, especially the young mothers, began to yearn for a more companionate style of love—a shared partnership. Some of their partners were not ready to leave their single lifestyle behind—hanging out and drinking with their friends, going to bars, seeing other women, and so forth. This led to inevitable strains in the relationship or to its dissolution. Young women, like Cori, came to understand that their infatuation had been just that. They decided that their partners were not good candidates for companionate love and so terminated the relationship.

> Cori: We did it twice or whatever and he gave me something [a sexually transmitted infection] and got me pregnant. . . . I found out after, when I found out I was pregnant five months later, I had chlamydia . . . and when I found out, I was so mad I wanted to kill him, I was so mad! Afterward, I found out that he was sleeping with my best friend. All my friends were sleeping with him. He was really cute. He was a gorgeous little thing. He was a *cholo*, but you know how girls like *cholos* . . . They like those little gangsters, little *cholo* guys. They get all those girls pregnant and they just leave, and they don't think of their kids . . . when they need to give them money, to the girl, to take care of the kid, they are not there.

Others discovered that they were now in relationships with men for whom they had feelings and upon whom they were economically dependent, but about whom they expressed a certain ambivalence. Silvia who was *super enamorada* (head over heels in love) with Luís when she got pregnant is rethinking her relationship.

Silvia: Now I don't know. It could be due to the problems we had when we got here [the United States]. He drank a lot. Maybe I lost a little of all that I felt for him. Now I love him and all, but not like we were before.

For some of the young fathers, too, having a baby made them reevaluate their relationship to their girlfriends. Rudy, Eva's partner, conceded that he did not know whether he really loved her.

Rudy: Well, see, I never loved someone, like really loved 'em. You know? I don't know why. I'm just like that. I do like Eva and everything, but like, I miss her, but I don't like, love her, you know. *Todavía no* [Not yet]. I don't know, we share a lot of things together, you know, but I don't know how to love someone.

Rudy and Eva's situation is further exacerbated by educational disparities. Eva was in college at the time of her last interview. Rudy had dropped out of school long ago when he was in ninth grade. He was employed on and off in construction. He was still involved with their child and helped out financially when he could, but their relationship had been rocky and their life trajectories seemed to be taking different courses. Rudy thinks that because Eva is in college and wants to be a doctor that her life will be, and in many ways already is, so different from his that "she's not going to want to hang around with me when she's a doctor."

Another young man, an eighteen-year-old college freshman, wants to be a father to his daughter, but he and his girlfriend, Traci, broke up when she was pregnant a year ago. She has another boyfriend now, and he only sees his daughter from time to time. Was he in love with Traci?

Tomás: I could say I cared about her a lot, but I can't, I don't know about love. Love is just a word right now. I don't really know what it is. I mean I want to see more of my kid and I want to take care of her and to be a part of her life. I want to make it successful so I could give her a good life, you know, have a decent job, a house, a car, a family. But, what's bad is that you are in school and you got to drop out to get a job, but you got to stay in to get a really good job to support [a family]. I don't regret it [having a baby] cuz I know I have a kid and I am not really ready for it, but

I can't say the kid messed up my life, cuz for me nothing has changed that much.

For many young fathers and mothers, the baby became a catalyst for evaluating their lives and a motivation to better themselves—to go back to school, to begin job training, to learn English, to stop drinking, to take parenting classes, and to try to be a family. Some were able to transform their passionate love into the companionate style so much more compatible with child-rearing demands. Juan and Julia, for example, enjoy a warm, close, nurturing love. Juan finished high school and has a job, and they are hoping to buy a house in a few years. Jessica and Lalo also have a loving companionate-style relationship, but theirs is threatened by his continued unemployment and their dependence on his mother. Other young men, like Rudy and Tomás, seemed not to have felt that passionate love for the mothers of their children. Now, they want to have contact with their children, but their different life trajectories make it unlikely that they will ever be a united family.

Low education levels, language difficulties, and legal status in the United States limit employment opportunities for both young men and women, but it is the stories of the young men that speak to this issue poignantly. Their role as a father and husband, and thus their self-esteem, were both tied to being able to provide for their family. Only 61% of the partners of the teen mothers had a steady job, and many worked several jobs to make ends meet. Young couples were forced to live with parents, relatives, or friends in order to afford housing. Sometimes the economic stress led to relationship problems that could force couples apart. Sometimes the young mothers and their children returned to their natal families. The importance of maintaining kin ties under marginal economic conditions cannot be stressed too highly. Some teen mothers verbalized this explicitly when talking about their decisions concerning their boyfriends. If they go with their partners against their parents' wishes, they might be cut off from future support should the relationship fail. As Yesenia, a U.S.-born teen mother, notes:

> Yesenia: Family is very, very important, cuz even though my family is just like messed up, like they say "blood is thicker than water." Don't ever leave your family, cuz if you leave 'em in the dark, when your boyfriend or your mate leaves you, your family's gonna say "Know what, you preferred him over us, forget you."

DISCUSSION

The love stories told by the young people in this study suggest that early childbearing was not, for the most part, a planned event, but rather the result of how the intense emotions of love, passion, and desire played out within a context of sexual and contraceptive ignorance, silence regarding discussion of sexual matters, and the constraints of social norms that require women to resist and men to insist on sexual intercourse (Erickson 1998–99). The script for romantic love among these young Latinos allows young women to retain their purity and relinquish their virginity at the same time, but it does so at great potential cost. When this script is enacted in the contemporary world of incurable sexually transmitted diseases and the social and economic burdens of early parenthood, it places young men and women at enormous risk. Unfortunately, this cultural script for romantic relationships and appropriate female behavior makes love a dangerous pleasure.

In a sense, the script is also unfinished. It does not indicate to young people how or when to transform passionate love into companionate love. The script is detailed when it comes to courtship and the management of sexuality, but it simply ends at "get married and live happily ever after." All of the young people in the study held companionate marriage as the ideal for raising children, and they aspired to have a supportive partner, a good job, and a house, and to give their children the benefits of a good life. The developmental, social, and economic circumstances of most of the young people in this study, however, hampered their ability to transform passionate love relationships into companionate love relationships when faced with a pregnancy.

One barrier to the development of companionate love was the age, emotional maturity, and readiness for marriage and family formation of the individuals involved. Many of the younger partners of the teen mothers were simply not interested in taking on the responsibilities of marriage and family, and these couples eventually separated. Among the control cases, young women who were not ready for marriage and parenting chose to use contraception, to abort, or to abstain from sexual relations. Among the young mothers, those who were not ready for marriage and family, but were opposed to abortion, often fared the worst in their attempts to transform their relationships into companionate marriage. Not surprisingly, the young women who were ready for marriage and family, who were seeking pregnancy or at least not that worried about it, who had older partners, and who generally held more traditional values made the transition more easily. But even among the few couples who succeeded in developing a companionate relationship, lack of economic resources tended to undermine their ability to maintain it. Only those who had good jobs or whose families were particularly supportive were able to make a go of it.

These case studies raise important questions about whether modern love scripts are attainable for young people entering partnerships and having children under challenging temporal, social, and economic conditions. While youth worldwide may increasingly strive for the ideal of modern love and companionate partnerships, future research must address whether or not achieving this ideal is dependent on emotional maturity and economic security.

NOTES

1. The research was funded by the National Institute of Child Health and Development (HD32351).

2. The project received full review and was approved by the Human Subjects Protection Committees at both the University of Connecticut and the Los Angeles County—University of Southern California Medical Center.

3. About half of the young women had no partner at the time of recruitment or did not want us to contact him. Many men who were invited to participate declined due primarily to time constraints of employment. The nonmother controls included friends and relatives of the index mother when possible and nonmother family planning clients.

6

LOVE AND THE RISK OF HIV

COURTSHIP, MARRIAGE, & INFIDELITY
IN SOUTHEASTERN NIGERIA

Daniel Jordan Smith

Marriage has been a staple of anthropological study in sub-Saharan Africa since the colonial period (Radcliffe-Brown and Forde 1950; Colson 1958; Schapera 1966). More recent reexaminations of nuptuality in Africa have been important catalysts for rethinking anthropological theory (Comaroff 1980). The study of marriage has been central for understanding kinship and social organization (Fox 1967; Mair 1969), the developmental cycle of the household (Goody 1962; Guyer 1981), the social and cultural underpinnings of demographic processes (Bledsoe and Pison 1994; Feldman-Savelsberg 1999), and the significance of gender as an organizing social force and category of analysis (Potash 1986; Goheen 1996). Part of the impetus for a shift toward analytical perspectives that pay greater attention to women's agency (Bozzoli 1991) and to the strategic and performative aspects of marriage processes (Murray 1976; Karp 1987) has come from the changing nature of marriage itself (Caldwell 1968; Harrell-Bond 1975; Parkin and Nyamwaya 1987). As the introduction to this volume demonstrates, changes in courtship practices, in rituals establishing marriage, in marital ideologies, in household gender dynamics, and in the importance of conjugality vis-à-vis other kinship relationships must be understood in the context of broader social transformations.

In this chapter, I examine how changing patterns of courtship and marriage are affecting HIV risk among Igbo-speaking people in southeastern Nigeria. In particular, I aim to explain how a complex intersection of changing marital ideals and practices combine with continuing gender inequality to shape patterns of sexual behavior and condom use across a spectrum of premarital, marital, and extramarital relationships. Similar to trends in many other parts of the world (e.g., Hollos and Larsen 1997; Hirsch 2003), men and women in Nigeria increasingly privilege the conjugal bond relative to other social relationships. The idea that marriage should be a partnership sustained by the private personal and emotional attachment of two people has grown significantly over the past several decades (Obiechina 1973; Smith 2000, 2001). The rise of forms of marriage that have been described in this volume as companionate is sometimes interpreted as part of a larger movement toward individualism and gender equality. Indeed, among the population that I studied in Nigeria, most young women and many young men explicitly desired and promoted marital ideals that privilege conjugality, romance, and individual relationships as the bedrock of marriage, deploying these ideals in their negotiations with suitors and spouses as well as with their extended families. But these emerging ideals and patterns of marriage unfold in a context of continuing gender inequality, such that expectations about fidelity, romantic love, and intimacy are placing women at risk of contracting HIV from their partners. The combination of changing relationship ideals and behaviors and continuing gender inequality is making it difficult for women, married or not, to negotiate safe sex.

In sub-Saharan Africa, where 25 million people are estimated to be HIV positive (UNAIDS 2004), 55% of adult infections are in women (WHO 2000). For most women in Nigeria, as in much of the world, the behavior that puts them at greatest risk of infection from HIV is having sex with their husbands (Federal Ministry of Health 1999). In Nigeria, the most recent sentinel sero-prevalence survey of pregnant women (Federal Ministry of Health 2004) indicated that approximately 5% were HIV positive. Extrapolations from this data suggest that more than three million Nigerians are currently infected with HIV. Projections predict that in the next two to three years nearly five million Nigerians will be infected. The ethnographic study of sexual relationships, marriage, and gender dynamics elucidates how the rise of love as a relationship ideal combines with the social construction of male gender and its manifestation in multiple extra-marital sexual relationships to shape patterns of HIV risk in Africa's most populous country.

SETTING AND METHODS

The setting for the research that forms the basis for the analysis presented here is Igbo-speaking southeastern Nigeria. Igbos are the third largest of Nigeria's nearly 250 ethnic groups, numbering approximately 20 million. I have lived and worked periodically in Nigeria since 1989. During that time, I conducted more than three years of field research in southeastern Nigeria in a semirural community located just eight miles from Umuahia, the capital of Abia State. Data for this chapter have been accumulated while undertaking a variety of research projects carried out over the past ten years. Research methods included participant observation, semistruc-tured interviewing, extended case studies, village household surveys of women of reproductive age and their husbands, large sample surveys of secondary school and university students, and multiple interviews with adolescent and young adult rural-urban migrants. Over the years, I have spent most of my time doing participant observation, and it is, I think, the source of the most interesting and valuable data. Participant observation has meant attending all manner of local social events and ceremonies—marriage rites, burials, chieftancy installation ceremonies, family meetings, gatherings to resolve local disputes, child-naming ceremonies, and so on. But perhaps more important, it has entailed accompanying and spending time with people as they went about their everyday lives—farming, fetch-ing water, cooking, trading in the market, drinking palm wine or beer, going to church, and traveling to town. It has also meant listening to, and often participating in, the conversations, negotiations, and gossip that unfolded in all of these different settings and contexts. Much of what I know about Igbo marriages and about Igbo sexual relationships, marital infidelity, and the negotiation of condom use comes from observation and participation in the kinds of informal conversations and exchanges of gos-sip that can best be achieved through extended fieldwork.

ROMANTIC LOVE AND MARRIAGE IN WEST AFRICA

The question of whether or not romantic love is universal has intrigued researchers for a long time (Murstein 1974; Kurian 1979; Endleman 1989;

Jankowiak 1995). In one of the few anthropological studies of romantic love, Jankowiak and Fischer (1992) set out to test the question by examining Murdock and White's (1969) Standard Cross-Cultural Sample looking for the existence (or not) of romantic love in ethnographic data collected from nearly two hundred cultures. They preface their study with this assertion.

> The anthropological study of romantic (or passionate) love is virtually nonexistent due to the widespread belief that romantic love is unique to Euro-American culture. . . . Underlying these Eurocentric views is the assumption that modernization and the rise of individualism are directly linked to the appearance of romantic notions of love. (Jankowiak and Fischer 1992:149)

Defining romantic love as "any intense attraction that involves the idealization of the other, within an erotic context, with the expectation of enduring for sometime in the future" (1992:150), Jankowiak and Fischer conclude from their analysis that romantic love *is* a cross-cultural universal, or at least that it is *nearly* universal. They stress, however, that even if some form of romantic love is nearly universal across cultures, there is a need to understand "its emic manifestations within a variety of cultural settings" (154).

Like a number of scholars (e.g., Hatfield and Rapson 1996), Jankowiak and Fischer distinguish between romantic love, which is defined as passionate and erotic, and what they call "companionship" love (1992:150), which emerges over the long evolution of a relationship. As indicated in the introduction to this volume, terms such as *companionate marriage* are sometimes defined in different ways by different scholars. Falling in love, marrying for love, and staying married because of love are not the same thing. Regardless of terminology, it is important to recognize and explain the ways in which ideas and expectations about love are implicated in the social construction of marriage in contemporary Igbo-speaking Nigeria. My findings support the argument in this volume's introduction that changes in marriage in Nigeria, as in many settings, are intertwined with larger trends such as the rise of more explicit notions of an individualized self, the growing importance of commodity consumption as a means of self-fashioning, and the emergence of discourses about gender relations as a way to claim (or contest) modern identities. Further, I show how these same dynamics contribute to the configuration of premarital and extramarital sexual relationships. Specifically, I explore how the contemporary construction of marriage articulates continuities and changes in gender dynamics, and particularly how male gender and the structure of gender inequality continue to be expressed in patterns of extramarital sexual behavior.

Evidence from Nigeria (Obiechina 1973; Okonjo 1992) and across Africa (Mair 1969; Little 1979; van der Vliet 1991) indicates that Africans are increasingly likely to select marriage partners based, at least in part, on whether they are "in love." The emergence of romantic love as a criterion in mate selection and the increasing importance of conjugality in marriage relationships should not be interpreted to mean that romantic love itself has only recently emerged in Nigeria. When I asked elderly Igbos about their betrothals, about their marriages, and about love, I was told numerous personal stories and popular fables that indicated a long tradition of romantic love. A number of men and women confessed that they would have married a person other than their spouse had they been allowed to "follow the heart." Scholars have documented the existence of romantic love in Africa long before it became a widely accepted criterion for marriage (Bell 1995; Plotnicov 1995; Riesman 1972, 1981). Uchendu (1965) confirms the existence of passionate love in his study of concubinage in traditional Igbo society. Interestingly, both men and women were reportedly accorded significant institutionalized extramarital sexual freedom and a related proverb survives to the present: *uto ka na iko* (sweetness is deepest among lovers). As Obiechina notes: "The question is not whether love and sexual attraction as normal human traits exist within Western and African societies, but how they are woven into the fabric of life" (1973:34).

Exactly when Nigerians in general and Igbos in particular began to conceptualize marriage choices in more individualistic terms, privileging romantic love as a criterion in the selection of a spouse, is hard to pinpoint. In some parts of Igboland and in many parts of Nigeria the social acceptance of individual choice in mate selection is still just beginning. Certainly these changes occurred first in urban areas among relatively educated and elite populations (Marris 1962; Little and Price 1973). Obiechina's (1973) study of Onitsha pamphlet literature indicates that popular Nigerian literature about love, romance, and modern marriage began to emerge just after World War II. Historical accounts suggest that elements of modern marriage began even earlier in the twentieth century (Mann 1985). By the 1970s, a number of monographs about modern marriage in West Africa had been produced (e.g., Oppong 1974; Harrell-Bond 1975).

In contemporary Igboland, young people increasingly value choosing their own spouses. In my village sample of just over 200 married women of reproductive age, over 60% reported that their marriages were choice marriages rather than arranged marriages, and, not surprisingly, the percentages were higher among younger women and lower among older women. The expectation to choose one's spouse is almost universal among young persons still in school. In my sample of 775 students drawn from 19 secondary schools, over 95% said they expected to choose their marriage partners themselves, and the expectation was universal among 420 university students I surveyed. Among married people who chose their own spouses and among young people anticipating choosing a spouse, love is frequently mentioned as one important criterion, though not the only one. Individual choice in mate selection and love as a relationship ideal are connected, but one is not the equivalent of the other.

PREMARITAL SEX AND CONTEMPORARY IGBO COURTSHIP

To understand the emergence and spread of the expectation that marriage partners should be selected by individual choice based, at least in part, on romantic love, it is necessary to know something about premarital sexual relationships and patterns of courtship in contemporary Igbo society. Indeed, certain patterns and expectations about gender roles are established in premarital relationships, and these expectations create difficulties for women to negotiate safe sex after marriage, when the roles of wife and mother become paramount.

Premarital sexual relationships are increasingly common in contemporary Nigeria (Nichols et al. 1986), including in the Igbo-speaking southeast (Feyisetan and Pebley 1989; Makinwa-Adebusoye 1992; Smith 2000). Driven by the spread and acceptance of formal schooling as valuable for both boys and girls and the growth of nondomestic work opportunities for women, average age at marriage for females in southeastern Nigeria has increased from approximately sixteen years old at independence in 1960 to around twenty-one years old at present (Isiugo-Abanihe, Ebigbola, and Adewuyi 1993). A significant proportion of young women now remain single into their late twenties. Most men marry around the age of thirty, the later age at marriage for men attributed to their need to secure themselves economically in order to be able to pay bridewealth and support a family. Concurrent with and also contributing to later age at marriage, more and more single young people are migrating to Nigeria's cities (Oucho and

Gould 1993; Gugler and Ludwar-Ene 1995). In the city, young people are less subject to the discipline of their village relatives and more likely to be exposed to peer and media messages about the appeal and acceptability of premarital sex.

Related to demographic changes such as age at marriage and levels of urban migration is a changing conception of the nature of male-female relationships. In addition to simply having more time before marriage to try sex, young people value male-female intimacy to a degree their parents and grandparents did not. Premarital sexual relationships are places where young people construct their identities, very often in self-conscious opposition to traditions they perceive as "bush," "backward," and "uncivilized"—their words, not mine (Smith 2000). Sex is being socially constructed as an appropriate expression of intimacy, but also as a statement about a particular kind of modern identity. The place of sex in this creation of a modern Igbo identity and the relationship between modern sexual identities and commodity consumption are very much evident in practices of courtship (Smith 2001; Cornwall 2002). The case briefly described here exhibits many of the patterns that are now common in contemporary Igbo courtship.

Chinyere Nwankwo met her husband Ike in the town of Owerri in southeastern Nigeria, where she attended a teachers college after completing secondary school in her village community. Ike was eight years her senior, and when they met he was doing very well as a building contractor—well enough to own a used car, a prized symbol of wealth and success. On their first date he took her to the disco at the Concorde Hotel, at that time the fanciest in town. In addition to being educated, Chinyere was a beautiful young woman and consequently had many suitors. Her courtship with Ike lasted almost two years. During that time they often dined out and went dancing together. Among the more memorable events of their courtship were a weekend outing to the Nike Lake resort near Enugu and a trip to Lagos during which they attended a performance by Fela Ransome-Kuti, a famous Nigerian musician. During their courtship, each bought the other Hallmark-like cards on birthdays, and for Ike's birthday, Chinyere baked him a cake. They went to many social events together and acknowledged to their peers that they were a couple. Not long into their relationship, Chinyere and Ike began sleeping together. Many months before they decided to marry, they were sexually intimate. Prior to approaching Chinyere's people and his own family about their getting married, Ike asked Chinyere. They agreed together to get married and then began the process of including their families.

For Chinyere and Ike, as for many unmarried young Igbos, sexual intimacy constituted an integral part of their relationship, a relationship that they thought of as a romance. Chinyere described her decision to marry Ike this way: "A lot of things are important in deciding whom to marry. You need a good husband who can provide for the family and it's important to find a man who is progressive. I would never marry a man who just wanted a wife to cater to him like a servant. There are a lot of things, but if you are not in love what's the point, really?" Later, in talking more specifically about sex and intimacy she added: "For a good marriage husband and wife need to be compatible. Sex is part of it. A big part. If you are not compatible in bed how intimate can you really be?"

Premarital sex, symbolic commodities such as greeting cards, and public displays of being a "couple" are bound together in the performance of modern courtship in southeastern Nigeria. While young people engage in premarital sexual relations for a variety of reasons, what is striking is the degree to which most young Igbos expect and accept that sex is and should be a part of the process of courtship. Of course there are many competing and sometimes critical discourses about young people's sexual behavior in Nigeria (especially young women's sexual behavior), including those in the idiom of religious morality (Smith 2004a). Nevertheless, the degree of acceptance that sex is appropriate when two people are "in love" is most striking (Smith 2004b).

Equally important is recognizing the degree to which premarital romances tend to support a relatively egalitarian gender dynamic, at least with regard to expectations of fidelity. During courtship, when the couple's relationship is based primarily on their personal emotional relationship to each other, both persons feel an obligation to fidelity. While this obligation is not necessarily observed, an individual who cheats on his or her lover and gets caught knows there is a good chance that the other person will end the relationship. It was my impression that young unmarried Igbo men cheated more than young unmarried Igbo women, but not dramatically so. But most important for the case I want to make, the sanctions each faced were similar. Infidelity during courtship was a personal violation and the consequences had to be negotiated between the individuals involved. Of course young people often enlisted friends to plead their cases, but the grounds for "making up" almost always included a pronouncement of continued love. The patterns and consequences of infidelity that emerge after marriage are quite different, and they result from a very different construction of gender roles that emerges in marriage. The contrast between courtship and marriage is tied to the ways in which conjugal relationships are much more deeply embedded in larger kinship structures and relationships to extended family and community than premarital relationships (Smith 2001).

A final note about Igbo courtship and premarital sexual relationships is the way in which contraceptive use, particularly condom use, is (or is not) negotiated. Young people I interviewed in surveys in local secondary schools, at a local university, and in two large cities were split fairly evenly among those who thought that contraception was a man's responsibility, a women's responsibility, or a joint responsibility. But those numbers obscure the degree to which young people feared broaching the subject at all, an anxiety exacerbated by increasing awareness of the AIDS epidemic. Most contraceptive and condom negotiations took place under the aegis of concern over preventing unwanted pregnancies (Smith 2004a,b). Particularly in relationships self-described as romantic, few young people dared discuss condom use in the context of AIDS prevention because of the insinuation that they or their partners were unsafe (Smith 2003; cf. Preston-Whyte 1999 for South Africa, and Adih and Alexander 1999 for Ghana). While almost all young Igbos know that HIV/AIDS is transmitted sexually, a majority associated AIDS risk with various forms of immoral sexual behavior. Thus, to suggest condom use with a partner implies that one or the other has previously engaged in such wayward or promiscuous sex. In addition, there is a fairly widespread feeling among young Igbos (both men and women) that condoms inhibit intimacy, and it is precisely in love relationships that intimacy is most valued. Incredibly high rates of unsafe illegal abortions attest to widespread failure to use effective contraception in premarital relationships. Popular stories of young women resorting to abortion are legion in southeastern Nigeria and must be interpreted with caution because these stories are part of a critical public discourse about the role of gender and sexuality in social change. Nonetheless, in my sample of 420 university students, 40% of the women who had engaged in sexual intercourse (which was 80% of the sample) reported having had an abortion. As I will explain, ideals of monogamy and intimacy combine with the continued paramount importance of fertility in marriage to inhibit women's ability to negotiate condom use, even in instances where women know or suspect their husbands are unfaithful.

MARRIAGE, PARENTHOOD, AND MALE INFIDELITY

There is no doubt that both the ideals and practices of Igbo marriage have changed over the past generation. The strength of the conjugal relationship has grown vis-à-vis other family and community relationships. Young couples are far more likely than their parents to share one bedroom, eat together, maintain a single household budget, and live in town away from the compound of the husband's family, which is the traditional place of residence. The quality of a young couple's personal relationship, including the degree of emotional intimacy and sexual compatibility, is more likely to figure in their private assessments of the state of their marriage than was the case with their parents.

But once a couple is married, and certainly once they have children, the importance of their personal relationship as a measure of the state of the marriage recedes in comparison to the tremendous emphasis on successful parenthood. The place of children in adult relationships is central to understanding the whole social fabric of Igbo society. As Meyer Fortes argued quite some time ago, it is "parenthood that is the primary value associated with the idea of family in West Africa" (1978:121). "Parenthood," Fortes says, "is regarded as a *sine qua non* for the attainment of the full development of the complete person to which all aspire" (1978:125). Having children is not only a means to individual personhood, but also a fulfillment of one's obligations to kin and community. Biological reproduction is also social reproduction. Once a couple has children together, particularly once they have a son, there are few socially acceptable reasons for them to divorce. Disputes and incompatibilities that lead to fissures and separations are almost always mediated by extended family members on both sides who see it as their duty to bring the couple back together—most often with the welfare of the children explicitly voiced as the obligation that must reunite the couple. Deteriorating personal relationships are not generally sufficient grounds for divorce. A married woman with children will be on much firmer ground in complaining about her marriage if she can show that her husband fails to support his children than if she complains of personal problems with him.

The striking thing that I want to describe and explain is the dramatic

Fig. 6.1. Although many Igbo couples now marry for love, fertility and successful parenthood remain paramount social values. (Photo by Daniel J. Smith.)

shift in gender dynamics between man and woman that occurs in the transition from courtship to marriage and parenthood (Smith 2001). A more patriarchal gender dynamic emerges after marriage. It is in the expectations about and consequences of marital infidelity that this inequality is most profound, and the sad irony is that even as women continue to deploy ideals of intimacy and love to influence their husbands' sexual behavior, these very ideals prevent the negotiation of safe sex.

SUGAR DADDIES, HANDBAGS, AND RAZOR BLADES: GENDER AND MARITAL FIDELITY

In premarital relationships, the social rules about fidelity are largely the same for men and women, as I indicated earlier. In Igbo marriages the rules about fidelity are quite different. An older wealthy Igbo man once said to me, when I asked about the consequences of extramarital affairs for men and women: "If I catch my wife, she is gone; if she catches me, she is gone too." In other words, not only was it not acceptable for her to have extramarital sex, it was also not acceptable for her to object to his having extramarital sex. The levels of acceptance of extramarital sexuality are much more contested than my informant's bold statement suggests, but the idea that Igbo men can and do have extramarital partners is widely acknowledged. A man who cheats on his wife risks little social condemnation, assuming he continues to provide for his wife and children, and does not do something "foolish" like propose to leave his wife for his lover. In fact, among Igbo men there is a certain pride in taking lovers. It is primarily in the way that men construct masculinity in their male peer groups that taking lovers becomes so significant. Being able to have lovers is sign of continuing masculine prowess and of economic success, because, increasingly, women expect their lovers to "perform" economically as well as sexually (Cornwall 2002; Hunter 2002).

When I lived in the town of Owerri ten years ago, people used to lament (but also laugh about) the plethora of cars parked outside the gates of Alvin Ikoku Teachers College on Friday and Saturday nights—cars belonging to married men who were there to meet young female lovers. Patterns of marital infidelity are structured along the dimensions of age, gender, and social class. Alvin Ikoku Teachers College has male students as well. But it was inconceivable that married women would park en masse outside the college waiting for young male lovers. Nor was it possible to imagine that poor men would be waiting outside on foot or with their bicycles. The following example illustrates some of the ways that men's extramarital sexual relationships are organized along various dimensions of inequality.

John Ezigbo is forty-seven years old. A married father of five, he runs a successful business raising poultry and selling animal feed. Most every night John leaves his house about 5 P.M. bound for Umuahia Club, where he plays an hour of tennis, drinks a few beers, and socializes with the other well-to-do Igbo men who are members of the club. Many evenings, after a postgame beer, he drives off to pick up a young lady friend whom he brings back to entertain, offering her drinks and something to eat from the club's kitchen. Though spouses are honorary members once their husbands are inducted, John knows that he and his girlfriend will not encounter any wives at the club, women who might report him to his own spouse. There is an unwritten rule among the men that wives are not welcome, except on specially designated occasions. The club is a safe place to bring one's girlfriend.

John's girlfriends are typically secondary school graduates, who are either attending one of several tertiary institutions in town or seeking employment in some kind of urban office or business. All of them are young, educated, modern girls who wear makeup, straighten their hair, sport fashionable clothes, and see school and the city as means to a better life. John is one of the more blatant philanderers in the club. It is rare to see the same lady in his company for more than a few weeks.

Other men keep much more steady lovers; many do not bring their girlfriends to the club at all, preferring to keep their sexual affairs more private. Indeed, some men do not have extramarital lovers at all. But keeping outside women (that is, outside of marriage) is accepted, indeed socially rewarded, among elite Igbo men (cf. Karanja 1987; Hunter 2002; Luke 2005). Bringing a pretty young lady to the club is done proudly. Many men want their male peers to know that they have extramarital affairs. They tell each other stories about sexual conquests, sometimes including the graphic details. One of the wealthiest guys in the club, who also had the reputation of attracting the most beautiful women, was known by the nickname "One Man Show." No doubt there is much male bravado in all this. Surely some men exaggerate their sexual exploits to their own social benefit. But the fact that perceived extramarital sexual activity is socially rewarded is precisely what I want to emphasize. Most Igbo men share a sense that real manhood implies continued sexual desire and new sexual conquests after and outside marriage.

Perhaps not surprisingly, given the economic inequalities in Nigerian society, the ability to have new women is a marker of economic status as well as virility. Men who own cars, belong to social clubs, rent expensive hotel rooms, and have the resources to give women substantial amounts of money and gifts are by far the more desirable married lovers. Such attributes define "sugar daddy." Much as men expect sexual intercourse and an attractive partner to display to their peers, the young women require and exact from their married lovers any number of kinds of assistance (Cornwall 2002; Hunter 2002; Smith 2002). On dates or outings, young ladies pressure their sugar daddies to buy them the most expensive beer, order them special food, and reserve rooms at the fanciest hotels. They routinely

Fig. 6.2. Settings of mostly all-male sociality, such as this sports club, contribute to strong positive peer-group pressure about extramarital sexuality. (Photo by Daniel J. Smith.)

ask their sugar daddies for money to pay school fees, start businesses, help their parents, or assist with rent. They also expect their men to buy them gifts—clothes, shoes, jewelry, and even electronics and appliances.

Unlike in their premarital relationships with their wives, few sugar daddies, and indeed few of their lovers, view these relationships as romances. Most men like to see themselves as masters of these extramarital relationships, in charge of their lovers in the same way they want to be in charge of their married households and their money. In male discourse, young female lovers are objectified—discussed as if they are not persons. When the men of the sports club travel to neighboring towns and cities to play tennis tournaments—as they do eight to ten weekends a year—these trips are viewed as great opportunities to meet (and display) their young lovers. In anticipation of a weekend on the road, men ask each other whether they are "carrying a handbag," a reference to taking a young female lover. I often traveled with the club to these tournaments and was struck by how widely this term was used and recognized, in Igbo cities all over the southeast. Even many of the young women knew the meaning of the term, and while they did not appreciate its derogatory connotations, they did not seem too bothered by it—perhaps because they knew very well that women have more power in these relationships than one would guess from male rhetoric.

Yet even men acknowledge, perhaps unwittingly, the degree to which young female lovers have some control over relationships with their sugar daddies. Men often complained that these young women would "bleed" them—manipulating them for money, and even, ironically, for sex. This brief dialogue in Nigerian Pidgin English is typical of married men's discussions about their young lovers.

Chuks: How e de go wit dat new girl from Alvin? E be like say you de busy too much.
Charles: Dat uman no de taya. These girls today na war-o. Di girl done bleed me finish. Na real razor blade.
Chuks: Take am easy-o.

The terms *bleeding* and *razor blade* in reference to sexual relationships have multiple meanings. First, there is the clear reference to economic extraction. Razor blades cut men to bleed them of their money. Second, and perhaps more interesting, is an implication that women are extracting sex; that somehow, even as men view themselves as the aggressors in sexual relationships, they see women as insatiable—reservoirs of bottomless and dangerous sexual desires that can wear men out. Finally, the terms are often used in connection with romance and love, such that women are able to manipulate men's hearts to get their own sexual and material gratification. Much as many men eschew the idea that they are vulnerable to love in these extramarital relationships, they participate in a common countervailing discourse in Igbo society that women have "love medicine" and are capable of manipulating men sexually and romantically (see Wardlow, this volume, regarding similar beliefs in Papua New Guinea).

"Razor blades" and "handbags" imply very different notions of women's agency, one active and dangerous, the other passive and under control, both objectifying, and neither particularly attractive. But these contrasting images reflect well the conflicting representations of women in Igbo men's discourse. And each is, to some extent, representative of the real status of unmarried young women in their sexual relationships with sugar daddies. They are clearly used by men; yet they clearly also use men.

EXTRAMARITAL SEX AND THE RISK OF HIV

Extramarital sexual relationships pose increasing risks given the spread of HIV/AIDS in Nigeria. When I first lived in Nigeria, from 1989 through 1992, few of the men I knew took seriously the risk of AIDS. Most men believed they were not personally at risk because they viewed AIDS as a "gay" disease, a white man's disease, or something that could only be contracted from prostitutes. Among these same men, other STDs were not taken to be too seriously. Indeed, I remember one conversation with some male friends in which they told me that anyone who had not experienced gonorrhea at some time in his life was not yet a man. Easy access to over-the-counter antibiotics led to widespread self-medication for STDs (no doubt increasing drug-resistant strains). During fieldwork from 1995 through 1997, little had changed about people's perceptions of their own risk for contracting HIV/AIDS, and many men in extramarital sexual relationships still preferred to rely on their girlfriends to prevent (or terminate) pregnancy rather than use "pleasure-inhibiting" condoms. While young women were certainly concerned about preventing pregnancy and about the possible effects on their own future fertility of contracting STDs, even among women who had such concerns, negotiating condom use proved difficult in these economically unequal relationships. However, over the past several years, I have noticed the beginnings of a change in the attitude toward AIDS. The change was due in part to widespread publicity in the wake of Nigeria's 1999 and 2003 sero-prevalence surveys. But it is probably more important that some people now knew or had heard about individuals with HIV/AIDS.

Still, in a great many of these extramarital relationships condom use remains difficult to negotiate. Even among the most educated and elite classes—like my tennis buddies—AIDS continues to be represented as a disease of immorality spread through reckless sex with wayward or evil strangers (Smith 2003). Yet almost all real sexual relationships are between people who know each other—one's lover is not a stranger. In sugar daddy relationships even negotiations for money take place in a personal or kinship idiom. Young women rarely ask directly for money for sex. Women often defer their requests for money specifically not to coincide with a recent sex act. A woman's requests are made in terms of needing money for rent or transportation, or even more characteristically so that she can help a sibling pay school fees or assist her parents with a problem in the village. Sugar daddies almost always know the community of origin of their lovers,

Fig. 6.3. Public health communication about HIV/AIDS in Nigeria has risen dramatically in recent years, including messages about the risks of extramarital sex. (Photo by Daniel J. Smith.)

and likewise the girls know the same about their men. After one's name, one's place of origin is the first question Igbos ask in ordinary conversation. People are always placed in the context of the networks of social relationships that constitute Igbo society. As disparagingly as my elite male Igbo friends seemed to talk about their "handbags," the reality is far more complex. Even as peer-reinforced ideas of masculinity seem to create in sugar daddies the need to possess and control their lovers as objects, other notions of manhood require that they fulfill social obligations to these lovers—obligations that the girls can manipulate by exploiting men's sense of themselves as patrons and providers.

I have provided ethnographic evidence primarily about elite men, relatively educated young women, and a distinctly urban-oriented population. One might wonder how sexual dynamics play out in courtship and marriage among poorer men and less educated women who live mostly in rural areas. Certainly the people I have focused on are not the lowest common denominator. Men who cannot afford to belong to a tennis club are not as well placed to secure young women aspiring to a better life. Nevertheless, similar patterns of sexual relations play out in courtship and marriage among less privileged Igbos. An old adage about social hierarchy in sub-Saharan Africa says that everyone is a patron to a lesser person and a client to a more powerful person (d'Azevedo 1962). A similar nesting of power characterizes patterns of sexual relationships, so that while the young lovers of my tennis buddies expect, for example, that their sugar daddies will offer them Guinness Stout to drink, sexual relationships among poorer people are negotiated with, for example, Coca-Cola. In other words, while the level of expectations regarding economic support and conspicuous consumption is lower, sexuality and sexual intimacy are markers and means of being modern among poorer Igbos, just as they are among the more educated and well off. With regard to HIV/AIDS, the salient point is that because AIDS has been socially constructed as a fearful disease spread by immoral sexual relations with variously constructed others, few people see their own sexual liaisons as fitting into this risky category.

LOVE, MARRIAGE, AND HIV

To conclude, I want to bring attention back to the risks that this situation poses to married women and explain how it is that the very ideals that provide women with significant leverage over their husbands also prevent them from negotiating condom use. Igbo women know that, in general, married Igbo men often seek "outside" women. Many married women certainly suspect, and may even know, that their own husbands do so. When a woman discovers that her husband has a lover, it often leads to terrible rifts—especially among younger couples where the basis for marriage included pronouncements of love, feelings of intimacy, and promises of sexual fidelity. Young Igbo women want their husbands to be faithful. To keep their husbands in line, women deploy discourses about love and call upon Christian concepts of monogamy and fidelity (see van der Vliet 1991 for a similar account about South Africa). In addition, as more women in urban areas are employed outside the home, they are controlling economic resources that give them certain kinds of leverage in their marriages. Anecdotes I heard in conversations among friends suggest that men who are more financially dependent on their wives may be more cautious in initiating extramarital relationships. But overall, women's increasing participation in the formal economy has not dramatically changed the domestic division of labor and the dynamics of power in the household. Even among the most elite women, the roles of wife and mother remain highly valued.

In contemporary Igbo-speaking Nigeria, extramarital sexuality is largely conceived of as a contest between husbands who want to be and think they are entitled to extramarital sexual relationships and wives who mostly want to rein in their husbands' extramarital activities. In many cases the women's strategies, combined with the strength of conjugal relationships, are effective. Not all Igbo men cheat on their wives. But women find it difficult to appeal to their kinfolk and affines for help and can expect little sympathy from society if they leave a man simply because he has had sex outside the marriage, especially if he has been relatively discreet.

Marriages among the current generation in Igboland are likely to be contracted first between individuals, with love and emotional intimacy as part of the criteria of spousal choice, and with monogamy as the expectation. While most people are aware of the prevalence of male marital infidelity, and of the fact that HIV/AIDS is transmitted through sexual intercourse, a number of factors combine to make it difficult for women to negotiate condom use with their husbands. First, as I have emphasized earlier, despite the rise of a companionate marriage ideal, the collective interests in marriage as an institution continue to emphasize the importance of parenthood in social reproduction. Thus, for a woman to suggest condom use (or any other contraception) for the sake of preventing pregnancy is itself potentially problematic. But more to the point in the context of the AIDS epidemic, a woman's expectation that marriage should be based on love and intimacy, with sexual fidelity as the ideal, means that any suggestion that her husband use a condom can be interpreted by him as undermining intimacy and trust and implying his (or her) infidelity. The irony is that because women rely on ideals of love and intimacy to negotiate relationships with their husbands, trying to protect themselves through condom use is seen as undermining the very thing they wish to preserve. Rather than protecting women, love marriages may contribute to the risk of contracting HIV from their husbands.

Part Three

GENDER POLITICS
& IMPLICATIONS

7

"HE CAN BE SAD LIKE THAT"

LIBERDADE & THE ABSENCE OF ROMANTIC LOVE
IN A BRAZILIAN SHANTYTOWN

Jessica Gregg

Danda intimidated me. During the eighteen months I spent in her community, a *favela* (shantytown), in northeastern Brazil, I was never entirely at ease in her company. At twenty-nine, she was only a few years older than I was, but she had a confident, lazy air that made my own eager awkwardness seem almost adolescent. She loved to talk about sex, and she liked best to talk about my sex life. She loved to fluster me. A favorite activity was to bring by lingerie catalogs and speculate about what I could do with different purchases. She once showed me black lace underwear that had no material in the crotch area. "It's easier to screw that way. You don't even have to take them off. I'm going to get you a pair, Jessica. Raimundo [my then-boyfriend] will love them. Wear them with a miniskirt."

Danda herself had had several boyfriends and one pregnancy, which she had aborted. She had never married and was adamant that she never would, neither for love nor money. As we watched a telenovela (a Brazilian soap opera) one evening, the two young lovers on screen stared longingly into each other's eyes and then suddenly embraced and kissed passionately. Danda looked at me and asked, "Do you think there is love like that? There is no such love. It doesn't exist. It's just a thing they put on TV." Men, she told me, are all *safado* (shameless) and would inevitably mistreat any woman who was good to them. The best tactic, she would explain, was for a woman to keep her *liberdade*, her liberty, and to never stay too long with any one man. Rather, she should get as much as possible—money, food, clothes, jewelry—from that man and then just move on.

While this volume is dedicated to the exploration of companionate marriage as a core ideology of modernity, I argue in the present chapter that, for many women in impoverished northeastern Brazil, the bleak state of gender relations, and of the economic system, often made marriage in any form undesirable. While young women often rejected "traditional" models of gender relations and marriage, they did not instead endorse an alternative of romantic love. Rather, they pursued lives of *liberdade*, or liberty, which provided them not only with independence but also with an avenue of protest against the current gender system.

To make this argument, I will first frame it in terms of what Deniz Kandiyoti (1988) has termed an economic and ideological "patriarchal bargain" and in terms of what has classically been termed an honor/shame complex. I will then suggest that, in my community, with the demise of that bargain, and with a clear understanding that values consistent with honor and shame were no longer tenable, women sought economic alternatives through wage work and sought ideological alternatives through an ideal of *liberdade* and a negation of love.

THE PATRIARCHAL BARGAIN

Deniz Kandiyoti has argued that women in male-dominated societies strategize within the constraints of what she has termed a "patriarchal bargain." These bargains, she suggests, arise out of the patriarchal culture, defining what, ideally, is the role of each gender in society. The bargain set within what she terms "classic patriarchy" is that male support and protection of women is exchanged for control of female sexuality and appropriation of women's labor and progeny. She further argues that the bargain set by classic patriarchy only works when men have the land or other resources available to support women. When, in landless and impoverished households, women need to work for wages to ensure the survival of the family, male economic protection of women becomes a myth, the bargain crumbles, and women must seek economic and ideological alternatives.

HONOR AND SHAME IN THE SHANTYTOWN

Kandiyoti's notion of a bargain helps in the understanding of gender relations in the shantytown. Though the term *marriage* was defined quite broadly in the community, and included any relationship that involved both sexual activity and moderate- to long-term financial support, the set of rules defined by classic patriarchy were largely the rules by which men and women defined appropriate marital behavior. The assumption was that before a woman was sexually active, her well-being (including control of her sexuality) was the responsibility of her parents. When she married, that control was turned over to her husband.

The rules of the patriarchal bargain are also consistent with standards of sexual propriety consistent with what has been termed an "honor and shame" complex. Several authors have described an honor/shame complex that appears to permeate the value systems of nearly all Mediterranean cultures (Pitt-Rivers 1965, 1977; Ortner 1978). Within this paradigm, a woman's status is directly linked to her sexual "purity" (or, alternatively, her shame to impurity), while a man's honor derives in large part from guarding and controlling that purity. The paradigm suggests that once she becomes sexually active, a woman may assume one of two roles: that of wife/mother or that of prostitute. Only by retaining her virginity until marriage, when she transfers control of her sexuality from her parents to her husband, and by remaining faithful to her husband thereafter, can a woman achieve the proper status of wife and mother. When a man loses control over that sexuality, he becomes a cuckold (*corno*); his honor is sullied and his masculinity questioned (Parker 1991). Fundamental to this system, then, is the idea that women are defined in terms of their sexual behavior.[1]

In Brazil, values consistent with an honor/shame complex have been traced to Portuguese colonization of the country in the sixteenth century. Colonists, emulating habits of the nobility in their native country, adopted the customs of female seclusion and patriarchal rule (Bruschini 1990; Schwartz 1985). The Catholic Church also played a large role in reinforcing these attitudes, focusing on female status as achieved through sexual restraint, preservation of virginity, and marriage (Vainfas 1989; Lavrin 1989).

In twentieth-century Brazil, historic and ethnographic evidence suggests that these values continue to dominate discourse surrounding gender relations. For example, in his classic work *A Casa e a Ru*a (The House and the Street), Brazilian anthropologist Roberto Da Matta notes that the gendered division between women's secluded domain "of the house" and the male domain "of the street" continues to divide the moral world in Brazil (1987). Similarly, Cynthia Sarti argues that women in impoverished São Paolo continue to be defined in terms of their sexuality: "the principal accusation against a woman is that she is a 'whore'" (1995:122). Anthropologist Linda-Anne Rebhun, while acknowledging the limitations of the honor/shame complex, also acknowledges that values associated with the complex describe an idealized vision of Brazilian womanhood in the Brazilian town of Caruaru. She explains that these values prevent women from ever living alone, as women alone "because they are neither virgins nor coupled . . . are sexually suspect" (1999a:159). Further, she argues that a girl's loss of virginity is still sufficient reason for her family to insist on marriage to salvage her honor, and she notes that some men are afraid to have daughters due to the fear of the potential dishonor they may bring to the family. Clearly, values associated with honor and shame continue to strongly influence attitudes and behaviors regarding gender and sexuality.

Similarly, for women in the *favela* virginity and fidelity were often noted to be quite important to avoiding shame. Ideals consistent with an honor/shame paradigm were espoused constantly. Individuals were clear about the need for girls to maintain their virginity before marriage and for women to be faithful to their spouses. One woman in her midtwenties explained to me in a casual conversation that mothers "imprison" their daughters in the house so that men can't seduce them and "take their value. Well, there are other things, like their lives, that are valuable too, but virginity has value." A sixteen-year-old girl noted in another conversation that "a *moça* (adolescent girl) who loses her virginity [outside of marriage] has no value. No one respects her."

Respect was due to women whose sexuality was controlled by fathers or husbands. This, women explained, was one of the reasons that, even if a man was abusive, "a house without a man is terrible." One woman told me in casual conversation that when a girl in the *favela* lost her virginity or when a woman separates from her husband, other men "are on top of her right away." Another explained that "if you have a man in the house you have company and you have more respect. Especially within this community, if you are alone, men say things as you pass by, they are always behind you trying to mount you. If you have a man you have respect." And as Renata, forty-seven, explained, "They want a woman to stay in the house, hidden." In fact, to not "hide" could be dangerous. Maria Teresa, forty-four, referring to her husband, noted, "He won't let me out of the house alone. I can't even go to the plaza. He would kill me if I give him horns. And I don't want to die."

The situation for men was far different. Men were considered responsible for their own sexuality and were generally expected to be unfaithful to their partners. In fact, a man who was faithful might be considered not fully a man. I once asked a friend why married men cheat on their wives. She explained to me that if a woman wants a man, she approaches him, and if he rejects her advances, she taunts him, saying that he must be gay or dominated by his wife, until finally he gives in. A fifty-five-year-old male acquaintance told me the same thing. He was at the house one night while we were all watching a soap opera in which three women were in love with the same man. The one woman that the man actually loved was angry with him because she thought he was having sex with the other two. My acquaintance commented to me that if a woman chases a man and he doesn't sleep with her, he is not a man. So the woman shouldn't be angry with her lover. He should be expected to sleep with other women if they chase him.

The situation was summed up for me one night as I approached my neighbor Marta's house and heard a heated argument going on inside. Marta saw me as I hesitated outside her doorway and called me in. She then turned back to continue arguing with her former "husband," Ton, a thin man who sold newspapers in the street for a living. Ton had recently left Marta to return to live with his first wife, Rosana, and their three children. As I entered the room, Marta was vehemently denying that she had been with any other men since he had left her two weeks before. I asked why he cared, given that he had left Marta anyway. He said that he was involved with four women, including Marta. He "helped" them all financially, and he expected them to be faithful. "That," he said, "is the way it is in Brazil."

And when men were a primary, stable source of household income, that generally was the way that marital relationships functioned.

ECONOMIC CONSIDERATIONS

Significantly, however, men were often not the primary or stable sources of income. A poor man in Recife often simply did not have the resources to assume that role. Most did not own land, only a fortunate few held steady, salaried work, and economic conditions in the northeast did not offer anyone much hope for the future.

Conditions in the northeast had not always been so bleak. Though it is

one of the poorest, most economically depressed regions of Brazil
(Schneider, Lenz, and Petry 1990), the northeast actually functioned as
the hub of the Brazilian economy during the heyday of sixteenth-century
sugar cultivation (Freyre 1986; Rodrigues 1967; Frank 1967). Fortunes
only began to change in the nineteenth century as competition from European beet sugar drove sugar prices down (Galloway 1968), and as
increased dependence on coffee cultivation in the southern regions of
Brazil drew investment away from the north (Rodrigues 1967). The twentieth century heralded a focus on industrialization that cemented the
decline of the northeast. Most investment in industry took place in the
south, and the industrialization that did occur in the north generally
occurred within the sugar industry, reducing the need for peasant labor
and contributing to the influx of rural workers to cities like Recife in
search of wage labor (Forman 1975). While workers came in search of
wages, most ended up living in *favela*s and working in the informal economy. Indeed, the "Brazilian economic miracle" of the 1960s and 1970s,
while temporarily improving economic conditions in the south, nearly
destroyed the northeast, and some scholars now refer to the northeast as a
"colony" of southern metropolitan Brazil (Rodrigues 1967).

The rapid growth of *favela*s in Recife was not only the result of the
migration of sugarcane workers to the city but was also the result of devas-
tating droughts in the rural *sertão* (arid backlands), coupled with marked
changes in the system of agriculture in the more fertile zones (known as the
agreste). The traditional system of agriculture in the *agreste* revolved
around a *latifundio-minifundio* complex, in which peasants rented small
plots of land from large landowners. This system was often cruel and
forced peasants to survive under incredibly harsh conditions. However,
when the large estates began to shift from an emphasis on labor-intensive
farming to one that depended more on machines and capital outlay, peasants lost what little they did have. Plantation estates, which had formerly
depended on peasant labor to both grow and process sugarcane had, by the
early twentieth century, given up control of sugar production to central-
ized and mechanized *usinas*, or sugar factories. Looking to increase land
available for sugar cultivation, and not dependent on peasant labor, the *usinas* then began the process of evicting, or simply driving off, peasant farm-
ers (Scheper-Hughes 1992).

Many of these displaced peasants migrated to Recife, squatting where
they could, filling the *favela*s to capacity and beyond, and helping to create
what has been described as "a distinctive kind of wretchedness not found

anywhere else in Brazil" (Page 1995:191). In 1992, a third of the economically active population of Recife made a minimum wage or less a month,[2] and only 38% of the population of the city could boast indoor plumbing (Ferraz et al. 1992). In my community of about 1,500 residents, there was no school, no health clinic, no garbage pickup, no paved roads, and no sewage system. Electricity was illegally funneled off from city sources.

During my research, which occurred on and off from 1993 through 1996, the minimum salary in Recife ranged from about 45 dollars to about 100 dollars per month. A *cesta basica*, groceries sufficient to feed a family of four to six people for a month, cost two to three minimum salaries. A 1990 survey of the community by the urban planning department of Recife found that 64.5% of male heads of household made one minimum salary or less a month, and that 91% of female heads of household made one minimum salary or less (Empresa de Urbanização do Recife 1990). There were 316 households, 180 households (57%) headed by males and 136 (43%) headed by females. Further, in 1990, about half of the employable population of women (the term "employable" was not defined) was engaged in wage labor. The most common female employment was that of domestic worker. Notably, domestic work is poorly remunerated, and domestics rarely receive the signed work cards that guarantee a minimum salary, social security benefits, illness compensation, and retirement pensions.

In 1995, when I surveyed thirty households in the community, little had changed. Not quite one-third of households ($n = 9$) made one salary or less, and just over half of all households ($n = 16$) made one and a half to two minimum salaries. Few households ($n = 4$) made more than two minimum salaries a month. Fourteen households were headed by males, and sixteen were headed by females. Generally, the primary source of income was the informant ($n = 12$) or her partner ($n = 13$). As often as not, then, men in the *favela* were not the primary sources of income for their families, and in fact were not functioning as heads of households. Instead, women were supporting themselves and their children.

RESENTMENT, ANIMOSITY, AND THE DEMISE OF THE PATRIARCHAL BARGAIN

As predicted by Kandiyoti, the bargain, in these circumstances, was crumbling. Women in my research, especially younger women, often made clear to me their belief that guarding their virginity in order to marry well was an outdated notion, and that what was more important was the guardianship of their *liberdade*. They noted that within the shantytown, long-term male support was uncertain at best, and that most women, even with male support, had to work for wages to ensure the survival of the family. For example, one young woman, seventeen years old and a new mother, told me that the father of her child was not going to be involved with its care, and that she preferred it that way. She lived at home with her mother and said that she had an on- and-off boyfriend, which was just right. "I want my life free . . . I want to do what I want to do. If I want to go to the beach, I just go. If I want to work, I work." I asked her if that was better than being married and having a man help at home. She replied that her *liberdade* was much more important to her than the security a man might provide. "Besides security isn't really so secure. You may have help for awhile, but then he is gone." And for Danda, the woman whose story began this chapter, to have her freedom and to use her sexuality for extras like beer and barbecue made sense. As a maid she had a relatively reliable source of income, and she had no one trying, as she put it, to step on her foot and control her.

It is probably not surprising that, when faced with the knowledge that men would not provide sufficiently for them, women found wage work. What is perhaps more interesting is that when faced with that knowledge, many women chose to reject monogamy altogether. Rather than embracing a notion of romantic love, unencumbered by traditional economic considerations, or rather than simply attempting to increase their share of power within monogamous relationships, women often opted instead for the freedom of *liberdade*, rejecting the notions of love and monogamy altogether and ultimately embracing an ideal of sex as vengeance.

LOVE LOST

When I first arrived in my community, I was struck by the bitter feelings women seemed to hold toward men. While I didn't ask everyone in my interview sample if they loved their current partners, of the seven that I did happen to ask, only one professed love for her partner. And in no casual conversations did any woman tell me of her love for her partner. In fact, love between men and women, I was often told, simply did not exist in the *favela*. One evening, my friend Sielma was trying to convince Fatima, the woman I lived with, that she should not be so angry with her husband João for cheating on her. She said that Fatima should be grateful that he was not always out chasing women, and that she should understand that when other women chased him, sometimes he was weak and gave in. She pointed out that he had never propositioned me, and how many men would have a young, single woman living in their house and not proposition her? Fatima, clearly agitated, replied,

> Look, I am the mirror of my mother. I won't ever let a man make me suffer the way my father made her suffer. He felt so bad when she died, and he died just a month later, which is just what he deserved. He would be out in the plaza buying presents for his girlfriends while we were home with my mother, who was a saint, and we didn't even have enough to eat. You know what I'm saying is true, Sielma. Besides, men and women don't love each other. If someone tells you that she loves her husband and you ask her why, she'll tell you such and such and you'll see that they don't love each other, they are just used to each other. João is used to me. He knows when I am sad, when I am angry, when it is better not to talk to me. That's why I stay with him. But I don't love him. Love is what you feel for your mother or your sisters.

Stepping on women's "silliness" and leaving wives and children hungry, men neglected to be protectors and lost the right to be loved and trusted. Indeed, women were clear that the reason love between men and women did not exist was because men destroyed it. For instance, Carla, thirty-nine, was raped when she was sixteen, beaten by her first partner, and abandoned by her second partner when she got pregnant, and she had had about eight other casual sexual partners before meeting her current husband. These experiences, she believed, simply broke her capacity to love a man. Even so, at the time of our interview she had been with the same man for over ten years and had legally married him. I asked why she thought her marriage lasted when so many didn't. "We match. He doesn't like to go to other people's houses, and I don't like him to. He doesn't want me going out alone and I don't like him going out alone. We go together. We are always together."

I asked if she loved him.

"No. I like him a lot. But, love, I was already so deceived by my early life, so hurt. But I like and respect him very much."

Why, I asked her, did she think that love for men seemed so rare in the *favela?*

"Men are so aggressive here. Love comes from inside, but if you are humiliated or hurt you lose that affection. The worst thing in the world is to be humiliated. The enchantment of love is broken."

Carla believed that the abuse she had suffered at the hands of individual men caused her to lose the ability, or the desire, to love men in general. Similarly, Fatima spoke of her father's behavior, and not just João's, as the reason that she did not love her husband.

My friend Marta also blamed early experiences for her inability to love her present partner. One afternoon, I was talking to her about why she was considering leaving her new partner Ton (the newspaper vendor), just after he had finally decided to leave his wife again and move in with Marta for good. I asked, didn't she like Ton, or even love him? "I don't trust men. My [first] husband made me suffer so much. They will always hurt you. It is always better to like them, but from a distance. Men lie too much and say things to you and then leave."

"But," I persisted, "why leave a man you like, who likes to go out with you and drink and dance?"

"Because I like to be by myself."

"Won't he be sad?"

"Was he sad when he left his wife and three children and one on the way? Did that make him sad when he left her for me? He can be sad like that."

Thus, though Ton hadn't caused Marta any suffering, he would bear the consequences of the fact that her husband had. And as Marta pointed out, Ton had certainly caused his own share of suffering with other women and could now "be sad like that." Because men in general would invariably hurt and disappoint women, no specific man deserved love.

ANIMOSITY

But women did not simply feel an absence of love. They felt the presence of animosity. When I asked one woman, in an interview, what was the worst thing about men, she replied, "There are so many terrible things, I can't even say."

"Then what is the best thing about men?"

"There are so many terrible things, I can't even say."

Two other women in my interview sample had similar responses when I asked them to tell me what, for them, was the best thing about men. One informant, in her seventies, replied that there was nothing good about men. "They are the worst. My *marido* was good for me at first, but after he started with other women, he became terrible." Another stated simply, "I think there is nothing good about men." Even Dona Renata, who at forty-three was a widow, and who constantly lamented the loss of her husband, clearly had ambivalent feelings about men in general. The best thing about men, according to Renata, was their "affection (*carinho*)." The worst was that "there are a lot of bad men out there, but I had a good *marido*." When I then asked Renata whether it was better to work or have a man provide, she said, "I think it's better to work than to break your head over men who just want to exploit you." I told her that I was surprised to hear her say that, given that she spoke so often about how much better things were when her husband worked and provided for her. "But there aren't many men like him," she replied. "I would never find another. Better just to work." Even for Renata, then, who had, by her own account, a good relationship, men in general could not be trusted to protect rather than to exploit a woman.

And men weren't considered to be simply irresponsible or lazy or somehow otherwise just not up to par. They were, rather, considered malicious. Explaining to me why men leave when women get pregnant, one woman said, "Some men just like to ruin women's lives. They get them pregnant and leave." Similarly, telling me why a woman should never move into a man's house, Marta explained, "Men humiliate women more than women humiliate men. A man will suddenly decide he doesn't want you and leave you in the street. Women have more pity. They don't humiliate men so much." And explaining to me why women don't love men, Fatima said, "Men here are *ruim* (wicked, terrible). Women may start out loving them, but men make women suffer too much here." According to Fatima, men hurt women not because they are irresponsible but simply because they want to. Sielma told me much the same thing: "They [men] are egoists. I want to live alone and just have a man when I really need one, like they do with us." And again, "Men here are *ruim, safado*."

RESISTANCE

Given this degree of animosity, it is perhaps not surprising, then, that women felt that to love a man was folly. But for women who chose *liberdade*, not only was to love folly, but so too was fidelity. While married women almost never were unfaithful, women who chose *liberdade* flaunted their multiple partners. Indeed, for many women a large part of the point of *liberdade* was the ability to *botar galha*, or make cuckolds of men. Women engaged in *liberdade* resisted the unstated rules of gender relations in the shantytown.

Resistance and Sexuality

That women in Brazil might use their sexuality as a form of resistance makes sense given that male honor, and indeed Brazilian male identity, is closely tied to male control of female sexuality. Anthropologist Richard Parker, in his work on sexuality in Brazil, found that fear of cuckoldry pervaded men's lives: "the possibility that one's *mulher* might at any instant be betraying one seems to haunt the Brazilian male" (1991:49). Though I had no formal interviews with men and far less contact with men in my community than with women, it was also clear to me that men in my community were obsessed with the idea that they might be made a cuckold, and they talked about it constantly. And whether men in the community truly felt shamed by women's cheating or whether they simply used protection of their own honor as a convenient excuse for constraining women's freedom (or both), fear of cuckoldry was cited as the reason for many male behaviors. My friend Sielma once pointed out her neighbor's black eye to me, explaining, "She wouldn't have sex with her husband so he said that she had another man and hit her." Many women explained that they didn't work because their husbands were afraid to let them be out alone around other men all day.

Parker suggests that because of male fear of female infidelity, "recognizing that women can be seen at once as fundamentally inferior, as desirable, and as threatening and dangerous is crucial to any full understanding of the Brazilian system" (1991:41). Women who cheat on their partners are threatening to men. Through infidelity, women attacked men's sense of self and masculinity.

Resistance and Liberdade

Of course, women who chose *liberdade* were not, ultimately, unfaithful. That is, they were not in committed monogamous relationships and therefore were not fully expected to be faithful. Even so, however, they were aware of the ire and discomfort they provoked in their male partners when they had more than one partner—and they relished it. For instance, Danda once told me of a conversation she'd had with an on-again, off-again boyfriend. She reported that upon seeing him again after a long absence, she taunted him, informing him, "I've eaten so many good men since you left." When he accused her of being shameless (*safada*), she retorted that men just want what is good for themselves and want women to sit on the side and wait for them.

The fact that Danda said that she had "eaten" so many good men was interesting. According to Parker, and as I generally observed in the community, to "eat" someone sexually is a rather gender-specific activity in heterosexual relationships. Men, the active sexual partners, "eat" women sexually, while women give (*dar*) passively. Danda turned the dynamic inside out, claiming her ability to "eat" (*comer*) and taunting her partner for his inability to constrain her.

That Danda was then accused of being *safada* is also interesting. Danda, and other women who chose *liberdade*, did not consider themselves, nor were they generally considered, *sem vergonha*, or shameless. Rather they were *safada* and engaged in *safadeza*. This is an important distinction. Women and men often used the word *safado* (shameless, scoundrel) rather than the more precise phrase *sem vergonha* (without shame) to describe a man or woman who lacked shame. This phrasing, and the fact that it applied both to men and to women, invested significantly different social and personal meaning in loss of shame. Both men and women, when either engaged in some disreputable behavior, or when simply considered to be generally disreputable characters, might, in the *favela*, be labeled *safado(a)*. And while *safado* is often translated as "shameless," it means more than simply a lack of shame. It suggests a certain intent, malicious or mischievous, attached to that lack of shame. Therefore it is not, as shame is, something simply to be lost. *Safadeza* is an intentional assertion, a flaunting of norms, something achieved.

So women, when angry at individual men for ignoring their responsibilities to home and family, or when describing the ways in which men take advantage of women, invariably referred to male *safadeza*. They were referring to men's intentional and even malicious disregard for the well-being of the family. At the same time, however, women would sometimes describe their attraction to a man in terms of his *safadeza*, his rather exciting and mischievous disregard for social norms. Similarly, many women, when engaged in sexual activity for revenge or as an assertion of sexual independence, would describe their own behavior as *safadeza*. It was deliberate, chosen behavior leading to a reputation, *safada*, intentionally gained, rather than to a quality, *vergonha*, irrevocably lost.

In this construction, then, women proudly denied shame and shame-lessly claimed pride. And in doing so, they simultaneously denied men in the community access to control of female sexuality.

Significantly, while many women engaged in infidelity simply in an attempt to upset individual men, there was also the sense that men in general were the target. For instance, when I asked twenty-nine-year-old Maria Jose why women cheated on men so frequently in the *favela*, she replied, laughing, "That's our job."

"Why?"

"Because men are *safado* and deserve it."

Later, in another conversation, I asked Maria Jose if she'd been with a lot of different men.

"A *montão*. So many."

I asked why.

"We have fun with men. And when one leaves us, we get another, and then he leaves and we arrange another and it keeps going. When I separated from Marcello [the father of her children] he went out with so many women. I think after just one month, he had been with at least ten. He was with all my friends (*colegas*). So I did the same thing with the men."

"Here" she continued, "it is a war. The men all have other women and the women have other men. We refuse to be beneath them. We won't let them step on us."

More than just an individual act of revenge, Maria Jose sees her actions toward her partner as her "job" and part of a "war." This is not to suggest that women were consciously engaged in collective resistance or that they actually joined forces in any way as a result of their animosity toward men. But it does suggest that some women considered the problems that they had with men to be part of something larger than just their individual experiences. It suggests an awareness of their need and ability to resist.

It is important to note that Danda, Maria Jose, and other women were not protesting that their partners refused to protect or support them. They were not asking men to hold up their part of the patriarchal bargain, and their actions were not an attempt to force male compliance. Instead, they were protesting what, under the traditional bargain, was basically a male right—male infidelity. They were questioning the very basis of the bargain, showing by their actions, and by the motivation for their actions, that they no longer saw that bargain as tenable. Thus they denied both that men had the right to control female sexuality and that men had the right to virtually uncontrolled sexuality themselves.

Just before I left, Danda told me about a party that some of the women who hung around the local bar were going to have. Surprisingly, it was to include both men and women, and invitations were being sent out. It was to be a "*cornos*" (cuckold's) party. She said that each invitation referred to the person with whom one's partner had cheated. For example, one woman's boyfriend got an invitation addressed to the "*corno da boca rica*," the cuckold of rich mouth. This is because the woman had evidently been seen around with a man who had a mouthful of gold teeth. Another man was the *corno de couscous*, because even though he knew he was being cheated on, he didn't admit it. Instead he just put a lid on it and steamed.

I never found out how the party went, or if it even happened, but the idea of it fascinated me. Pointing out the humor of their own infidelity, the women highlighted their collective disregard for norms of honorable female behavior, while simultaneously suggesting the foolishness of the men who might expect that behavior from them. They sent the message that they didn't accept an ideology that would keep them at home, protected and faithful, and they made clear that they didn't expect to be taken care of, at least not by any of the men who were invited to the party. By challenging the very structure of the gender system, and by doing so as a group, they were moving beyond protest, beyond struggle within the boundaries of ideology, and toward resistance and the questioning of the boundaries themselves.

Resistance and Reinforcement

However, while sexual activity by these women may have proved their power to resist male sexual control and even to undermine fundamental male notions of masculinity, it was only effective because all the players shared the same worldview. That is, only because everyone agreed that men's honor depended on control of female sexuality, and only because everyone agreed that blatant infidelity by a woman was a slap in the face for a man, was women's behavior so effective. By seeking a strong reaction, then, to their behavior, women who chose *liberdade* reinforced the fact of that general worldview even as they undermined individual men's place in it.

Further, this clearly served to reinforce the idea that a woman's social role was determined almost entirely via her sexual activity with men. She wrought her revenge only by having sex with another man. As Parker points out, although she may undermine her partner's social status, "she confirms the fundamental virility and masculinity of her illicit partners" (1991:51). And, following from that, her limited form of power also demanded that a woman adopt a specific social role in order to defy the sexual hierarchy. A woman who was married and wanted to remain married could not be defiant, a woman who was not sexually active could not be defiant, and a prostitute, because she was not capable of infidelity, could not be defiant. And married women actually rarely cheated. So, generally, only a woman who was neither married nor single, neither monogamous nor completely sexually undiscriminating could defy male expectations. And this of course dilutes the defiance considerably—suggesting that only women who had no male commitment to lose were willing to throw away male approbation.

Nevertheless, women who engaged in *liberdade* were defiant. They were aware that the rules governing gender relations were no longer tenable within an economic system that had crippled male earning power and that had made land ownership for the poor virtually impossible. And they used their own sexuality to demonstrate that defiance.

Unfortunately, while women engaged in *liberdade* might have engaged in effective protest against an ideology of gender that had failed them, their protest did not ultimately address the root causes of that failure. Political corruption, unfair land practices, and an unstable economy that privileges the wealthy have all contributed to a situation in which men cannot support wives and in which the scarcity of male employment encourages male mobility and makes transitory sexual relationships in Brazilian shanty-towns the norm. In the best case scenario, women's resistance to gendered expectations, the search for *liberdade*, will ultimately afford them more ability to creatively confront other, less gender-specific political issues. In the worst case scenario, women will collectively change an unfair system of gender only to find that the expected reward for their efforts is equal opportunity misery.

NOTES

1. I should note here that the honor/shame model has also been validly critiqued as a somewhat simplistic gloss. Critics argue that it has too often been used to describe any system that privileges female chastity and male protection of that chastity, while ignoring subtle (and not so subtle) variations in class and gender experience as well as important historical and cross-cultural differences (Herzfeld 1980; Lever 1986; Corbin 1987; Cole 1991). Nevertheless, the fact remains that an astonishing array of cultures define women in terms of their sexual behavior, define

men in terms of their control over female sexuality, and privilege female virginity and sexual fidelity. To ignore the ubiquity of these values, or to assume that ostensibly similar values cannot be compared across cultures and time, seems limiting. It seems most reasonable to neither ignore the complex nor to assume that it tells the whole story (Delaney 1987:35–36). As such, the honor/shame paradigm can serve both as a useful guide toward understanding intra- and intercultural gender systems and as a foil against which one can more clearly make distinctions between those systems across and within cultures.

2. Wages in Brazil are generally measured in "minimum salaries."

8

THE BONDS OF LOVE

COMPANIONATE MARRIAGE & THE DESIRE FOR INTIMACY AMONG HIJRAS IN HYDERABAD, INDIA

Gayatri Reddy

It was a hot summer afternoon in Hyderabad, the South Indian city where I did my fieldwork among hijras—the so-called "eunuch-transvestites" or "third sex" of India (Nanda 1990; Sharma 1989; Vyas and Shingala 1987). I was sitting with Shanti in the shade of her hut while she systematically plucked out the stray hairs on her chin. She was the only hijra awake at this time, all the others catching up on their sleep after a busy night of sex work. Shanti was in a contemplative mood, talking about her life in the hijra community and idly speculating about her future. In the course of conversation, we began to talk about relationships with men and more specifically her ideals of marriage, when she had this to say: "It is a different thing . . . It is not [sexual] desire. Now it is a companion through life . . . It is companionship and the hope that the person will be there with you later." Drawing on statements such as Shanti's, this article will focus on hijras' constructions of intimacy and desire as they articulate with and interpret the global ideology of companionate marriage.

EMERGING DESIRES: COMPANIONATE MARRIAGE
AND THE ATTACHMENTS OF SEXUALITY

The companionate marriage ideal—with its construction of relationships built on sexual and emotional intimacy rather than solely on a reproductive mandate—is emerging as an important value of modernity, as several scholars have cataloged in different regions of the world (Collier 1997; Inhorn 1996; Kendall 1996; Hirsch 2003; Hirsch et al. 2002; Hoodfar 1997; Rebhun 1999a; Simmons 1979). While the institution of marriage retains its salience and symbolic valence (perhaps never more so than at the present moment, with the recent debates and controversy regarding gay marriage), roughly over the space of a generation, the *meanings* attributed to this institution and the cultural significance of the marital bond appear to have changed rather dramatically. Drawing on her multigenerational study of gender and sexuality among migrants in western Mexico and Atlanta, Hirsch (1999a:2) for instance, notes that there has been a "transition from marriages of duty and obligation (marriages of *respeto* or respect) . . . to marriages of love and intimacy (relationships of *confianza* or trust and closeness)." As she elaborates on this transformation:

> Older couples talk about marriage in terms of mutual respect, gendered work obligations, and bonds of marriage that are reinforced through reproduction. Younger couples, in contrast, present an ideal of companionate marriage marked by a significant amount of "helping" with previously gendered tasks, increased heterosociality, and greater emphasis on trust, emotional warmth, and communication than on obligation and respect. (1999a:1)

Through this ideology of companionate marriage, men and women are constructing new ways of understanding their relationships to one another, increasingly premised on sexual and emotional intimacy and pleasure rather than merely a shared responsibility for reproduction. In other words, marital bonds are increasingly predicated on such intimacy, with companionship emerging as an important and articulated goal, transforming perceptions of marriage as well as the role of sexuality in this process—from a reproductive role to a more productive function in establishing the ties that bind.

How does one account for this seemingly universal (albeit variously

elaborated) discursive reality? What is the foundation of this new understanding? While most theorists acknowledge this "transformation of intimacy" (Giddens 1992), this shift in marital ideals that *emphasize* emotional
and sexual intimacy, as a peculiarly "modern" phenomenon dating variously from the mid-eighteenth to the early twentieth century, the basis for
this transformation in people's narratives of self, and subsequently in their
constructions of love and marriage, has been variously theorized.[1] Michel
Foucault, for instance, emphasizes new *constraints* in the form of the disci-
plining knowledge of the sexual sciences and the punishing practices of
modern states in people's search for intimacy (1977, 1978, 1980). Anthony
Giddens, on the other hand, stresses the increasing *choices* facilitated by the
production of new reproductive technologies that allowed women to
become the "emotional revolutionaries of modernity" (1992:130)—facilitating the emergence of what he terms "plastic sexuality" or "decentered
sexuality, freed from the needs of reproduction" (1992:2). In one of the
first non-Euro-American theorizations of fertility transition, John Caldwell (1976) accounts for the fertility decline and accompanying transformations of intimacy in Nigeria as resulting primarily from cultural
influences, including the impact of religious missionaries. Jane Collier
(1997), in turn, argues that the transformations of intimacy that she
observes in Los Olivos, the Andalusian village she returned to in the 1980s,
twenty years after her first fieldwork experience there, can be related to
cultural and economic changes in households and the members' relationships to one another through work—the transition from the experiences of
property ownership (being "co-owners") to wage labor (being "co-work-
ers," as she terms it).

More recent ethnographic explorations of this transformation "from
duty to desire," to use Collier's (1997) evocative title, have drawn on the
insights of these theorists, increasingly emphasizing the "mutually reinforcing structural and cultural forces" (Hirsch 1999a:17) that underlie the
shift in "modern" discourses of love and marriage (Jankowiak 1995; Hirsch
1999a, 2003; Rebhun 1999a; Wardlow, this volume; see also the introduction to this volume). As these authors (among others) argue, it is important
not to interpret these changes merely as an *inevitable* product of industrialization, one that all countries experience in a similar fashion as they "mod-
ernize." Marriage and the meanings of this institution for the inhabitants
of each country are historically, culturally, and socially variable, these
authors contend. While there may be structural parallels in these processes
across the world today, the interpretations of these changes and the man-

ner of their incorporation into people's lives are not only culturally specific, as most authors have noted, but also differentially related to the political and economic structures of their local contexts. These changes and the resulting configurations of "companionate marriage" are seen as the complex result of individual/national/transnational economic, social, cultural, and political forces; it is the totality of these mutually constitutive and dialectic forces that account for any one culturally specific interpretation of marriage.

In this chapter, my focus is not so much on accounting for the basis of this change in India (beyond noting its seeming ubiquity and increased intensity since the liberalization of the Indian economy and media apparatus in the early 1990s) as documenting the ethnographic details of a particular elaboration of this phenomenon. I address one interpretation of this "global" discourse of companionate marriage—among hijras in the South Indian city of Hyderabad. I argue that hijras serve as a particularly interesting and instructive case study through which to examine this ideology owing to their defiance of the centrality of procreative sexuality, and the fact that traditionally marriage has *not* been the fulcrum of relatedness or the central institution within this community. A brief introductory note will provide background before I expand on this theme.

"THIRD-SEXED" HIJRAS AND THE HETERONORMATIVE BOUNDS OF MARRIAGE

Hijras are perhaps the most commonly encountered contemporary figures in the narrative linking of India with sexual difference. As mentioned earlier, hijras are individuals often described in the literature as the "third sex" (Nanda 1990) or "eunuch-transvestites" (Vyas and Shingala 1987) of India. For the most part, they are "men" who wear female clothing and sacrifice their genitalia in return for the power to confer fertility, and as such, hijras have long been social pariahs, stigmatized and set apart on the basis of their apparently transgressive gender identification and their location beyond the domain of procreative sexuality. "Real" hijras are said to be like ascetics or *sannyasis*, having renounced sexual desire. They are asexual beings, "neither men nor women," as the title of Serena Nanda's (1990) popular ethnography proclaims, being reborn as hijras by virtue of an ideal (but not always realized) complete physical genital excision and are subsequently believed to be endowed with the power to confer fertility on newlyweds or newborn children. As Amir *nayak*, one of the hijra leaders stated, a "real" hijra is one whose "[sexual] body has no strength, and who has no mental or physical desire for men whatsoever . . . We are like ascetics. This is what is important." This ideology of asexuality with the associated implications of celibacy[2] is instantiated by and through the defining hijra practice of genital excision or *nirvan*—the moment of rebirth as a "real" hijra.[3] In the case of hijras, however, this invocation of celibacy/asexuality emphasizes not the retention of semen and masculine "life-force," but its irrevocable expelling through the act of physical emasculation.[4] Subsequently, all hijras are expected to "have no mental or physical desire whatsoever," as Amir *nayak* stated previously; they are reborn as "men minus men," to invoke O'Flaherty's (1980) colorful phrase, without the need or imperative to fulfill any reproductive mandate.

Despite this avowed asexuality, however, several hijras not only express sexual desire for men, but also act on this desire by actively engaging in sex work. As one hijra sex worker phrased it, "All hijras desire men. Otherwise why do they become hijras? Those who say 'we do not do this,' they are lying." To some extent, this appears to be a life-developmental course with the apparently "asexual" senior hijras having engaged in sex when they were younger, and with many of the younger hijra sex workers actively aspiring toward a more "respected," asexual life in their later years. But, as many of the sex workers indicate, one of the reasons—if not the primary one as some maintain—individuals choose to become hijras is in order to express their desire and engage in sex with other men.[5] As such, many of the younger hijras earn their income primarily from sex work with other (non-hijra) men, and in addition, several of them establish sexual and emotional relationships with men whom they consider as their "husbands."

Given the discursive salience of sexual desire among hijras—whether in terms of its refutation or espousal—as well as the acknowledged disavowal of the reproductive imperative in hijras' relationship with their "husbands," it is particularly interesting and, I would argue, instructive, to examine hijra constructions of "marriage." For one thing, all hijras concur in their belief regarding the excision of their genitalia or *nirvan* as the quintessential (and idealized) marker of their identity. They are "neither men nor women" to invoke Nanda's popular phrase, making issues of reproduction and fertility incidental to their pleasure in relationships. For another, their "marriages" to non-hijra men are all to some degree "love" marriages—relationships that are predicated primarily on love or affection between the partners—rather than socially sanctioned "arranged" marriages, given that officially, marriage, whether to a man and/or especially to a woman, is proscribed within the hijra canon.[6] Knowledge on the part of the senior hijras of this rule's transgression is threatened by punishments ranging from a harsh fine to excommunication from the community. And yet, among the hijra sex workers at least, "marriage"—or a long-lasting and emotionally intimate relationship with a man—is perhaps the most longed-for relationship in their lives. In this chapter I hope to unpack hijras' understandings of such marriages and their intimate "bonds of love" with their "husbands," exploring the way these understandings incorporate, elaborate, and modify global ideologies of "companionate marriage," individuality, and modernity.[7]

REPRESENTATIONS OF CONJUGALITY AND INTIMACY IN CONTEMPORARY INDIA

Companionate marriages—with their construction of relationships built on sexual and emotional intimacy rather than reproduction—are emerging as important values associated with modernity in different regions of the world, as the introduction to this volume indicates. India appears to be no exception in this regard. Responding to the changing consumer dynamic of a new middle class in the throes of self-discovery, representations of intimacy in the media have been undergoing a rapid transformation in recent times. Perhaps the most striking and classic images emblematic of this change are the advertisements for condoms—from those of Nirodh in the 1970s to Kamasutra in the 1990s.

For a long time the only condom advertisements in the public or mass media were the regimented world of Nirodh. With its images of an inverted triangle (the Nirodh symbol) interposed between an explicitly non-intimate but "small" and "happy" family, this product was indelibly associated with the state and the Indian government's ubiquitous message of family planning. The classic Nirodh advertisement depicted stick figures of a couple and their two children and was accompanied by the slogan *do ya teen bus* or "two or three is enough," a message that was marginally changed in the 1990s to *hum do, hamare do* or "us two, our two." The principal message of these advertisements was fertility control in the service of "development"; the Nirodh advertisements were a principal tool in the state apparatus for addressing the problem of overpopulation, long believed to be the cause of the country's underdevelopment.

In marked contrast, the Kamasutra television advertisement, first launched in the early 1990s, depicts a man rowing ashore in the dead of night, walking into an unlocked house, and joining a woman in the shower where they both caress their almost naked bodies while a woman's voice whispers in English: "Kama Sutra. For the pleasure of making love."[8] Dramatically opposed to the Nirodh advertisement, the Kamasutra advertisements (both the television advertisement described here and similar magazine advertisements) signal a new public legitimation of consensual sexuality, highlighting the agency of men and to some extent women, and the possibility of their mutual pleasure.[9] Also notable in the Kamasutra advertisement is the absence of visible signs of the state, whether through images of the family or messages of "development" through family planning. Along with the modernization of the apparatus for population control, the condom has been resignified through such advertisements in the 1990s to connote the right to pleasure of the emerging middle class. In this context, the Kamasutra advertisement symbolizes not so much the "victory of sexual pleasure over that of fertility control, as a shift in the relative framing of sexuality and fertility" (John and Nair 1998:16) in contemporary society with new divisions and exclusions along urban/class/caste/religious lines.[10]

My interest here is not in analyzing these new alignments, fascinating as they may be, so much as pointing to the institution of *marriage*, which I believe is indelibly caught up with these resignifications. In this regard, perhaps the most interesting aspect of the Kamasutra advertisement is the marked absence of any explicit conjugal marker. At the very least, this advertisement conveys an ambiguity in the marital relationship between the couple, with the conscious elision of all markers of marriage as well as of Indian-ness, one might add. For instance, in the television advertisement, there is no *sindhur* in the woman's hair, no *mangalsutra* around her neck, nor is there a ring on either of their fingers; the couple *appear* to share the house but this message is left ambiguous. In the magazine advertisement depicted here, the couple in the throes of experiencing the "pleasure of making love" are not only scantily clad but are attired in what are commonly perceived to be Western outfits and do not exhibit any marker of either their ethnicity or their marital status. The subtext of the advertisement seems to be that public representations of sexual intimacy and desire are permissible between two consensual people as long as they do not *emphasize* and thereby adversely impact the construction of marriage and the meaning of the "family." That is, in representations of desire and sexuality (insofar as they are permitted in the mass media), the marital signifier needs to be consciously masked; while on the other hand, in depicting images of marriage, desire is often reformulated and cloaked in terms of the family and "Indian" tradition, as a television advertisement for a popular body lotion, Vicco Turmeric, indicates. Preparations for a wedding are the setting for the Vicco Turmeric advertisement, with scenes of a young Indian woman being made up by her family and friends for her impending marriage. The advertisement then ends with a shot of this coy, blushing Indian bride sitting on the wedding platform with her husband, while members of his family invoke kinship idioms as they look on approvingly at her and comment upon what a lovely couple they make.

STATE(D) CONVENTIONS AND THE LOGIC OF CENSORSHIP

Not surprisingly, the state plays a significant role in reinforcing and possibly shaping the legitimacy/illegitimacy of such images and the institution of marriage. As Madhava Prasad argues, it is in regimenting representations of the "private"—often symbolized by and through the conjugal couple—that the "modern" state's role is most apparent. In his recent book on the ideology of the Hindi film, Prasad (1998) examines the ban on scenes of kissing in Indian cinema,[11] arguing that this prohibition is symptomatic of the "new" regime of modern state authority. The very need to institute a prohibition is indelibly tied to the capitalist enterprise of the modern state, according to Prasad. Drawing a distinction between the representations of private sexual intimacy (in this case the kiss) and the public spectacle of the female body ("vulgar" dance scenes, for instance) in Hindi films, Prasad argues that the ban imposed on the former (and not on the latter) can only be understood as an elaboration of the modern (capitalist) state agenda to assume absolute authority and control over the realm of the private—in effect "inventing the couple" and the domain of the family whose representations it then regulates. As he notes, "The minimal unit of the private domain is the nuclear family, whose rise to pre-eminence coincides with the dissolution of pre-capitalist patriarchal enclaves and the emergence of the modern state as the sole supervising authority over the family as the site of biological reproduction and socialization" (1998:24). Notably, it is precisely the "kiss that seals the Christian marriage and inaugurates a zone of privacy . . . [that] is the very same kiss that is prohibited on the Indian screen, between Indian citizens" (1998:96).

At a related though more obvious level, the ban on kissing also invokes a nationalist politics of culture: "The most frequently offered justification of this informal prohibition has been that it corresponds to the need to maintain the Indian-ness of Indian culture. Kissing is described as a sign of Western-ness and therefore alien to Indian culture," Prasad writes (1998:88). As a case in point, when denying the hero a kiss, the heroine in the 1967 film *An Evening in Paris*[12] states, "I'm an Indian girl and according to Indian custom that . . . that's only after marriage." In such instances, the "Western" kiss threatens not merely the institution of marriage and the family, but also the very demarcation of national identity, through the explicitly gendered body of the woman.[13]

Perhaps the most important point to focus on in this context is the state's "incitement to marriage" as it were. It is through the marital signifier that legitimate and illegitimate markers of modernity, culture, and Indian-ness are "invented" and its representations regulated by the state. Specifically, it is in articulating its position with regard to the institution of marriage that state ideologies with respect to a "modern" image of desirous agency and erotic sexuality are most apparent. To use another recent example from the media, an extremely controversial full-page advertisement for Tuffs shoes depicting a nude man and woman wearing only shoes while embracing each other was forced to be withdrawn from circulation by the Maharashtra state government.[14] The ostensible reason for such censorship, as articulated by a government representative, centered precisely on the institution of marriage—it was because the two models used in the advertisement were about to get married in real life that the nudity was particularly problematic. As noted in *The Hindu*, a popular Indian daily, in responding to this advertisement, a minister in the government is reported to have said: "How can we allow anyone to pose in the nude with his *wife?*" (Sharma 1995, emphasis in original).

HIJRA "HUSBANDS" AND EMOTIONAL INTIMACY

Given these normative constructions of intimacy, sexuality, and marriage, how do hijras negotiate this divide—between the apparent legitimacy of intimate encounters only within the confines of the marital signifier, and its apparent illegitimacy in sexual encounters outside this sphere? On the one hand, hijras are officially located outside the bounds of marriage and "the family" through their image as non-reproductive "eunuchs." On the other hand, sexual desire and the need for emotional intimacy with non-hijra men is a very powerful motivating factor in their lives, with several hijras engaging in sex work as their primary occupation as well as engaging in intimate relationships with their husbands. How then do *these* hijras—

hijras who clearly articulate and enact their sexual desire, at the same time as they locate themselves outside the reproductive mandate—negotiate the "official" or normative ideologies of sexuality, marriage, and modernity? As I argue in the remainder of this article, the hijras in Hyderabad that I interacted with did not necessarily contravene the official discourse; they merely negotiated it by displacing their sexual desire onto a (less valorized) client relationship, while locating their need for emotional (more highly valued) bonds onto their relationships with their "husbands."

As noted in the opening vignette, talking about her ideals of men or "husbands" and marriage, Shanti said, "It is a different thing . . . It is not desire. Now it is a life companion . . . It is companionship and the hope that the person will be there with you later." As her statement makes evident, the hijras appear to differentiate between desire and lifelong companionship, displacing them onto different relationships—marital and non-marital. As several hijras reiterated, their clients or 'customers' as they referred to them could appease their desire. But their relationships with their "husbands," on the other hand, were "different." It was not just sexual pleasure that was the basis of this intimate relationship, but more importantly "companionship" and caring that were the ideals desired. In the hijras' local constructions of companionate marriage, emotional intimacy appears to be disengaged from sexual or corporeal intimacy, that is, the "bonds of love" in their intimate relationships are emotional rather than primarily or solely corporeal.[15]

Talking about Sharmila's husband who was currently visiting, another hijra sex worker, Jyoti, stated wistfully: "That Mohan [Sharmila's husband] is a good man. He comes every day to see her . . . At least once a week, he brings her something or the other." She added disgustedly, "Unlike this bastard Rajesh, who only comes here when he wants money for his drinking," referring to another hijra's husband who had just walked in, who was not only a drunkard, but also repeatedly beat his "wife" and took all her money. In a similar vein, according to Munira, the fact that her husband Zahid accompanied her on a religious trip to Ajmer despite difficulties at home was proof of his affection for her. As she stated proudly, "His work was not going so well. And at home, his brother's son was not well. But still he came with me when I asked him to."

In addition, Zahid was held up as an ideal husband not only because he looked after Munira and nursed her back to health following her all-important *nirvan* operation as well as her bout with typhoid, but also because of his openness with his family about his relationship with Munira.

According to her, because she was Zahid's *first* "wife," he not only asked Munira's *permission* before marrying his current "official" wife, but also supposedly told his wife's family and gained their acceptance of his relationship with Munira before agreeing to his second marriage.[16] This of course was Munira's rendition of the story, offered as proof that Zahid really cared for her. But whatever the veracity of this account, her emphasis on Zahid's trust, openness, and caring reveal these as important criteria defining a "good" husband in her estimation.

Interestingly, despite the hijras' engagement with sex work as well as their husbands' conjugal relations with their (other) wives as well as occasional visits with a female sex worker, lifelong commitment in their relationship was held up as the ideal to be striven for. As Munira stated explicitly, "On the road, how many [people] we meet who say come, I'll make you [mine]. But staying with one man only is good." In this respect, she invoked the strength of her relationship with her husband Zahid, saying, "My man beat me and did everything. To the point where he broke my hand . . . to the point where he threatened to set me on fire. But I shouldn't say like that . . . Why did he do like that? Because between us there is a bond [*jodi*], a relationship of love [*pyar ka rishta*]. Twice I ate rat poison . . . I did everything. Still I didn't leave him. I didn't leave him; he didn't leave me. It should be like that."[17]

Significantly, this ideal of companionate marriage appears to cross the boundary between the hijra community and that of society at large, being the ideal held up for *all* married couples. Almost the first question hijras would ask of me, irrespective of how well they knew me, was "When are you going to get married?" Without waiting for a reply, they would then dreamily imagine the scene: it would be a grand wedding with a big band, I would look very nice dressed in a silk sari with flowers in my hair, and they would all come and dance for me. Most important, my husband would be a handsome man who would not drink alcohol or beat me, and instead, would buy gifts for me, take care of me, and really love me throughout my life. It was this image—of love, caring, and emotional intimacy that lasts a lifetime—that was the important factor in the marital relationship, irrespective of the existence of multiple sexual partners. Hijras' fantasies of the ideal marital relationship appear to be conditioned not so much by sexual, bodily desire per se as by a caring relationship and emotional intimacy. This is not to imply that the ideal marriage *precluded* any experience of sexual desire, physical intimacy, and pleasure, but only that perhaps what was *most important* for the hijras in a marital relationship was companionship and emotional intimacy.

HIJRA CLIENTS AND SEXUAL INTIMACY

The hijras' relationships with their clients, on the other hand, were founded *primarily* on sexual or corporeal desire. In response to a direct question about sex work, Zarina had this to say to me: "Why do we do this [sex] work? Some . . . many . . . do this mainly because of desire for men . . . and to earn money of course! Everyone does it for that. There is a fondness for 'sex'[18] . . . I do not lie." In a similar statement, Aliya said, "*All* hijras desire men. Otherwise why do they become hijras and do this work. Those who say 'we do not do this,' they are lying." For the hijra sex workers, "this [sex] work" was not only their primary occupation, providing their only means of livelihood, but also served as an integral expression of the "truth" of "*all* hijras' desire." Although their lives would have been infinitely more comfortable in their leader's middle-class households, hijra sex workers preferred to lead a less "respectable" and somewhat precarious life facing the everyday threat of arrest, eviction, and the destruction of their makeshift huts that they had erected on government land—all so they could engage their "fondness for 'sex.'"

"Sex" for these hijras was a very important aspect of their identity and practice. For the most part, each of these hijras engaged in sex with between five and ten partners every night. They had their own hierarchy of sexual practices with different valences placed on specific acts. The most significant categorical difference was that between "real" and "false" sex— or *sees* and *kavdi*, respectively. While *sees* work included anal and oral sex, *kavdi* "sex" referred primarily to frottage, whether between the thighs or stimulation by hand. The particular sex act engaged in with a client or "customer" was a complex negotiation factoring in desire, beauty, monetary compensation, and sometimes, familiarity with the client. While "real" or *sees* work garnered a higher wage (with oral sex being more expensive relative to anal sex within this category), "false" or *kavdi* work was perhaps the more common practice. However, at least every other night, hijras engaged in *sees* work with at least one of their several clients, deriving sexual pleasure and "enjoy[ment]" from engaging "in this sex line."

On one occasion I was visiting the hijras in the afternoon. Most of the hijras were asleep. I was sitting on a mat in the shade of a hut with my hijra friends Radhika and Surekha, lazily reading a film magazine with them, when we saw Rani, another hijra, walking in from the direction of the railway tracks where the hijras usually engaged their clients.[19] She had a radiant smile on her face as she came and sat with us. Surekha gave her an amused glance as she asked, "where are you coming from, you pimp? . . . *Sees* or *kavdi?*" In response, Rani grinned slyly and replied, "*Sees* . . . A new 'customer.' He works in the railway [service]." She then added excitedly, "He is really handsome you know! He said he would come back tomorrow." "How much?" Radhika immediately asked. Rani looked a little sheepish, as she answered, "He didn't have that much money. But he said he would come back tomorrow evening, so I'll ask him for more then." Radhika just shook her head while Surekha playfully batted Rani, affectionately calling her a pimp and teasing her about her new man.

Why then do these hijras valorize the acquisition of a husband? What is the role these "husbands" play relative to the hijras' sexual "customers"? When I once asked Rekha why she continued to engage in sex work after marrying her husband given that he could presumably satisfy her sexual desire, she looked at me seemingly in utter bewilderment that I would ask such a simplistic and stupid question and said, "But that is different, Gayatri. A husband is different." This "difference" is manifested not only in the relative valence of corporeal and emotional bonds in the hijras' relationships with their "husbands" and clients respectively, but also in the specific sexual practices engaged in. While the *absolute* incidence and frequency of *sees* work and subsequent pleasure derived from these acts might be greater with their sexual clients, the *relative* incidence of "real" and "false" sex (irrespective of the pleasure they derive from the act) with their "husbands" perhaps reflects the importance of this relationship for the hijra sex workers. As they indicated to me, sex with their husbands is *always* "real" sex, while sex with their clients can be (and often is) "false." Although as noted earlier, hijras do in fact derive pleasure from sexual engagement with their clients and often with greater frequency than with their husbands, quite often these "customer" relationships are disparaged, and much is made of their monetary worth and the opportunity they provide to denigrate men. For instance, one of the hijra sex workers once told me quite proudly, "We make fools out of these customers. We say we will do the 'real' work, and we actually do 'false' [sex/work]. They are in such a hurry and they don't know anything . . . So we can easily make fools of them."

The bonds with their clients are not primarily emotional or affective bonds; rather, the relationship is premised, for the most part, on the cold calculus of monetary transactions. Coupled with the disparagement of men and their mocking of supposed male knowledge and power, hijras interpret these "customer" bonds, not surprisingly, through the lens of their monetary worth. The less a "customer" is willing or able to pay, the more disparaged he is, often incurring derogatory, abusive terms and even physical violence from the hijras on this account. Unless of course, the client is a particularly handsome or desirable young man—as with Rani and her railway worker—in which case sex, more often than not, is "real" sex that provides mutual sexual pleasure, irrespective of the payment proffered. However, even in these instances, there is often no respect for the men with whom they engage in sex. A couple of weeks after the incident where Rani had met her "handsome" railway worker, she was disparagingly telling Surekha how easily he could be manipulated and made to do whatever Rani wanted, something I never heard any of the hijras say about their husbands.

VIOLENCE AND THE REINSCRIPTION OF GENDERED IDEOLOGIES

The flip side of these constructions is the explicit gendering of hijras' marital relationships. Hijra "bonds of love" with their husbands are explicitly constructed in the image of normative heterosexual marital bonds with all of their often-problematic reinscriptions of gendered and patriarchal ideals, norms, and practices. In this relationship, domestic responsibilities such as cooking, cleaning, washing, and sewing are clearly the "wife's" (hijra's) duties. Every day, wherever Rajesh had spent the previous night, he would come back to the railway station where his hijra "wife" lived, and she would wash his clothes, make sure he was fed, selecting the choicest bits of meat or the largest helping of whatever dish she had prepared for him, lay out a mat for him to sleep on, and sometimes press his feet for him as he fell asleep.

A good wife, moreover, is likely to respect her husband, never act promiscuously in public when he is around (whatever one's occupation or behavior in contexts outside of their relationship), and always look after him and his needs, especially in times of trouble. Munira was extremely upset one day when she found out that Zahid had eaten at a hotel and slept with his friends on the road that night. She yelled at him when he came to see her the next day saying, "Don't you have a wife and home here? How will it look that you didn't come here? Won't people say his wife is probably not looking after him well?" Likewise, Surekha very proudly informed me that she had a "system" worked out with her husband. At eleven o'clock at night, she would descend from the "platform" [railway tracks where many of the hijras engaged their "customers"], immediately take off all makeup and flashy jewelry, have a bath, put on a nice clean sari, wear *sindhur* in her hair (a marker of marital status), and wait for her "husband" to arrive. This was the "system" that he had devised and instituted, she told me very proudly.

But, importantly, these relationships also incorporated an explicit trust, respect, and bond of intimate affection between the partners. Whenever Zahid was in financial and even emotional trouble he would come first to Munira, rather than his "legal" (female) wife or other friends. Likewise, it was Zahid and not the other hijras who helped Munira when she was sick, first with typhoid, and then after she had her (*nirvan*) operation. "When I had 'typhoid,' for at least two months I could not do anything or even get up and go to the bathroom. Then it wasn't these hijra pimps who helped me but my man, Zahid," Munira told me proudly. As Zahid once told me when we were both waiting for Munira to come back from the market, "[She] understands my troubles . . . and always tries to help me. For many years . . . we have both lived through a lot of difficulties together . . . and I know that [Munira] will help me any time."

Rajesh had a similar story to tell of his relationship with Surekha. "She must have spent over a lakh of rupees [a hundred thousand] on me in the past few years. Always, [Surekha] gave me money whenever I needed anything, [saying] 'go and get whatever you want.' I have complete trust in her." On another occasion Surekha told me, "My love [for Rajesh] is real love . . . whenever Rajesh needs anything, I will do whatever to help him, even if it means being beaten and thrown out by the hijras," she said, referencing a recent occurrence. Rajesh wanted to go to Bombay and see what it was like to live there. So Surekha had left Hyderabad without telling the other hijras (who she claimed would have protested and not allowed her to go) and left in the middle of the night for Bombay. When they came back a couple of months later, the hijras in Hyderabad beat her up and, for a few days at least, ostracized her from the community.

Further, when Rajesh was thrown in jail, it was Surekha (rather than his "blood" family) who worked extra hard despite having just had her operation so that she could earn enough money to post bail for him. Again, when Rajesh slept with another hijra within the same community, everyone urged Surekha to throw him out, but as she told me later, "I said no . . . this is my husband . . . How can I just throw him out?" She continued to look after him and give him money, often behind her (hijra) seniors' backs because they didn't want her to have anything more to do with him. Last year, when I went to visit Surekha, she had just returned from her husband's village in the neighboring state where she had helped to first set up an alliance and then helped to organize her husband's wedding to a woman, so that as Surekha happily told me, "now he can have children . . . and we can all live together in Hyderabad."

On another occasion, Nagalakshmi, who was only semiliterate, asked me to write a "love letter" to her husband Nagesh, who lived in a city about three hundred kilometers away. When I asked her what she wanted me to write, she first said shyly, "I don't know . . . You know all these love words and all that . . . how to say everything about love. So you say whatever you think will sound good." When I pressed her, she said, "Tell him that I really want to see him and am really suffering . . . I am dying . . . without him here. Also tell him I really, really love him and have never loved anyone so much. You tell him these things but in a way that will make him come here."

Despite the "official" injunctions against marriage and the establishment of intimate relationships with men, for the hijra sex workers I interacted with most closely, these relationships are perhaps the *most* important in their lives. Every single life history that I collected from these hijras overwhelmingly emphasized their relationships with their husbands. Although many of these relationships began as "customer" encounters, they were rapidly transformed into intimate emotional bonds according to the hijras. In this scenario "husbands" cared for their "wives," spent time with them, accompanied them on trips, got them gifts on special occasions, were not embarrassed to publicly acknowledge their relationships with the (stigmatized) hijras, and, perhaps most important, appeared to share an emotional bond with the hijras that was not premised on obligatory reproductive grounds so much as "bonds of love."

But this trust and confidence in one another does not always play itself out in these relationships. In fact, more often than not, accompanying these "systems" or (gendered) chaste behavioral scripts is a very unequal, gendered pattern of violence. Despite the fact that for the most part, hijras are fairly big and strong, with pronounced male musculature, they continue to suffer violence and abuse from their husbands. In fact any statement on my part indicating their ability to fight back or questioning their lack of resistance was greeted with absolute incredulity. "*Chi!* That is not possible," I was told in categorical terms. "How can we do that? This is our husband." There appeared to be an explicit re-gendering of relationships that held up the values of emotional security, trust, and respect as the ideals in a marital relationship despite the reality of abuse and suffering—the desire for companionship rather than sexual or corporeal appeasement, as Shanti stated in the opening vignette. Despite the repeated thwarting of such ideals, it is this *longing* for bonds of affection and emotional intimacy that motivates the hijras' eternal quest for ideal "husbands"—while also accounting for much of the pathos of their everyday lives. Ultimately, although (potentially) premised on powerful egalitarian ideals, clearly not all "companionate marriages" result in (and from) the empowerment of the "female" partner in the relationship as Giddens (1992) and others suggest.

In this context, perhaps the most telling practices that exemplify hijras' longing for intimate, caring relationships with their husbands are their attempts to commit suicide. Disturbingly, almost all of the hijra sex workers I met in Hyderabad had attempted suicide at least once (mostly unsuccessfully but for one instance), on account of abandonment, neglect, or abuse by their husbands. I end this article with one such dramatic account—a statement from Surekha explaining to me why she had slashed her wrists in an attempt to kill herself: "Last week, Rajesh [her husband] went back to Vijayawada . . . I told you, no? He has kept this other hijra there. Even that I was willing to bear with, as long as he spent some time with me also. You know what he said? [He said] why will I want to spend time with you now? I've been many years with you. You have become old and I no longer care for you. How will I feel? You tell me . . . what should I do when he says [things] like that? I thought . . . what is the point of this life if it is worth the same as death? So I tried to kill myself." Clearly, for the hijras today, a demonstration of affection and emotional intimacy—even more than sexual desire and corporeal pleasure—are perhaps the *most* important sentiments in constructing a "companionate" marriage, eminently worth dying for as Surekha's words—and actions—indicate.

NOTES

1. Importantly, the historical origin and class character of this companionate ideal is highly contested. Social historians have posited different developmental narratives, ranging from the eleventh century through the nineteenth century, with varied historical and social investments by different segments of society (see the introduction to this volume for an elaboration on these issues/contestations).

2. As recent literature notes, scholarship on (male) sexuality in India reflects a predominant theme of "semen anxiety," i.e., wherein loss of semen is equated with loss of masculine strength (John and Nair 1998; Srivastava 2001). Correspondingly, much of this literature valorizes celibacy as the most important (male) Hindu and/or Gandhian cultural ideal (cf. Alter 1992, 2000; Caplan 1987; Carstairs 1958; Lal 1999).

3. The term *nirvan* means rebirth and indexes the Hindu/Buddhist understanding of rebirth through enlightenment.

4. The marked difference between the Brahmanical/Hindu philosophical view that renunciatory celibacy produces masculinity or concentrated masculine vigor and the Buddhist view that celibacy leads to loss of virility or emasculation is pertinent here (cf. Chakravarti 1987).

5. Needless to say, this is a hotly debated issue both within the hijra community as well as in literature on the hijras (cf. Cohen 1995). Although there are dissenting voices, this somewhat problematic etiological referent remains, among other important threads in hijra articulations of their identity and practice.

6. See De Munck 1998 for an effective problematization of such binaries, i.e., love versus arranged marriages.

7. Here I will be drawing primarily on the experiences and articulations of the younger hijra sex workers. Marital bonds and their salience among the hierarchically senior hijras, who do not engage in sex work, would no doubt be somewhat different. An analysis of these differences however is beyond the scope of this article.

8. In conceiving of the Kamasutra advertisement, the contrast between Nirodh and Kamasutra was an explicit focus or target of the campaign. As the well-known advertising executive credited with this campaign, Alyque Padamsee, recently stated, "Long before Viagra, Gautam Singhania and myself created yesterday's Viagra: Kamasutra condoms. Our theory was simple: Nirodh is unsexy and anti-pleasure. It is a downer. So why not [introduce] something that perks a man up? Something that adds rather than subtracts from his pleasure? And that is how we created the sexy condom KamaSutra . . . 'For the pleasure of making love'" (transcript of live chat, June 19, 1999, www.indiatimes.com). Interestingly, gender is one axis that appears to explicitly play into this representation. By and large (although it varied with respect to the rural market; see endnote 9), condom advertisements are increasingly emphasizing the element of "pleasure" and "desire," while messages of family planning and birth control are being displaced onto advertisements of (female) contraceptive devices such as the Copper-T and oral contraceptive pills such as Mala-D—in effect representing women (and not men) as bearing the ultimate responsibility for "family planning," and one could add, implicitly representing sexual desire and "pleasure" as the legitimate pursuit of men (and not women).

9. The current Kamasutra advertisement can be viewed at http://manav .www9.50megs.com/vb.htm.

10. It is interesting to note that in positioning and targeting audiences for condoms, there is also an urban/rural divide corresponding to perceived class interests/needs in the vision of the advertising executives. For instance, commenting on the philosophy behind the introduction of a new condom (Durex) into the Indian marketplace and its comparison with existing condom brands (Kohinoor), Clive Kitchener, the director of strategy at London International Group (LIG) had this to say: "Thus while LIG is targeting the urban market with lifestyle, happiness, and pleasure themes, in the rural market, the stress is on safety and security . . . Kohinoor [targeted more at rural audiences] is positioned (and perceived) as the condom for the married couple and the underlying pitch is for family planning. With sexual

attitudes and mores in India changing with international trends, Durex will be positioned as a lifestyle product that is all about pleasure and fun" (*Hindu Business Line*, July 10, 1997).

11. As Prasad notes, the prohibition on kissing was based on a "unwritten rule" deriving from the British code of censorship and its more formal "written rules" prohibiting "excessively passionate love scenes," "indelicate sexual situations," and "scenes suggestive of immorality" (*Report*, 1969:93, quoted in Prasad 1998:88). Interestingly, although the government inquiry committee on film censorship that was examining this ban recommended it be lifted in the late 1960s, it wasn't until the mid-1980s that (even perfunctory) kissing scenes were introduced in Hindi films. In fact, a survey conducted in the 1960s indicated significant popular support for the ban, with 51% expressing the view that " 'kissing scenes should be deleted from Indian films even if kissing and embracing was a natural part of the story,' as against 33.3% who voted for a more liberal code" (quoted in Prasad 1998:89).

12. It is precisely on foreign shores that the uniqueness of the national (Indian) culture is highlighted, and the responsibility of the nation's citizens to uphold it is magnified. Following the logic of this argument, foreign films and the rules governing foreign actors' performances (even if they were acting in the same Hindi film) were censored according to a different code.

13. See Butalia 2000; Chatterjee 1993; Das 1998; Menon and Butalia 1998 for similar accounts wherein women's bodies serve as the singular locus that mark and are imprinted with "other"—ethnic, religious, and nationalistic—divisions.

14. The case is currently still in court with an initial trial date set for November 2004 although the two models in the advertisement are no longer engaged to be married.

15. Hijras use the phrase *pyar ke rishte* to refer to relationships with their husbands; it references the foundation of such relationships—love, *pyar*, or *mohabbat*. However, the phrase has also been used by non-hijras to refer to a variety of so-called fictive relationships, most notably sibling and parent-child relationships. Such relationships (much like relationships with their husbands to a certain extent) are premised on notions of volition or choice, in contrast to immediate consanguinal (and affinal) ties. The use of the term *fictive*, however, has increasingly been criticized, given the presumptions of authenticity and, implicitly, heterosexual normativity, that underlie such constructions (see Weston 1991).

16. Zahid is Muslim and can legally engage in polygamy.

17. Sudhir Kakar's (1989) invocation of the *jodi* as perhaps the most important ideal for women, about which there is "formidable consensus," is noteworthy in this regard. Also note valid critiques of this postulation—especially of the notion that there is a "formidable consensus" about this ideal among *all* women (Raheja and Gold 1996).

18. The English term *sex* was used. Henceforth, any English term employed will be indicated by quotation marks.

19. This area was close to the railway station. The hijras either engaged in sex work in the stray railway compartments that were parked in this area for repairs or, more often, out in the open along the railway tracks. Engagement in sex work was (and is) usually a nocturnal activity.

BIBLIOGRAPHY

Abdool, K. Q., J. E. Mantell, and E. Scheepers

    1996   South Africa's Response to Preventing HIV/AIDS and Other STDs in Women: Introducing Female Controlled Methods in the Public Sector. *International Conference on AIDS* 11 (July 7–12, Vancouver): 258 (abstract no. Tu.D.354).

Adih, William, and Cheryl Alexander

    1999   Determinants of Condom Use to Prevent HIV Infection among Youth in Ghana. *Journal of Adolescent Health* 24 (1): 63–72.

Ahearn, Laura

    1998   "Love Keeps Afflicting Me": Agentive Discourse in Nepali Love Letters. Paper presented at American Anthropological Association meetings, December 4, 1998, Philadelphia.

    2001   *Invitations to Love: Literacy, Love Letters, and Social Change in Nepal.* Ann Arbor: University of Michigan Press.

Alarcón, Norma, Ana Castillo, and Cherríe Moraga, eds.

    1993   *The Sexuality of Latinas.* Berkeley: Third Woman Press.

Alter, Joseph S.

    1992   *The Wrestler's Body.* Chicago: University of Chicago Press.

    2000   *Gandhi's Body: Sex, Diet, and the Politics of Nationalism.* Philadelphia: University of Pennsylvania Press.

Amadiume, Ifi

    1987   *Male Daughters, Female Husbands: Gender and Sex in African Society.* Atlantic Highlands, NJ: Zed Books.

Amaro, H.

    1995   Love, Sex, and Power: Considering Women's Realities in HIV Prevention. *American Psychologist* 50 (6): 437–47.

Appadurai, A.

    1996   *Modernity at Large: Cultural Dimensions of Globalization.* Minneapolis: University of Minnesota Press.

Awofeso, Niyi
  2002 Wedding Rings and the Feminist Movement. *Journal of Mundane Behavior* 3 (2): 1–16.
Bailey, Beth
  1987 Scientific Truth . . . and Love: The Marriage Education Movement in the United States. *Journal of Social History* 20 (4): 711–32.
Baker, Hugh
  1979 *Chinese Family and Kinship*. London: Macmillan.
Bell, Jim
  1995 Notions of Romantic Love among the Taita of Kenya. In *Romantic Passion: A Universal Experience?* ed. W. Jankowiak, 152–65. New York: Columbia University Press.
Benton, John
  1966 Clio and Venus: An Historical View of Romantic Love. In *The Meaning of Courtly Love*, ed. F. X. Neuman, 19–42. Albany: New York State University Press.
Bernard, R.
  1994 *Qualitative Research Methods*. Newbury Park: Sage.
Blackwood, Evelyn
  2005 Wedding Bell Blues: Marriage, Missing Men, and Matrifocal Follies. *American Ethnologist* 32 (1): 3–19.
Bledsoe, Caroline, and Gilles Pison, eds.
  1994 *Nuptuality in Sub-Saharan Africa: Contemporary Anthropological and Demographic Perspectives*. New York: Oxford University Press.
Bletzer, K. V.
  1995 Use of Ethnography in the Evaluation and Targeting of HIV-AIDS Education among Latino Farm Workers. *AIDS Education and Prevention* 7:178–91.
Bocock, Robert
  1993 *Consumption*. London and New York: Routledge.
Bolton, R.
  1992 AIDS and Promiscuity: Muddles in the Models of HIV Prevention. *Medical Anthropology* 14 (2–4): 145–223.
Borneman, John
  1996 Until Death Do Us Part: Marriage/Death in Anthropological Discourse. *American Ethnologist* 23 (2): 215–38.
  2001 Caring and Being Cared For: Displacing Marriage, Kinship, Gender, and Sexuality. In *The Ethics of Kinship: Ethnographic Inquiries*, ed. J. Faubion, 29–46. Lanham, MD: Rowman and Littlefield.
Bott, Elizabeth
  1957 *Family and Social Network: Roles, Norms, and External Relationships in Ordi-*
  (1971) *nary Urban Families*. New York: Free Press.
Bozzoli, Belinda
  1991 *Women of Phokeng: Consciousness, Life Strategy, and Migrancy in South Africa, 1900–1983*. Portsmouth, NH: Heinemann.
Bravo-Garcia, Enrique, and Carlos Magis-Rodríguez
  2003 El Sida en al área rural. In *La Otra Epidemia: El Sida en al área rural*, ed. Car-

los Magis, Enrique Bravo-García, and Ana María Carrillo. México: Centro Nacional para la Prevención y Control del VIH/SIDA (CENSIDA).

Bronfman, M., S. Camposortega, and J. Z. Izazola

1989 Distribución de la epidemia del SIDA. In *SIDA, Ciencia, y Sociedad en Mexico*, ed. J. Sepulveda-Arnor, M. Bronfman, G. Ruiz-Palacios, E. Stanislawski, and J. L. Valdespino. Mexico: Secretaria de Salud, Instituto Nacional de Salud Pública, Fondo de Cultura Economica.

Bronfman, M., and S. Lopez-Moreno

1996 Perspectives on HIV/AIDS Prevention among Immigrants on the U.S.-Mexico Border. In S. Mishra, R. Conner, and R. Magaña, eds., *AIDS Crossing Borders: The Spread of HIV among Migrant Latinos*, 49–76. Boulder: Westview.

Bronfman, M., and N. Minello

1995 Hábitos sexuales de los migrantes temporales Mexicanos a Los Estados Unidos de América: Prácticas de riesgo para la infección por VIH. In *Sida en Mexico: Migración, Adolescencia, y Genero*, by M. Bronfman, A. Amuchástegui, R. Martina, N. Minello, M. Rivas, and G. Rodriguez, 1–90. Mexico City, Mexico: Información Profesional Especializada.

Bronfman, M., G. Sejenovich, and P. Uribe

1998 *Migración y SIDA en México y América Central.* Mexico City, Mexico: Angulos del SIDA and CONASIDA.

Bruschini, Maria Cristina Aranha

Mulher, Casa e Família: Cotidiano nas Camadas Medias Paulinistanas. São Paulo: Editora Revista dos Tribunais Ltda, Edições Vértice.

Buss, David

1988 Love Acts: The Evolutionary Biology of Love. In *The Psychology of Love*, ed. R. Sternberg and M. Barnes, 100–118. New Haven: Yale University Press.

Butalia, Urvashi

2000 *The Other Side of Silence: Voices from the Partition of India.* Durham: Duke University Press.

Butler, Judith

1990 Gender Trouble, Feminist Theory, and Psychoanalytic Discourse. In *Feminism/Postmodernism*, ed. L. Nicholson, 324–40. New York: Routledge.

Caceres, C., and A. Rosasco

1993 An HIV/STD Prevention Program for Homosexually Active Men Who Do Not Necessarily Identify Themselves as Gay in Lima. *International Conference on AIDS* 9 (1, June 6–11, Berlin): 111 (abstract no. WS-D08-4).

Cacopardo, Alberto, and Augusto Cacopardo

2001 *Gates of Peristan: History, Religion, and Society in the Hindu Kush.* Rome: Istituto Italiano per L'Africa e L'Oriente.

Caldwell, John

1968 *Population Growth and Family Change in Africa: The New Urban Elite in Ghana.* Canberra: Australian National University Press.

1976   Toward a Restatement of Demographic Transition Theory. *Population and Development Review* 2 (3–4): 321–66.

Campbell, Catherine
1997   Migrancy, Masculine Identities, and AIDS: The Psychosocial Context of HIV Transmission on the South African Gold Mines. *Social Science and Medicine* 45 (2): 273–81.
2000   Selling Sex in the Time of AIDS: The Psychosocial Context of Condom Use by Sex Workers on a Southern African Mine. *Social Science and Medicine* 50:479–94.

Cancian, Francesca
1986   The Feminization of Love. *Signs: Journal of Women in Culture and Society* 11 (4): 693–709.

Caplan, Pat
1987   Celibacy as a Solution? Mahatma Gandhi and *Brahmacharya*. In *The Cultural Construction of Sexuality*, ed. P. Caplan. London: Tavistock.

CARA (Center for Applied Research in Anthropology), Georgia State University
1998   Hispanics in Georgia 1998: By County.

Cardenas-Elizalde, M. R.
1998   Migración y SIDA en México. *Salud Publica de Mexico* 30:613–18.

Carstairs, Morris G.
1958   *The Twice Born*. London: Hogarth.

CEDAW (Convention on the Elimination of All Forms of Discrimination Against Women).
1981   United National General Assembly. Full text available at http://www.un.org/womenwatch/daw/cedaw/cedaw.htm

Celentano, D. D., K. E. Nelson, C. M. Lyles, C. Beyrer, S. Eiumtrakul, V. F. Go, S. Kuntolbutra, and C. Khamboonruang
1998   Decreasing Incidence of HIV and Sexually Transmitted Diseases in Young Thai Men: Evidence for Success of the HIV/AIDS Control and Prevention Program. *AIDS* 12:F29–36.

Cerrutti, M., and D. S. Massey
2001   On the Auspices of Female Migration from Mexico to the United States. *Demography* 38 (2): 187–200.

Chakravarti, Uma
1987   *The Social Dimensions of Early Buddhism*. Delhi: Oxford University Press.

Chan, Ching Selina
1997   Negotiating Tradition: The Changing Pattern of Customary Succession in the New Territories in the 1990s. In Grant Evans and Maria Tam, eds., *Hong Kong: The Anthropology of a Chinese Metropolis*, ed. Grant Evans and Maria Tam, 151–74. Hawaii: Curzon.

Chatterjee, Partha
1993   *The Nation and Its Fragments: Colonial and Postcolonial Histories*. Princeton: Princeton University Press.

Chavez, L. R.
1984   Undocumented Immigrants and Access to Health Services: A Game of Pass the Buck. *Migration Today* 12:20–24.

Chavez, L. R., W. A. Cornelius, and O. Williams
  1985 Mexican Immigrants and the Utilization of U.S. Health Services: The Case of San Diego. *Social Science and Medicine* 21:93–102.
Chavez, L. R., E. T. Flores, and M. Lopez-Garza
  1992 Undocumented Latin American Immigrants and U.S. Health Services: An Approach to a Political Economy of Utilization. *Medical Anthropology Quarterly* 6:6–26.
Chen, Chung-min
  1985 Dowry and Inheritance. In *The Chinese Family and Its Ritual Behaviour*, ed. J. C. Hsieh and C. Y. Chuang, 117–27. Taipei: Institute of Ethnology, Academic Sinica.
Chisholm, James S.
  1995 Love's Contingencies: The Developmental Socioecology of Romantic Passion. In *Romantic Passion: A Universal Experience?* ed. W. Jankowiak, 42–56. New York: Columbia University Press.
Cohen, Lawrence
  1995 The Pleasures of Castration: The Postoperative Status of Hijras, Jankhas, and Academics. In *Sexual Nature, Sexual Culture*, ed. P. Abramson and S. Pinkerton, 276–304. Chicago: University of Chicago Press.
Cohen, M. S.
  1995 HIV and Sexuality Transmitted Diseases: The Physician's Role in Prevention. *Postgraduate Medicine* 98:52–58, 63–64.
Cole, Sally
  1991 *Women of the Praia: Work and Lives in a Portuguese Fishing Community.* Princeton: Princeton University Press.
Collier, Jane
  1997 *From Duty to Desire: Remaking Families in a Spanish Village.* Princeton: Princeton University Press.
Collins, Jan, and Thomas Gregor
  1995 Boundaries of Love. In *Romantic Passion: A Universal Experience?* ed. W. Jankowiak, 72–92. New York: Columbia University Press.
Colson, Elizabeth
  1958 *Marriage and Family among the Plateau Tonga of Northern Rhodesia.* Manchester: Manchester University Press.
Comaroff, John, ed.
  1980 *The Meaning of Marriage Payments.* New York: Academic.
CONASIDA
  1997 *Separata de la Revista SIDA/ETS (Enfermedades de Transmision Sexual): Situación Epidemiologica del SIDA & Situación Epidemiologica de las ETS, Datos Actualizados Hasta Tercer Trimestre de 1997.* 3 (3). Mexico, D.F.: Consejo Nacional de SIDA, Secretaria de Salud.
Connell, R. W.
  1987 *Gender and Power: Society, the Person, and Sexual Politics.* Stanford: Stanford University Press.

Coontz, Stephanie
2005 *Marriage, A History: From Obedience to Intimacy or How Love Conquered Marriage*. New York: Viking.
Corbin, M. P.
1987 Review of Sex and Gender in Southern Europe: Problems and Prospects. *Man* 22 (4): 756.
Cornelius, W.
1991 *Los migrantes de la crisis:* The Changing Profile of Mexican Migration to the United States. In *Social Responses to Mexico's Economic Crisis*, ed. M. González de la Roche and A. E. Latapi, 155–94. San Diego: Center for U.S.-Mexican Studies, University of California at San Diego.
Cornwall, Andrea
2002 Spending Power: Love, Money, and the Reconfiguration of Gender Relations in Ado-Odo, Southwestern Nigeria. *American Ethnologist* 29 (4): 963–80.
Da Matta, Roberto
1987 *A Casa e a Rua*. Rio de Janeiro: Editora Guanabara.
Das, Veena
1998 National Honor and Practical Kinship. In *Conceiving a New World Order: The Global Politics of Reproduction*, ed. R. Rapp and F. Ginsberg, 212–33. Berkeley: University of California Press.
d'Azevedo, Warren
1962 Common Principles and Variant Kinship Structures among the Gola of Western Liberia. *American Anthropologist* 64 (3): 504–20.
De la Peña, G.
1984 Ideology and Practice in Southern Jalisco: Peasants, Rancheros, and Urban Entrepreneurs. In *Kinship, Ideology, and Practice in Latin America*, ed. R. T. Smith, 204–34. Chapel Hill: University of North Carolina Press.
De Munck, Victor
1998 Lust, Love, and Arranged Marriages in Sri Lanka. In *Romantic Love and Sexual Behavior: Perspectives from the Social Sciences*, ed. V. de Munck, 285–300. Westport, CT: Praeger.
del Rio-Zolezzi, A., A. L. Liguori, C. Magis-Rodríguez, J. L. Valdespino-Gomez, M. L. Garcia-Garcia, and J. Sepulveda-Amor.
1995 La epidemia de VIH/SIDA y la mujer en Mexico. *Salud Publica de Mexico, Numero Especial: Doce Años de SIDA en Mexico* 37(6): 581–91.
Delaney, Carol
1987 Seeds of Honor, Fields of Shame. In *Honor and Shame and the Unity of Mediterranean*, ed. D. D. Gilmore, 35–48. Washington, DC: American Anthropological Association.
D'Emilio, John
1999 Capitalism and Gay Identity. In *Culture, Society, and Sexuality: A Reader*, ed. R. Parker and P. Aggleton, 239–48. London: UCL Press/Taylor and Francis.

Diaz-Santana, D., and A. Celis
  1989 AIDS and Migration in Jalisco, Mexico: Their Relation with Risk Factors. *International Conference on AIDS* 5:1057 (abstract number T.H.H.P.20).
Dixon-Mueller, R.
  1993 The Sexuality Connection in Reproductive Health. *Studies in Family Planning* 24:269–82.
Dubois, Ellen Carol
  1978 *Feminism and Suffrage: The Emergence of an Independent Women's Movement in America, 1848–1869.* Ithaca: Cornell University Press.
Durand, J.
  1994 *Más Allá de la Línea: Patrones Migratories entre México y Estados Unidos.* Mexico City, Mexico: Consejo Nacional para la Cultura y las Artes.
Dunn, Cynthia Dickel
  2004 Cultural Models and Metaphors for Marriage: An Analysis of Discourse at Japanese Wedding Receptions. *Ethos* 32 (3): 348–73.
Empresa de Urbanização do Recife, Diretora de Planejamento Urbano-DPU, Divisão de Estudos e Pesquisa
  1990 Relatorio de Pesquisa: João de Barros. Photocopied.
Endleman, Robert
  1989 *Love and Sex in Twelve Cultures.* New York: Psyche.
Engels, F.
  1985 *Origin of the Family, Property, and the State.* London: Penguin.
Erickson, Pamela I.
  1998 *Latina Adolescent Childbearing in East Los Angeles.* Austin: University of Texas Press.
  1998– Cultural Factors Affecting the Negotiation of First Sexual Intercourse
  99   among Latina Adolescent Mothers. *International Quarterly of Community Health Education* 18 (1): 121–37.
Errington, Frederick, and Deborah Gewertz
  1993 The Historical Course of True Love in the Sepik. In *Contemporary Pacific Societies: Studies in Development and Change,* ed. V. Lockwood, T. Harding, and B. Wallace, 233–48. Englewood Cliffs: Prentice-Hall.
Evans, C. A.
  1995 Immigrants and Health Care: Mounting Problems. *Annals of Internal Medicine* 122:309–10.
Farmer, P.
  1999 *Infections and Inequalities.* Berkeley: University of California Press.
Farmer, P., M. Connors, and J. Simmons, eds.
  1996 *Women, Poverty, and AIDS: Sex, Drugs, and Structural Violence.* Monroe, ME: Common Courage Press.
Federal Ministry of Health, Nigeria
  1999 *1999 HIV/Syphilis Sentinel Sero-Prevalence Survey in Nigeria.* Abuja, Nigeria: Federal Ministry of Health.
  2004 *2003 HIV Sero-Prevalence Sentinel Survey.* Abuja, Nigeria: Federal Ministry of Health.

Feldman-Savelsberg, Pamela
   1999   *Plundered Kitchens, Empty Wombs: Threatened Reproduction and Identity in the Cameroon Grassfields.* Ann Arbor: University of Michigan Press.
Felski, Rita
   1995   *The Gender of Modernity.* Cambridge: Harvard University Press.
Ferraz, A. G., A. S. Sales, J. A. do Nascimento Jr., M. H. Barcellos, M. G. da Silva, and M. S. Barbosa
   1992   Proposta de um Modelo Decentralizado de Vigilancia Sanitaria para a Cidade de Recife. Recife: Nucleo de Estudos em Saude Coletivo. Photocopied.
Feyisetan, Bamikale, and Anne Pebley
   1989   Premarital Sexuality in Urban Nigeria. *Studies in Family Planning* 20 (6): 343–54.
Fisher, Helen
   1995   The Nature and Evolution of Romantic Love. In *Romantic Passion: A Universal Experience?* ed. W. Jankowiak, 23–41. New York: Columbia University Press.
Flaskerud, J. H., and S. Kim
   1999   Health Problems of Asian and Latino Immigrants. *Nursing Clinics of North America.* 34:359–80.
Flores, Bettina R.
   1990   *Chiquita's Cocoon: A Cinderella Complex for the Latina Woman.* Granite Bay, CA: Pepper Vine Press.
Forman, Shepard
   1975   *The Brazilian Peasantry.* New York: Columbia University Press.
Fortes, Meyer
   1978   Parenthood, Marriage, and Fertility in West Africa. *Journal of Development Studies* 14 (4): 121–48.
Foucault, Michel
   1977   *Discipline and Punish: The Birth of the Prison.* New York: Pantheon Books.
   1978   *The History of Sexuality.* Vol. 1., *An Introduction.* New York: Pantheon Books.
   1980   *Power/Knowledge: Selected Interviews and Other Writings [1972–1977].* New York: Pantheon Books.
   1990   *The History of Sexuality.* Vol. 2, *The Use of Pleasure.* New York: Vintage Books.
Fox, Robin
   1967   *Kinship and Marriage: An Anthropological Perspective.* Baltimore: Penguin.
Frank, Andre Gunder
          Capitalism and Underdevelopment in Latin America. New York: Monthly Review Press.
Frankel, Stephen
   1986   *The Huli Response to Illness.* Cambridge: Cambridge University Press.
Freedman, Maurice
   1957   *Chinese Family and Marriage in Singapore.* London: Her Majesty's Stationery Office.
   1966   *Chinese Lineage and Society: Fukien and Kwangtung.* London: Athlone.

Freyre, Gilberto
  1986   *The Mansions and the Shanties: The Making of Modern Brazil.* Berkeley: University of California Press.
Fullilove, M. T., R. E. Fullilove III, K. Hayes, and S. Gross
  1990   Black Women and AIDS Prevention: A View towards Understanding the Gender Rules. *Journal of Sex Research* 27:47–64.
Gagnon, John H.
  1990   The Explicit and Implicit Use of the Scripting Perspective in Sex Research. In *Annual Review of Sex Research*, ed. J. Bancroft, C. David, and D. Weinstein, 1–44. Mt. Vernon, IA: Society for the Scientific Study of Sex.
Galloway, James H.
  1968   The Sugar Industry of Pernambuco during the Nineteenth Century. *Annals of the Association of American Geographers* 58 (3): 285–303.
Gayet C., C. Magis, and M. Bronfman
  2000   Aspectos conceptuales sobre la relación entre migración y SIDA en México. *Enfermedades Infecciosas y Microbiologia* 20:134–40.
Georgia Department of Human Resources, Division of Public Health.
  1994   *Access to Health Care by Limited English Proficient Populations in Georgia: A Report of the Bilingual Health Initiative Task Force*, Atlanta.
Giddens, Anthony
  1992   *The Transformations of Intimacy: Sexuality, Love, and Eroticism in Modern Societies.* Stanford: Stanford University Press.
Glasse, Robert M.
  1968   *Huli of Papua: A Cognatic Descent System.* Paris: Mouton.
  1974   Le Masque de la Volupté: Symbolisme et Antagonisme Sexuels sur les Hauts Plateaux de Nouvelle-Guinée. *L'Homme* 14 (2): 79–86.
Goheen, Miriam
  1996   *Men Own the Fields, Women Own the Crops: Gender and Power in the Cameroon Grassfields.* Madison: University of Wisconsin Press.
Goldman, Laurence
  1983   *Talk Never Dies: The Language of Huli Disputes.* London: Tavistock.
  1986   The Presentational Style of Women in Huli Disputes. Papers in New Guinea Linguistics 24:213–89.
Gonzalez, L.
  1974   *San José de Gracia: Mexican Village in Transition.* Trans. J. Upton. Austin: University of Texas Press.
Goode, William
       World Revolution and Family Patterns. New York: Free Press.
Goody, Jack, ed.
  1962   *The Developmental Cycle in Domestic Groups.* Cambridge: Cambridge University Press.
Gregg, Jessica
  2003   *Virtually Virgins: Sexual Strategies and Cervical Cancer in Recife, Brazil.* Stanford: Stanford University Press.

Grima, Benedicte
  1992 *The Performance of Emotion among Paxtun Women*. Austin: University of
        Texas Press.
Gugler, Josef, and Gudrun Ludwar-Ene
  1995 Gender and Migration in Africa South of the Sahara. In *The Migration
        Experience in Africa*, ed. J. Baker and T. Aina, 257–68. Uppsala: Nordiska
        Afrikainstitutet.
Gutmann, Matthew
  1996 *The Meanings of Macho: Being a Man in Mexico City*. Berkeley: University
        of California Press.
Guyer, Jane
  1981 Household and Community in African Studies. *African Studies Review*
        2–3:87–137.
Harrell-Bond, Barbara
  1975 *Modern Marriage in Sierra Leone: A Study of the Professional Group*. Paris:
        Mouton.
Hatfield, Elaine, and Richard Rapson
  1996 *Love and Sex: Cross-Cultural Perspectives*. Boston: Allyn and Bacon.
Herzfeld, Michael
  1980 Honor and Shame: Problems in the Analysis of Moral Systems. *Man*, n.s.,
        15:339–51.
Hetherington, S. E., R. M. Harris, R. B. Bausell, K. H. Kavanaugh, and D. E. Scott
  1996 AIDS and Prevention in High-Risk African American Women: Behav-
        ioral, Psychology, and Gender Issues. *Journal of Sex and Marital Therapy*
        22:9–21.
Higgins, Jennifer
  2005 The Pleasure Deficit. Doctoral dissertation, Atlanta, Emory University,
        Department of Women's Studies.
Hinkle, Y. A., E. H. Johnson, D. Gilbert, L. Jackson, and C. M. Lollis
  1992 African American Women Who Always Use Condoms: Attitudes,
        Knowledge about AIDS and Sexual Behavior. *Journal of the American
        Medical Women's Association* 47:230–37.
Hirsch, Jennifer
  1998 *Migration, Modernity, and Mexican Marriage: A Comparative Study of Gen-
        der, Sexuality and Reproductive Health in a Transnational Community*. Doc-
        toral dissertation, Baltimore, Johns Hopkins University.
  1999a *"Un Noviazgo despues de ser casados"*: Companionate Marriage, Sexual Inti-
        macy, and the Modern Mexican Family. Paper presented at IUSSP Sem-
        inar, Cairo, Egypt, September 16–18.
  1999b *En el Norte la mujer manda*: Gender, Generation, and Geography in a
        Mexican
        Transnational Community. *American Behavioral Scientist* 42:1332–49.
  2003 *A Courtship after Marriage: Sexuality and Love in Mexican Transnational
        Families*. Berkeley: University of California Press.
Hirsch, J. S., R. Albalak, and C. Nyhus
  2000 Masculinity, Sexuality, and AIDS Risk Behavior in a Mexican Migrant

Community. Paper presented at the annual meeting of the Population Association of America, Los Angeles, March 23–25.

Hirsch, Jennifer S., Jennifer Higgins, Margaret Bentley, and Constance Nathanson
2002 The Social Constructions of Sexuality: Marital Infidelity and STD/HIV Risk in a Mexican Migrant Community. *American Journal of Public Health* 92 (8): 1227–37.

Hirsch, Jennifer S., and Constance A. Nathanson
1998 Demografía informal: Cómo utilizar las redes sociales para construir una muestra etnográfica sistemática de mujeres mexicanas en ambos lados de la frontera. *Estudios Demograficos y de Desarollo Urbano* 12:177–99. Mexico, D.F.: El Colegio de Mexico.
2001 "Some Traditional Methods Are More Modern Than Others": Rhythm, Withdrawal, and the Changing Meanings of Gender and Sexual Intimacy in the Mexican Companionate Marriage. *Culture, Health, and Sexuality* 4 (3): 413–28.

Hirsch, J. S., K. Yount, H. Chakraborty, and C. Nyhus
n.d. 'Because he misses his normal life back home': Sexuality, Loneliness, and AIDS-risk Behavior among Mexican Migrants in Atlanta. Manuscript.

Holland, Dorothy C., and Margaret A. Eisenhart
1990 *Educated in Romance: Women, Achievement, and College Culture.* Chicago: University of Chicago Press.

Hollos, Marida, and U. Larsen
1997 From Lineage to Conjugality: The Social Context of Fertility Decisions among the Pare of Northern Tanzania. *Social Science and Medicine* 45:361–72.

Hondagneu-Sotelo, P.
1994 *Gendered Transitions: Mexican Experiences of Immigration.* Berkeley: University of California Press.

Hoodfar, Homa
1997 *Between Marriage and the Market: Intimate Politics and Survival in Cairo.* Berkeley: University of California Press.

Howard, Viki
2003 A "Real Man's Ring": Gender and the Invention of Tradition. *Journal of Social History* 36 (4): 837–56.

Hunter, Mark
2002 The Materiality of Everyday Sex: Thinking beyond "Prostitution." *African Studies* 61 (1): 99–120.
2005 Cultural Politics and Masculinities: Multiple-Partners in Historical Perspective in KwaZulu-Natal. *Culture, Health, and Sexuality* 7 (3): 209–23.

Illouz, Eva
1997 *Consuming the Romantic Utopia: Love and the Cultural Contradictions of Capitalism.* Berkeley: University of California Press.

Inhorn, Marcia
1996 *Infertility and Patriarchy: The Cultural Politics of Gender and Family Life in Egypt.* Philadelphia: University of Pennsylvania Press.

Institute of Medicine, Committee on the Elimination of Tuberculosis in the U.S., Division of Health Promotion and Disease Prevention

    2000   *Ending Neglect: The Elimination of Tuberculosis in the United States.* L. Geiter, ed. Washington, DC: National Academy Press.

Isiugo-Abanihe, U. C., J. A. Ebigbola, and A. A. Adewuyi

    1993   Urban Nuptuality Patterns and Marital Fertility in Nigeria. *Journal of Biosocial Science* 25:483–98.

Jankowiak, William

    1995   Introduction. In *Romantic Passion: A Universal Experience?* ed. W. Jankowiak, 1–19. New York: Columbia University Press.

Jankowiak, William, and Edward Fischer

    1992   A Cross-Cultural Perspective on Romantic Love. *Ethnology* 31 (2): 149–55.

Jettmar, Karl

    1986   *The Religions of the Hindu Kush.* Vol. 1, *The Religion of the Kafirs.* Warminster: Aris and Phillips.

John, Mary, and Janaki Nair

    1998   Introduction. In *A Question of Silence? The Sexual Economies of Modern India,* ed. Mary John and Janaki Nair, 1–51. New Delhi: Kali for Women.

Johnson, Patricia

    1981   When Dying Is Better Than Living: Female Suicide among the Gainj of Papua New Guinea. *Ethnology* 20 (4): 325–34.

Kakar, Sudhir

    1989   *Intimate Relations: Exploring Indian Sexuality.* New York: Penguin.

Kanaaneh, Rhoda Ann

    2002   *Birthing the Nation: Strategies of Palestinian Women in Israel.* Berkeley: University of California Press.

Kandiyoti, Deniz

    1988   Bargaining with Patriarchy. *Gender and Society* 2:274–90.

Karanja, Wambui

    1987   "Outside Wives" and "Inside Wives" in Nigeria: A Study of Changing Perceptions of Marriage. In *Transformations in African Marriage,* ed. D. Parkin and D. Nyamwaya, 247–61. Manchester: Manchester University Press.

Karp, Ivan

    1987   Laughter at Marriage: Subversion in Performance. In *Transformations in African Marriage,* ed. D. Parkin and D. Nyamwaya, 137–54. Manchester: Manchester University Press for the International African Institute.

Katz Rothman, B.

    1986   *The Tentative Pregnancy: Prenatal Diagnosis and the Future of Motherhood.* New York: Penguin.

Keiser, Lincoln

    1986   Death Enmity in Thull: Organized Vengeance and Social Change in a Kohistani Community. *American Ethnologist* 13 (2): 489–505.

Kendall, Laurel

    1996   *Getting Married in Korea: Of Gender, Morality, and Modernity.* Berkeley: University of California Press.

Kipnis, Laura
  1998   Adultery. *Critical Inquiry* 24 (2): 289–327.
  2005   Love or Money: The Matrimonial Mystique. *Harper's Magazine* 310
         (June): 83–88.
Kline, A., E. Kline, and E. Oken
  1992   Minority Women and Sexual Choice in the Age of AIDS. *Social Science
         and Medicine* 34:447–57.
Knauft, Bruce
  1997   Gender Identity, Political Economy, and Modernity in Melanesia and
         Amazonia. *Journal of the Royal Anthropological Institute* 3 (2): 233–59.
  2002   Critically Modern: An Introduction. In *Critically Modern: Alternatives,
         Alterities, Anthropologies*, 1–54. Bloomington: University of Indiana
         Press.
Kollontai, Alexandra
  1978   *Love of Worker Bees*. Trans. Cathy Porter. Chicago: Cassandra Editions,
         Academy Press Limited.
Kurian, George, ed.
  1979   *Cross-Cultural Perspectives on Mate-Selection and Marriage*. Westport, CT:
         Greenwood.
Lal, Vinay
  1999   Nakedness, Non-Violence, and the Negation of Negation: Gandhi's
         Experiments in *Brahmacharya* and Celibate Sexuality. *South Asia*, n.s., 22
         (2): 63–94.
Lane, Sandra, Robert Keefe, Robert Rubinstein, Brooke Levadowski, Michale
Freedman, Alan Rosenthal, Donald Cibula, and Maria Czerwinski
  2004   Marriage Promotion and Missing Men: African American Women in a
         Demographic Double Bind. *Medical Anthropology Quarterly* 18 (4):
         405–28.
Lantz, Herman
  1982   Romantic Love in the Pre-Modern Period: A Sociological Commentary.
         Journal of Social History 15 (3): 349–70.
Larkin, Brian
  1997   Indian Films and Nigerian Lovers: Media and the Creation of Parallel
         Modernities. *Africa* 67:406–40.
Lash, Scott, and Jonathan Friedman
  1991   Introduction: Subjectivity and Modernity's Other. In *Modernity and Iden-
         tity*, ed. S. Lash and J. Friedman, 1–30. Oxford: Blackwell Publishers.
Lauman, Edward O., and Robert T. Michael
  2000   *Sex, Love, and Health in America: Private Choices and Public Policies*.
         Chicago: University of Chicago Press.
Lavrin, Asunción
  1989   Introduction: The Scenario, the Actors, and the Issues. In *Sexuality and
         Marriage in Colonial Latin America*, ed. A. Lavrin, 1–46. Lincoln: Univer-
         sity of Nebraska Press.
Lever, Alison
  1986   Honor as a Red Herring. *Cultural Anthropology* 1 (2): 83–106.

Lindholm, Charles

1981   The Structure of Violence among the Swat Pakhtun. *Ethnology* 20 (2): 147–56.

1982   *Generosity and Jealousy: The Swat Pukhtun of Northern Pakistan.* New York: Columbia University Press.

1995   Love as an Experience of Transcendence. In *Romantic Passion: A Universal Experience?* ed. W. Jankowiak, 57–71. New York: Columbia University Press.

Little, Kenneth

1979   Women's Strategies in Modern Marriage in Anglophone West Africa: An Ideological and Sociological Appraisal. In *Cross-Cultural Perspectives on Mate Selection and Marriage*, ed. G. Kurian, 202–17. Westport, CT: Greenwood.

Little, Kenneth, and Anne Price

1973   Some Trends in Modern Marriage among West Africans. In *Africa and Change*, ed. C. Turnbull, 185–207. New York: Knopf.

Loude, Jean-Yves, and Vivian Lievre

1988   *Kalash Solstice.* Trans. Grahame Romaine and Mira Intrator. Islamabad: Lok Virsa.

Luke, Nancy

2005   Confronting the "Sugar Daddy Stereotype": Age and Economic Asymmetries and Risky Sexual Behavior in Urban Kenya. *International Family Planning Perspectives* 31 (1): 6–14.

MacCormack, C., and A. Draper

1987   Social and Cognitive Aspects of Female Sexuality in Jamaica. In *The Cultural Construction of Sexuality*, ed. P. Caplan, 143–65. London: Routledge and Kegan Paul.

Magaña, J. R., O. de la Rocha, and J. L. Ansel

1996   Sexual History and Behavior of Mexican Migrant Workers in Orange County, CA. In *AIDS Crossing Borders: The Spread of HIV among Migrant Latinos*, ed. S. Mishra, R. Conner, and R. Magaña, 77–94. Boulder: Westview.

Maggi, Wynne

2001   *Our Women Are Free: Gender and Ethnicity in the Hindukush.* Ann Arbor: University of Michigan Press.

2003   Kalasha. In *South Asian Folklore: An Encyclopedia*, ed. M. Mills, P. Claus, and S. Diamond, Routledge: New York.

Magis-Rodríguez, C., A. del Rio-Zolezzi, J. L. Valdespino-Gomez, and M. L. Garcia-Garcia

1995   AIDS Cases in Rural Mexico. *Salud Publica de Mexico* 37:615–23.

Magis-Rodríguez, C., E. B. Garcia, E. R. Nolasco, P. U. Zuñiga.

1998   Rural AIDS Cases in Mexico. Abstract presented at the International Conference on AIDS 12:164, Geneva, June 28–July 3, 1998 (abstract no. 13389).

Magis-Rodríguez, C., E. B. Garcia, E. R. Nolasco, and P. U. Zuñiga

2000   *Rural AIDS Cases in Mexico.* Mexico City: CONASIDA.

Magis-Rodríguez, C., Cecilia Gayet, Mirka Negroni, Rene Leyva, Enrique Bravo-Garcia, Patricia Uribe, and Mario Bronfman
    2004   Migration and AIDS in Mexico: An Overview Based on Recent Evidence. *Journal of Acquired Immune Deficiency* 37 (4): S215-S226.

Mahoney, Rhona
    1996   *Kidding Ourselves: Babies, Breadwinning, and Bargaining Power.* New York: Basic Books.

Mair, Lucy
    1969   *African Marriage and Social Change.* London: Frank Cass.

Makinwa-Adebusoye, Paulina
    1992   Sexual Behavior, Reproductive Knowledge, and Contraceptive Use among Young Urban Nigerians. *International Family Planning Perspectives* 18 (2): 66–70.

Mann, Kristin
    1985   *Marrying Well: Marriage Status and Social Change among the Educated Elite in Colonial Lagos.* Cambridge: Cambridge University Press.

Marris, Peter
    1962   *Family and Social Change in an African City.* Evanston: Northwestern University Press.

Mason, K. O.
    1994   HIV Transmission and the Balance of Power between Women and Men: A Global View. *Health Transition Review* Supp. 4, 217–40.

Massey, D. S., R. Alarcon, J. Durand, and H. Gonzalez
    1987   *Return to Aztlan: The Social Process of International Migration from Western Mexico.* Berkeley: University of California Press.

Massey, D. S., J. Arango, G. Hugo, A. Kouaouci, A. Pellegrino, and J. Taylor
    1993   Theories of International Migration: A Review and Appraisal. *Population and Development Review* 19:431–66.

Massey, D. S., and J. Durand
    1998   Historical Dynamics of Mexican Migrant Destinations, 1920–90. Paper presented at the meeting of the Latin American Studies Association, Chicago, September.

McCoy, C. B., L. R. Metsch, J. A. Inciardi, R. S. Anwyl, J. Wingred, and K. Bletzer
    1996   Sex, Drugs, and the Spread of HIV/AIDS in Bella Glade, Florida. *Medical Anthropology Quarterly* 10:83–93.

Menon, Ritu, and Urvashi Butalia
    1998   *Borders and Boundaries: Women in India's Partition.* Delhi: Kali for Women.

Michael, Robert T., and Kara Joyner
    2000   Choices Leading to Teenage Births. In *Sex, Love, and Health in America: Private Choices and Public Policies,* ed. E. O. Lauman and R. T. Michael, 72–104. Chicago: University of Chicago Press.

Miles, M. B., and A. M. Huberman
    1994   *Qualitative Data Analysis: An Expanded Sourcebook.* Newbury Park: Sage.

Miller, L. C., B. A. Bettencourt, S. C. DeBro, and V. Hoffman

1993   Negotiating Safer Sex: Interpersonal Dynamics. In *The Social Psychology of HIV Infection*, ed. J. B. Pryor and G. D. Reeder, 85–123. Hillsdale, NJ: Lawrence Erlbaum.

Mishra, S., R. Conner, and R. Magaña, eds.
1996   *AIDS Crossing Borders: The Spread of HIV among Migrant Latinos.* Boulder: Westview.

Mohanty, Chandra
1991   Cartographies of Struggle: Third World Women and the Politics of Feminism. In *Third World Women and the Politics of Feminism*, ed. C. Mohanty, A. Russo, and L. Torres, 1–47. Bloomington: Indiana University Press.

Morril, A., J. Ickovics, V. Golubchikiv, S. Beren, and J. Rodin
1996   Safer Sex: Social and Psychological Predictors of Behavioral Maintenance and Change among Heterosexual Women. *Journal of Clinical Psychology* 64:819–28.

Muñiz-Martelon, M., J. Baez-Villasenor, C. del Rio, J. Guzman, R. Figueroa
1996   Mexican Migrant HIV Issues: Problems and Strategies. *International Conference on AIDS* 11 (July 7–12, Vancouver): 256 (abstract number Tu.D.246).

Murdock, George, and Douglas White
1969   Standard Cross-Cultural Sample. *Ethnology* 8 (4): 329–69.

Murray, Collin
1976   Marital Strategy in Lesotho: The Redistribution of Migrant Earnings. *African Studies* 35 (2): 99–121.

Murstein, Bernard
1974   *Love, Sex, and Marriage through the Ages.* New York: Springer.

Nanda, Serena
1990   *Neither Man Nor Woman: Hijras of India.* Belmont: Wadsworth.

Nathanson, Constance A.
1993   *Dangerous Passage: The Social Control of Sexuality in Women's Adolescence.* Philadelphia: Temple University Press.

Nichols, Douglas, O. A. Lapido, John Paxman, and E. O. Otolorin
1986   Sexual Behavior, Contraceptive Practice, and Reproductive Health among Nigerian Adolescents. *Studies in Family Planning* 17 (2): 100–106.

Obiechina, Emmanuel
1973   *An African Popular Literature: A Study of Onitsha Market Pamphlets.* Cambridge: Cambridge University Press.

Obwogo, B. S.
1996   Modeling Safe-Sex Practices among Medical Students through Peer Education. *International Conference on AIDS* 11 (July 7–12, Vancouver): 467 (abstract no. Pub.C.1184).
1998   Sexual Practices among Nairobi University Freshmen. *International Conference on AIDS* 12 (June 28–July 3, Geneva): 1015 (abstract no. 60079).

O'Flaherty, Wendy Doniger
1980   *Women, Androgynes, and Other Mythical Beasts.* Chicago: University of Chicago Press.

Okonjo, Kamene
  1992   Aspects of Continuity and Change in Mate-Selection among the Igbo
         West of the River Niger. *Journal of Comparative Family Studies* 13 (3):
         339–60.
O'Leary, A., L. S. Jemmott, F. Goodhart, and J. Gebelt
  1996   Effects of an Institutional AIDS Prevention Intervention: Moderation by
         Gender. *AIDS Education and Prevention* 8:516–28.
Oppong, Christine
  1974   *Marriage among a Matrilineal Elite.* Cambridge: Cambridge University
         Press.
Ortner, Sherry B.
  1978   The Virgin and the State. *Feminist Studies* 4 (3): 19–37.
Orubuloye, I. E., J. C. Caldwell, and P. Caldwell
  1997   Perceived Male Sexual Needs and Male Sexual Behavior in Southwest
         Nigeria. *Social Science and Medicine* 44 (8): 1195–1207.
Oucho, J. O., and W. T. S. Gould
  1993   Internal Migration, Urbanization, and Population Distribution. In *Demo-
         graphic Change in Sub-Saharan Africa,* ed. K. Foote, K. Hill, and L. Mar-
         tin, 256–96. Washington, DC: National Academy Press.
Page, Joseph A.
  1995   *The Brazilians.* Menlo Park, CA: Addison-Wesley.
Parker, Richard
  1991   *Bodies, Pleasures, and Passions: Sexual Culture in Contemporary Brazil.*
         Boston: Beacon.
  1999   *Beneath the Equator: Cultures of Desire, Male Homosexuality, and Emerging
         Gay Communities in Brazil.* New York: Routledge.
Parkes, Peter
  1983   Alliance and Elopement: Economy, Social Order, and Sexual Antagonism
         among the Kalash (Kalash Kafirs) of Chitral. PhD dissertation, Univer-
         sity of Oxford.
  1994   Personal and Collective Identity in Kalasha Song Performance: The
         Significance of Music-making in a Minority Enclave. In *Ethnicity, Identity,
         and Music: The Musical Construction of Place,* ed. Martin Stokes, 157–83.
         Oxford: Berg.
  1997   Kalasha Domestic Society: Practice, Ceremony, and Domain. In *Family
         and Gender in Pakistan: Domestic Organization in a Muslim Society,* ed.
         Hastings Donnan and F. Selier, 25–63. New Delhi: Hindustani Publish-
         ing.
  2000   Enclaved Knowledge: Indigent and Indignant Representations of Envi-
         ronmental Management and Development among the Kalaasha of Pak-
         istan. In *Indigenous Environmental Knowledge and Its Transformations: Crit-
         ical Anthropological Perspectives,* ed. Roy Ellen, Peter Parkes, and Alan
         Bicker, 253–91. Amsterdam: Harwood Academic.
Parkin, David, and Nyamwaya David, eds.
  1987   *Transformations in African Marriage.* Manchester: Manchester University
         Press.

Pashigian, Melissa
2002　Conceiving the Happy Family: Infertility and Marital Politics in Northern Vietnam. In *Infertility around the Globe: New Thinking on Childlessness, Gender, and Reproductive Technologies*, ed. M. Inhorn and F. van Balen, 134–51. Berkeley: University of California Press.

Pavich, Emma Guerrero
1986　A Chicana Perspective on Mexican Culture and Sexuality. *Journal of Social Work and Human Sexuality* 4 (3): 47–65.

Pérez, M. A., and K. Fennelly
1996　Risk Factors for HIV and AIDS among Latino Farmworkers in Pennsylvania. In *AIDS Crossing Borders: The Spread of HIV among Migrant Latinos*, ed. S. Mishra, R. Conner, and R. Magaña, 137–56. Boulder: Westview.

Person, Ethel S.
1988　*Dreams of Love and Fateful Encounters: The Power of Romantic Passion.* New York: Penguin.

Petchesky, R., and K. Judd, eds.
1998　*Negotiating Reproductive Rights: Women's Perspectives across Countries and Cultures.* London: International Reproductive Rights Action Group and Zed Books.

Pineda, T., B. Loeza, R. Heredia, N. Vazquez, and V. Hernandez
1992　Perfil del michoacano emigrado a Los EUA y el impacto de la epidemiologia del VIH/SIDA en la región. III Congreso Nacional de Investigación Sobre Salud, Mexico.

Pitt-Rivers, Julian
1965　Honour and Social Status. In *Honour and Shame: The Values of Mediterranean Society*, ed. J. G. Peristiany, 19–77. Chicago: University of Chicago Press.
1977　*The Fate of Shechem or the Politics of Sex: Essays in the Anthropology of the Mediterranean.* Cambridge: Cambridge University Press.

Plotnicov, Leonard
1995　Love, Lust and Found in Nigeria. In *Romantic Passion: A Universal Experience?* ed. W. Jankowiak, 128–40. New York: Columbia University Press.

Potash, Betty
1986　*Widows in African Societies: Choices and Constraints.* Stanford: Stanford University Press.

Prasad, Madhava
1998　*Ideology of the Hindi Film: A Historical Construction.* Delhi: Oxford University Press.

Preston-Whyte, Eleanor
1999　Reproductive Health and the Condom Dilemma: Identifying Situational Barriers to Condom Use in South Africa. In *Resistances to Behavioral Change to Reduce HIV/AIDS Infection in Predominately Heterosexual Epidemics in Third World Countries*, ed. J. Caldwell, P. Caldwell, J. Anarfi, K. Awusabo-Asare, J. Ntozi, I. O. Orubuloye, J. Marck, W. Cosford, R. Colombo, and E. Hollings, 139–55. Canberra: Australian National University.

Pulerwitz, Julie, Jose-Antonio Izazola-Licea, and Steven L. Gortmaker
   2001   Extrarelational Sex among Mexican Men and Their Partners' Risk of
          HIV and Other Sexually Transmitted Diseases. *American Journal of Pub-
          lic Health* 91:1650–52.
Radcliffe-Brown, Alfred, and Daryll Forde, eds.
   1950   *African Systems of Kinship and Marriage*. London: Oxford University Press.
Raheja, Gloria, and Ann Gold
   1996   *Listen to the Heron's Words: Reimagining Gender and Kinship in North India*.
          Delhi: Oxford University Press.
Rebhun, Linda-Anne
   1999   a*The Heart Is Unknown Country: Love in the Changing Economy of Northeast
          Brazil*. Stanford: Stanford University Press.
   1999   bFor Love and for Money: Romance in Urbanizing Northeast Brazil.
          City and Society 11 (1–2): 145–64.
Reilly, Kevin
          Love and Devotion. In *The West and the World: A Topical History of Civi-
          lization*, 183–204. New York: Harper and Row.
Report of the Enquiry Committee on Film Censorship
   1969   Chaired by G. D. Khosla. New Delhi, Government of India.
Riesman, Paul
   1972   Defying Official Morality: The Example of Man's Quest for Woman
          among the Fulani. *Cahiers d'Etudes Africaines* 11 (44): 602–3.
   1981   Love Fulani Style. In *Anthropological Realities*, ed. J. Guillemin, 9–25. New
          Brunswick, NJ: Transaction Books.
Robbins, Joel
   1998   Becoming Sinners: Christianity and Desire among the Urapmin of Papua
          New Guinea. *Ethnology* 37 (4): 299–316.
Rodrigues, Jose Honorio
   1967   *The Brazilians: Their Character and Aspirations*. Austin: University of
          Texas Press.
Rohde, David
   2005   A World of Ways to Say "Islamic Law." *New York Times*, Week in
          Review, March 13:4.
Rubin, Gayle
   1975   The Traffic in Women. In *Toward an Anthropology of Women*, ed. R.
          Reiter, 157–210. New York: Monthly Review Press.
Rumbaut, R. G., L. R. Chavez, R. J. Moser, S. M. Pickwell, and S. M. Wishnik
   1986   The Politics of Migrant Health Care: A Comparative Study of Mexican
          Immigrant and Indochinese Refugees. *Research in the Sociology of Health
          Care* 7:143–202.
Ryan, Peter
   1991   *Black Bonanza: A Landslide of Gold*. South Yara, Australia: Hyland House.
Santarriaga, M., C. Magis, E. Loo, J. B. Villasenor, C. del Rio
   1996   HIV/AIDS in a Migrant Exporter Mexican State. *International Conference
          on AIDS* 11 (July 7–12, Vancouver): 414 (abstract number Tu.D.2906).

Santelli, J. S., A. C. Kouzin, D. R. Hoover, M. Polascek, L. G. Burwell, and D. D. Celentano

  1996   Stage of Behavior Change for Condom Use: The Influence of Partner Type, Relationship, and Pregnancy Factors. *Family Planning Perspectives* 28:101–7.

Santelli, J. S., R. Lowry, N. D. Brener, and L. Robin

  2000   The Association of Sexual Behaviors with Socioeconomic Status, Family Structure, and Race/Ethnicity among US Adolescents. *American Journal of Public Health* 90:1582–88.

Sarti, Cynthia A.

  1995   Morality and Transgression among Poor Families. In *The Brazilian Puzzle: Culture on the Borderlands of the Western World*, ed. D. J. Hess and R. A. DaMatta, 114–33. New York: Columbia University Press.

Saussure, Ferdinand de

  1974   *Course in General Linguistics.* London: Collins.

Schapera, Isaac

  1966   *Married Life in an African Tribe.* Evanston: Northwestern University Press.

Scheper-Hughes, N.

  1992   *Death Without Weeping: The Violence of Everyday Life in Brazil.* Berkeley: University of California Press.

Schneider, Jane, and Peter Schneider

  1995   *Festival of the Poor: Fertility Decline and the Ideology of Class in Sicily, 1860–1980.* Tucson: University of Arizona Press.

Schneider, Jose Odelso, Matias Martinho Lenz, and Almiro Petry

  1990   *Realidade Brasileira: Estudo de Problemas Brasileiros.* Porto Alegre: Sulina.

Schneir, Miriam

  1972   *Feminism: The Essential Historical Writings.* New York: Vintage Books.

Schwartz, Stuart B.

  1985   *Sugar Plantations in the Formation of Brazilian Society: Bahia, 1550–1835.* Cambridge: Cambridge University Press.

Scrimshaw, Susan C. M.

  1978   Stages in Women's Lives and Reproductive Decision Making in Latin America. *Medical Anthropology* 2 (3): 41–58.

Sharma, Kalpana

  1995   The Message Is the Medium. *Hindu*, August 17.

Sharma, Satish

  1989   *The Labeled Deviants.* New Delhi: Vikas Publications.

Simmons, C.

  1979   Companionate Marriage and the Lesbian Threat. *Frontiers* 4 (3): 54–59.

Singer, M.

  1994   AIDS and the Health Crisis of the U.S. Urban Poor: The Perspective of Critical Medical Anthropology. *Social Science and Medicine* 39 (7): 931–48.

Singer, M., C. Flores, L. Davison, G. Burke, Z. Castillo, K. Scanlon, and M. Rivera

  1990   SIDE: The Economic, Social, and Cultural Context of AIDS among Latinos. *Medical Anthropology Quarterly* 4 (1): 71–114.

Singer, M., and L. Marxuach-Rodríguez
  1996 Applying Anthropology to the Prevention of AIDS: The Latino Gay Men's Health Project. *Human Organization* 55:141–48.

Skolnik, A.
  1991 *Embattled Paradise: The American Family in an Age of Uncertainty.* New York: Basic Books.

Smith, Carol
  1995 Race-Class-Gender Ideology in Guatemala: Modern and Anti-Modern Forms. *Comparative Studies in Society and History* 37:723–49.

Smith, Daniel Jordan
  2000 ""These Girls Today Na War-O": Premarital Sexuality and Modern Identity in Southeastern Nigeria. *Africa Today* 47 (3–4): 141–70.
  2001 Romance, Parenthood, and Gender in a Modern African Society. *Ethnology* 40 (2): 129–51.
  2002 "Man No Be Wood": Gender and Extramarital Sex in Contemporary Southeastern Nigeria. *Ahfad Journal* 19 (2): 4–23.
  2003 Imagining HIV/AIDS: Morality and Perceptions of Personal Risk in Nigeria. *Medical Anthropology* 22 (4): 343–72.
  2004a Youth, Sin, and Sex in Nigeria: Christianity and HIV-related Beliefs and Behaviour among Rural-Urban Migrants. *Culture, Health, and Sexuality* 6 (5): 425–37.
  2004b Premarital Sex, Procreation, and HIV Risk in Nigeria. *Studies in Family Planning* 35 (4): 223–35.

Sobo, Elisa
  1993 Bodies, Kin, and Flow: Family Planning in Rural Jamaica. *Medical Anthropology Quarterly* 7:50–73.
  1995a *Choosing Unsafe Sex: AIDS-risk Denial among Disadvantaged Women.* Philadelphia: University of Pennsylvania Press.
  1995b Finance, Romance, Social Support, and Condom Use among Impoverished Inner City Women. *Human Organization* 54:115–28.

Soler, H., D. Quadagno, D. F. Sly, K. S. Riehman, I. W. Eberstein, and D. F. Harrison
  2000 Relationship Dynamics, Ethnicity, and Condom Use among Low-Income Women. *Family Planning Perspectives* 32 (2): 82–88, 101.

Srivastava, Sanjay
  2001 Introduction: Semen, History, Desire, and Theory. *South Asia*, vol. 24, Sexual Sites, Seminal Attitudes: Sexualities, Masculinities and Culture in South Asia, special issue, September.

Stansell, M. Christine
  2000 *American Moderns: Bohemian New York and the Creation of a New Century.* New York: Metropolitan Books.

Stoler, Ann
  1995 *Race and the Education of Desire: Foucault's* History of Sexuality *and the Colonial Order of Things.* Durham: Duke University Press.

Stone, Lawrence
      The Family, Sex, and Marriage in England, 1500–1800. New York: Harper and Row.

Stout, David
  2001   A Nation Challenged: The First Lady: Mrs. Bush Cites Women's Plight
         under Taliban. *New York Times*, late edition, November 18:1B, 4.
Sturzenhofecker, Gabriella
  1998   *Times Enmeshed: Gender, Space, and History among the Duna of Papua New
         Guinea*. Stanford: Stanford University Press.
Susser, I., and Z. Stein
  2000   Culture, Sexuality, and Women's Agency in the Prevention of
         HIV/AIDS in Southern Africa. *American Journal of Public Health*
         90:1042–48.
Tapper, Nancy
  1990   *Bartered Brides: Politics, Gender, and Marriage in an Afghan Tribal Society*.
         Cambridge: Cambridge University Press.
Tennov, Dorothy
  1979   *Love and Limerence: The Experience of Being in Love*. New York: Stein and
         Day.
Thompson, Sharon
  1995   *Going All the Way: Teenage Girls' Tales of Sex, Romance, and Pregnancy*.
         New York: Hill and Wang.
Thornton, Arland
  2001   The Developmental Paradigm, Reading History Sideways, and Family
         Change. *Demography* 38 (4): 449–66.
Trawick, Margaret
  1990   *Notes on Love in a Tamil Family*. Berkeley: University of California Press.
Trimberger, Ellen
  1983   Feminism, Men, and Modern Love: Greenwich Village, 1900–25. In
         Powers of Desire: The Politics of Sexuality, ed. A. Snitow, C. Stansell, and S.
         Thompson, 131–52. New York: Monthly Review Press.
Tuzin, Donald
  1997   *The Cassowary's Revenge: The Life and Death of Masculinity in a New Guinea
         Society*. Chicago: University of Chicago Press.
Uchendu, Victor
  1965   Concubinage among the Ngwa Igbo of Southern Nigeria. *Africa* 35 (2):
         187–97.
UNAIDS
  2000   Men and AIDS—a Gendered Approach: 2000 World AIDS Campaign.
  2004   *AIDS Epidemic Update: 2004*. Geneva: UNIAIDS.
U.S. Census Bureau
  2000   Population by Race and Hispanic or Latino Origin, for the 15 Largest
         Counties and Incorporated Places in Georgia: 2000. Census 2000 Redis-
         tricting Data (P.L. 94–171) Summary File, Table PL1.
Vainfas, Ronaldo
  1989   *Trópico dos Pecados: Moral, Sexualidade e Inquisição no Brasil*. Rio de Janeiro:
         Editora Campus.

Vance, Carol S.
  1991   Anthropology Rediscovers Sexuality: A Theoretical Comment. *Social Science and Medicine* 33:875–84.
van der Vliet, Virginia
  1991   Traditional Husbands, Modern Wives? Constructing Marriages in a South African Township. *African Studies* 50 (1–2): 219–41.
Van Every, Jo
  1996   Heterosexuality and Domestic Life. In *Theorizing Heterosexuality: Telling It Straight*, ed. D. Richardson, 39–54. Buckingham: Open University Press.
Vyas, M., and V. Shingala
  1987   *The Lifestyle of the Eunuchs*. New Delhi: Anmol Publications.
Wardlow, Holly
  1996   "Bobby Teardrops": A Turkish Video in Papua New Guinea. Reflections on Cultural Studies, Feminism, and the Anthropology of Mass Media. *Visual Anthropology Review* 12 (1): 30–46.
  2001a The Mt. Kare Python: Huli Myths and Gendered Fantasies of Agency. In *Mining and Indigenous Life Worlds in Australia and Papua New Guinea.*, ed. A. Rumsey and J. Weiner, Adelaide, Australia: Crawford House.
  2001b "Free Food, Free Food!" Traditional Rituals of Modern Manhood among the Huli of Papua New Guinea. Paper presented at the Third Conference of the International Association for the Study of Sex, Culture, and Society, Melbourne, Australia, October 1–3. Part of the session entitled "Contemporary Masculinity in Melanesia" organized by Gilbert Herdt.
  2002a Headless Ghosts and Roving Women: Specters of Modernity in Papua New Guinea. *American Ethnologist* 29 (1): 5–32.
  2002b Giving Birth to *Gonolia*: "Culture" and Sexually Transmitted Diseases among the Huli of Papua New Guinea. *Medical Anthropology Quarterly* 16 (2): 151–75.
  2002c "Hands-Up-ing Buses and Harvesting Cheesepops: Gendered Mediations of Disjuncture in a Melanesian Modernity. In *Critically Modern: Alternatives, Alterities, Anthropologies*, ed. B. Knauft, 144–72. Bloomington: University of Indiana Press.
  2004   Anger, Economy, and Female Agency: Problematizing "Prostitution" and "Sex Work" in Papua New Guinea. *Signs: Journal of Women in Culture and Society* 29 (4): 1017–40.
  2006   *Wayward Women: Sexuality and Agency in a New Guinea Society*. Berkeley: University of California Press.
Wasonga, J.
  1996   Role of Publications in Disseminating Correct AIDS/HIV Information and Influencing Behavior among the Youth. *International Conference on AIDS* 11 (July 7–12, Vancouver): 499 (abstract no. Pub.D.1393).
Watson, Rubie
  1985   *Inequality Among Brothers*. Cambridge: University Press.

Watt, Ian

1987 Love and the Novel: "Pamela." In *The Rise of the Novel: Studies in Defoe, Richardson, and Fielding*. London: Hogarth [1957].

Weatherby, N. L., H. V. McCoy, L. R. Metsch, K. V. Bletzer, C. B. McCoy, and M. R. de la Rosa

1999 Use of Ethnography. *Substance Use and Abuse* 34:685–706.

Weeks, J.

1981 *Sex, Politics, and Society: The Regulation of Sexuality Since 1800*. New York: Longman.

Weeks, R. W., J. J. Schensul, S. S. Williams, M. Singer, and M. Grier

1995 AIDS Prevention for African-American and Latina Women: Building Culturally and Gender-Appropriate Intervention. *AIDS Education and Prevention* 7:251–63.

Weiss, E., and G. G. Rao

1994 The Need for Female-Controlled HIV Prevention. *International Conference on AIDS* 10 (August 7–12, Yokohama): 46 (abstract no. SS9).

Weiss, E., G. R. Gupta, and D. Whelan

1995 Findings from the Women and AIDS Research Program. *HIV Infection in Women Conference* (February 22–24, Washington), P115.

Weller, Susan C., and A. Kimball Romney

1988 *Systematic Data Collection*. Qualitative Research Method. Series 10. Newbury Park: Sage.

Weston, Kath

1991 *Families We Choose: Lesbians, Gays, Kinship*. New York: Columbia University Press.

WHO (World Health Organization)

2000 Women and AIDS. Fact Sheet 242. June 2000. Available at http://www.who.int/inf- fs/en/fact242.

William, P., and C. Britton

1999 Understanding the Culture of Masculinity and Creating Effective Prevention Messages. National HIV Prevention Conference (August 29–September 1, Atlanta) (abstract no. 116).

Williams, Norma

1990 *The Mexican-American Family; Tradition and Change*. New York: General Hall.

Wolf, Aurthur, and Huang Chieh-shan

1980 *Marriage and Adoption in China, 1845–1945*. Stanford: University Press.

Yan, Yunxiang

1997 The Triumph of Conjugality: Structural Transformation of Family Relations in a Chinese Village. *Ethnology* 36:191–212.

2003 *Private Life under Socialism: Love, Intimacy, and Family Change in a Chinese Village, 1949–1999*. Stanford: Stanford University Press.

Young, Katherine

1995 *Understanding Marriage: A Hong Kong Case Study*. Hong Kong: University Press.

Zavella, Patricia
   1997 Playing with Fire: The Gendered Construction of Chicana/Mexicana Sexuality. In *The Gender/Sexuality Reader: Culture, History, and Political Economy*, ed. R. N. Lancaster and M. di Leonardo, 392–408. New York: Routledge.
Zeldin, T.
   1973 *France, 1848–1945*. Vol. 1, *Ambition, Love, and Politics*. Oxford: Clarendon.
Zierler S, and N. Krieger
   1997 Reframing Women's Risk: Social Inequalities and HIV Infection. *Annual Review of Public Health* 18:401–36.

CONTRIBUTORS

MARGARET E. BENTLEY, professor of nutrition and associate dean for global health at the University of North Carolina at Chapel Hill, is a medical anthropologist whose research focuses on women and infant's nutrition, infant and young child feeding, behavioral research on sexually transmitted diseases, HIV, and community-based interventions for nutrition and health. She has expertise in both qualitative and quantitative research methods and the application of these for program development and evaluation. She currently is working on an HIV behavioral intervention prevention study in Chennai, India; on a community-based intervention to improve child growth and development in Andhra Pradesh, India; and on an intervention to decrease maternal to child transmission of HIV during breastfeeding in Malawi. In addition, she directs a five-year longitudinal study to examine risk factors for the development of pediatric obesity in North Carolina.

SELINA CHING CHAN has a DPhil in social anthropology from Oxford University. She taught in the department of sociology at the National University of Singapore and is currently associate professor in the department of sociology and associate director at the Contemporary China Research Center at the Hong Kong Shue Yan College. Her areas of research include the study of Chinese family, kinship, cultural identity, and religion in Hong Kong, Singapore, and China. Her work has been published in international journals such as *Ethnology, China Information*, and *Modern China*.

PAMELA I. ERICKSON, DrPH, PhD, is associate professor in the departments of anthropology and community medicine at the University of Connecticut, where she teaches medical anthropology, ethnomedicine, international health, and qualitative research methods. Her research interest centers on sexual and reproductive health issues among adolescents and young adults broadly construed to include the related issues of relationship violence, ATOD use, and other risk-taking behaviors. She has worked on youth reproductive health, sexuality, and gender issues in the United States, Nepal, and the Philippines. For fifteen years her research focused on understanding the Latina teen mother experience in East Los Angeles. Her current research in Hartford addresses how the social and cultural context of sexual and romantic relationships among inner city African American and Puerto Rican youth affects communication and negotiation of risk reduction behaviors. She has also done more traditional anthropological field-based research on warfare and fertility among the Waorani of eastern Ecuador. She is the current editor of the *Medical Anthropology Quarterly*.

JESSICA GREGG is a medical anthropologist and physician whose primary interests are in cancer prevention among underserved populations and in disabusing medical educators of the idea that teaching "cultural competence" is an effective way of addressing health disparities among poor and minority populations. She lives in Oregon with her husband and son.

JENNIFER HIGGINS recently finished her PhD in women's studies and MPH in global health at Emory University in Atlanta, Georgia. In the fall of 2005, she began a postdoctoral fellowship at Columbia University's HIV Center in New York City. She is interested in gender, sexuality, and reproductive health, especially the interface between pregnancy prevention and HIV prevention. Her latest research project explored the association between sexual pleasure and contraceptive use in the United States.

JENNIFER S. HIRSCH is associate professor in the department of sociomedical sciences at Columbia University's Mailman School of Public Health. She was initially drawn to anthropology via an interest in how cultural factors shape contraceptive use decision making, and in fact began her doctoral training in a multidisciplinary population studies program at Johns Hopkins University before shifting midway to a joint degree in public health and anthropology, which she earned in 1998. She has published widely from her dissertation, a comparative study of gender, sexuality, and reproductive health among Mexican transnational families, including the 2003 volume *A Courtship after Marriage: Sexuality and Love in Mexican Transnational Families*. Her current research interests include the intersections between HIV, migration, and sexuality; gender; the applications of anthropological theory and methods in public health; and, of course, the anthropology of love. She lives in New York City with her husband, John, and their two sons.

WYNNE MAGGI is the author of *Our Women Are Free: Gender and Ethnicity in the Hindukush* (2001). She is currently CFO of EnergySmiths, Inc., a residential energy services company in northern Colorado, where she lives with her family. She is still in contact with her friends in the Kalasha Valleys through letters and e-mail, and she misses them.

CONSTANCE A. NATHANSON is a sociologist and professor of clinical sociomedical sciences at Columbia University's Mailman School of Public Health. Major relevant recent publications include *Dangerous Passage: The Social Control of Sexuality in Women's Adolescence;* "A bargaining theory of sexual behavior in women's adolescence," with Robert Schoen (Proceedings of the IUSSP International Population Conference, Montreal, August 1993); and "The Impregnable Myth of Teenage Pregnancy," in John Bancroft (ed.), *The Role of Theory in Sex Research.* Current work includes completion of a manuscript on the comparative politics of public health in the United States, Canada, Britain, and France and consultation on the development of protocols for comparative cross-national research on the politicization of sexuality.

GAYATRI REDDY is assistant professor in the gender and women's studies program and department of anthropology at the University of Illinois at Chicago. Her research lies at the intersections of sexuality, gender, health, and the politics of identity formation in India, and more recently, within the immigrant South Asian community in the United States. She is the author of *With Respect to Sex: Negotiating Hijra Identity in South India* (2005), a book that problematizes representations of hijras as the so-called third sex of India and challenges the sufficiency of sexuality and gender performativity as adequate glosses on hijra identification and practice. Her research locates such figures of sexual difference and the domain of sexuality more generally within a broader field of difference or intersectionality, exploring the intersections of gender and sexuality with religion, race, ethnicity, and class in South Asia and its diaspora.

DANIEL JORDAN SMITH is the Stanley J. Bernstein Assistant Professor in the Social Sciences and assistant professor of anthropology at Brown University. He began working in southeastern Nigeria from 1989 through 1992 on a public health program and conducted dissertation research for his PhD in anthropology in the same region from 1995 through 1997. He received his doctorate from Emory University in 1999 and has continued an active research agenda in Nigeria. His current research interests include understanding the intersection of social change, population processes, and public health, particularly as these unfold in the arena of sexual relationships in the context of Nigeria's HIV/AIDS epidemic. He has published widely on these topics. He is also interested in the culture of politics, and his book, *A Culture of Corruption: Everyday Deception and Popular Discontent in Nigeria,* is forthcoming with Princeton University Press.

HOLLY WARDLOW, PhD, MPH, is assistant professor in the department of anthropology at the University of Toronto, where she teaches classes in medical anthropology, international health, gender, sexuality, and cultural anthropology. She is the author of *Wayward Women: Sexuality and Agency in a New Guinea Society* (2006). Her current research interests include sexual and reproductive health, violence, gendered risks for HIV, and Christian responses to the AIDS pandemic, particularly as these intersect with postcolonial nationalism.

INDEX